STUDIES IN VEDĀNTA PHILOSOPHY

STUDIES
IN
VEDĀNTA PHILOSOPHY

Edited By
Dr. R. K. Panda

BKP

BHARATIYA KALA PRAKASHAN
DELHI (INDIA)

First Published : 2002

Published by **C.P. Gautam**
BHARATIYA KALA PRAKASHAN
3421-A, IInd Floor, Narang Colony, Tri Nagar,
Delhi-110035. Phone : 7153083

ISBN : 81-86050-82-5

Laser Type Setting by
A-ONE GRAPHICS
X-4, Street No. 2, Brahmapuri, Delhi-110053
Phone : 218 3470

Printed at
Santosh Offset Press
Delhi

PREFACE

R.K. Panda

The present work, *Studies in Vedānta Philosophy* is an excellent contribution to Indian philosophical literature in general and Vedāntic school in particular. It contains thirty one well-studied articles which are written not by professonal academicians only but also by the great modern interpreters like swami Satprakashananda, swami Vireswarananda, swami Tapasyananda, swami Swahananda, swami Gnaneswarananda and Swami Vimalananda who have really realised the essence of Vedānta in their life. Great academicians like A.G. Krishna Warrier, M.P. Pandit, Roma Chaudhuri, P.K. Sundaram, M.K. Venkatarama lyer, Anima sen Gupta and others have also enriched this volume by their valuable articles. We have here research papers on the major schools of Vedāntic thought such as Advaita Vedānta, Dvaita Vedānta, Viśiṣṭādvaita Vedānta, Śuddhādvaita Vedānta and Dvaitādvaitavedānta. Some articles even explicate the difficult problems of Vedānta. So it is expected that the book will be very much useful to the students as well as scholars.

These articles are selected and collected from different published works with a view of creating a source book which will focus on various aspects of the Vedāntic systems. Since most of the articles of this book are not written by the professonal academicians but by the well-known saints and visionaries, it has a special importance in the sense that the book explores some unknown or a little-known facts relating to Vedāntic thoughts expounded mainly by the great Acharyas of India.

The first article is *An Introduction to the Vedāntism* by R.K. Panda.

The second article is *The Spiritual Heritage of India.* It deals with the paramount question— what is that by knowing which everything in this universe is known and how the search for the ultimate Truth has found expression in multifarious forms of religious attitude and devotional feeling that are characterstic of the soul of India. As it is known, the spiritual heritage of India is like a mighty stream, to which several tributaries, big and small, have contributed their own quota. But our author has focussed only on the major tributaries, leaving out of consideration of minor brooks and rivulets which have no doubt contributed in no insignificant measure to the enrichment of the variegated culture of the Indian people. The author is of the view that the mind of India is ever a thirst for an understanding and expressing the ultimate Truth that underlies everything in this universe and that is the spiritual heritage of India. And it has been expressed in the hymns of the Vedic sage who praised the deities presiding over the natural phenomena in the flashes of spiritual insight of the Upaniṣadic seer which penetrated into the core of Reality, in the depiction of mythological personalities who were the embodiments of great moral principles and spiritual truths and in the devotional fervour that became the dominant feature of the latter-day religious schools.

The third article from the pen of swami Vimalananda is *on the peace invocations of the vedas* which expounds the idea of peace in a fantastic manner. The author analyses very carefully the vedic *mantras* and comes to the conclusion that these *mantras* express the outstanding principles of Vedāntic thoughts.

The fourth article, *The Vedic concept of the Karma*

Doctrine, is written by Prakash Dubey who has prepared an exhaustive study of the Vedic concept of *karma*. He has given the meaning of the word and has traced its roots in the *saṁhitās* of the Vedas. He says that the idea was fully developed in the form of rebirth and transmigration which gave rise to the doctrine of *karma*. He has also tried to trace its rudiments in the Brāhmaṇa and Upaniṣadic literature. Thus the paper is comprehensive and critical. It makes us sufficiently clear why and how the doctrine of *karma* has a special role in the scheme of *puruṣārtha*. I am sure, a reader will find sufficient material in this article to revise his understanding of the Vedic doctrine of *karma*.

The fifth article, *The Grandest Discovery of the Upaniṣads,* is from the pen of M.K. Venkatarama lyer. The author has thrown lights on various aspects of Upaniṣadic thoughts which centres around the concept of *Brahman* and its different states like *jāgrat, swapna*, *suṣupti* and *Turīya*.

The sixth article, *The concept of māyā in the Upaniṣ ads* written by the same author will be very interesting to academic philosophers. The author has presented a clear picture of *māyā*, a binding and blinding force and its related concepts in very clear terms. The author concludes by saying that any attempt to explain the teachings of the Upaniṣads without reference to the cencept of *māyā* will mean either ignoring several important passages or placing a most unnatural interpretation on them.

Again, the author has contributed another article entitled *The Methodology of the Upaniṣads.* This article has brought to light the Upaniṣadic methodology which is very much useful for the understanding of supreme Reality. No doubt, a sincere reader will know about some important methods propounded by the Upaniṣadic thinkers.

V. Perumal in his article, *An Analytical Approach to the Bhagavadgītā* discusses the relevance of the *Gītā* and its usefulness in human life. The author holds the view that the *Gītā* does not contain dry and vague philosophy which can be divorced from human life. The *Gītā* is a spiritual reference book which contains the sum and substance of advanced thought, explained and illustrated in an easy flowing language. The article is very much useful to the scholars interested in the *Gītā* which is accepted as one of the *prasthānas* of Vedānta system. The author has not only presented an analytical approach but also the physical aspect, the mental aspect, the social aspect, the intellectual aspect, the spiritual aspect, the moral aspect etc., in this paper.

Vidya Chaitanya's article, *Śrīkṛṣṇa and the ideal of life* is equally important one. The author tries to clarify why there was a need of the *Bhagavadgītā* and what kind of role the Lord Kṛṣṇa played in singing this immortal song. He is of the view that the charm, rhythm and dignity of the Upaniṣadic language were appealing but unintelligible and incomprehensible to the general people. A concrete representation of Truth, Beauty and Goodness was necessitated for a meaningful blend of the doctrine and its realization, the ideal and the real. The conception of the decent of a Godhead into our emperical world is thus neither a myth nor a legend but a prudential necessity which undertook to bridge over the sult between the transcendent and the immanent, between the impersonal and the personal, between religion and philosophy. The paper ends with the conclusion that Śrīkṛṣṇa in the *Gītā* gives a correct interpretation of the Upaniṣadic thought. It is a concretised Upaniṣad and Śrīkṛṣṇa is the embodiment of the Upaniṣadic ideal.

Here is another article, *On the Advent of Śrīkṛṣṇa* from the pen of a great scholar M.V. Sridatta Sarma. He has analysed the etymological meanings of the word Kṛṣṇa and presented different interpretations of this word. In the light of the Upaniṣadic statements the author has discussed the matter of the advent of Kṛṣna and says that the supreme Lord represents the mighty force or form which remains neither split nor unsplit. He serves as a sigh of the collective unit or the universal spirit. From the point of view of the collective unit or the aggregate of all parts, He serves the purpose of a single whole or integral part. Each part in turn remains consubststially the same with the whole.

Mallika Clare Gupta in his article, *Kurukshetra*—the Land of the *Bhagavadgītā* deals with the history of Kurukshetra where the Lord Kṛṣṇa had sung the song of *Gītā* and has taught the immortal truth to Arjuna. Kurukshetra is as hoary with history as it is with legend and tradition. The reader will find a lot of valuable material of history in this article.

The great Swamiji Gnaneswarananda has contributed his article, *God of Human life according to jñānayoga*. The highest goal of human life has been considered by the jñānayogis as total absorption into the infinite substance. Unity is the goal of *jñānayoga*. The article is rich in profound thought and philosophic insights. The author has suggested also some methods for achieving that goal.

The article, *The Gītā and the Gaṅg*ā by R. Ramakrishnan compares the *Gītā* with the great river Gaṅgā. The author has clearly analysed the viewpoints of swami Vivekananda who had a great reverence for the both. He is of the view that Hindu society and the Indian community is *Gītā*-nourished and Gaṅgafed. And those of us who aspire to be truly Hindu or genuinely Indian will be near to the fulfilment of our aspiration to the extent to which we make ourselves Gaṅgā-soaked and Gītā- inspired.

Harold Barry Phillips's article. *'The six systems of Hindu philosophy'* gives a brief outline of the six systems of philosophy belonging to orthodox school. The author is of the view that philosophy is an insight into the nature and meaning of the universe. So all these six systems are six 'insights' and grouped into three entirely distinct groups: (i) The Nyāya-Vaiśeṣika; (ii) the Sāṁkhya - yoga; and (iii) the Pūrva and Uttara Mīmāṁsā. This well-written article would be very much useful to the beginners of philosophy. It presents before us the main tenets of these philosophical systems.

After having a good background one can enter into the system of Advaita Vedāna. This background is necessary for better understanding of Vedāntic systems. So we have here an article, entitled *The sum and substance of Advaita Vedānta* from the pen of a great authority, Swami Satprakashnanda. Swamiji has given us a tonic of Advaitic thoughts. He highlights the main tenets of Advaitism and explains the prominent doctrines in such a manner that even a layman will not find any difficulty in understanding them in full.

Next to it, is the article, *A New Angle on the Problem of Unreality in Advaita* written by A.G. Krishna Warrier who is well-known in the circles of philosophy-teachers for his significant cantribution. He is the author of an important work, *the concept of Mukti in Advaita Vedānta*. He has tried to clear some alleged acosmisms developed by both well-informed and ill-informed critics of Advaita. He has given his own arguments along with those of modern scholars like S. Radhakrishanan and others. He has clarified the concept of unreality in easy and interesting manner, without having any kind of complicacy. I am sure, a reader of this article will not be confused of Advaitic unreality after a thorough reading of Warrier's paper.

In the same spirit Professor Roma Chaudhuri has

analysed the Advaitic concept of the soul in her article *Advaita Vedānta Conception of Soul*. After her, comes Prof. P.K. Sundaram, a well-known authority on Advaita Vedānta, with his paper, *The conception of soul in Śaṅkara's Sūtra-bhāṣya.* Though both the articles deal with the same topic, still there is something new in boh the papers. While Prof. Chaudhuri discusses the issue in general, Prof. Sundaram restricts his discussions and limits only to the commentary of Śaṅkarācārya written on the *Brahmasūtras*.

In the same line comes again Anima sen Gupta who has written the article, *Madhusūdhana Saraswatī*. The paper is a critical exposition of the text, *Advaitaratnarakṣaṇam* written by Madhusūdana Saraswati, the great Advaitin of post-śaṅkara period. The article is erudite and the presentation is systematic.

In his article, *The philosophy of Rāmānuja : Some Salient Features,* Dr. R.K. Panda has given us the gist of Rāmānuja's Philosophy.

Then we have Swamiji Vireśwarānanda who has written on *Śrībhāṣya* of Rāmānujācārya. This will be interesting for the students of Viśiṣṭādvaita system propoundeed by Śrī Rāmānujācārya.

We have another article, *Sataduṣaṇī of Vedānta Deśika* written by B.H. Kapadia on the Viśiṣṭādvaita system of Vedānta. The paper gives some important information about the life and works of Vedānta Deśika who is one of the greatest promulgators of Viśiṣṭādvaita and his *Sataduṣaṇī* attempting at discussing a hundred topics. The main object of this work is to refute the doctrines of Śaṅkara and his followers. Dr. Kapadia has really made a good work by presenting the arguments of Deśika against Śaṅkara's Advaitavāda. It is really difficult to work on such topics for the reason that the text written in dialectical manner is not so easy to understand.

But for us Professor Kapadia has been of great help for the understanding of Deśika's viewpoints.

After Viśiṣṭādvaita we have to enter into the system of Madhvācārya, an uncompromising critic of the Advaita of Śaṅkara, known as *Dvaitavāda*. Sri Kowlagi Seshacharya has reviewed an important work of Madhva i.e. Śrimad *Viṣṇu-tattva-vinirṇaya* in his article *Śrīmad Viṣṇutattva-Vinirṇaya of Śrī Madhvācārya*. The review article is an eye-opener of the great Acārya's contribution to Indian philosophy in general and Dvaita Vedānta in particular.

Then Dr. Roma Chaudhuri has given an interesting paper on *Brahman-Jiva-Jagat* relation. Prof G.H. Bhatt's article on the school of Vallabhācārya is exhustive and critical. Swami Tapasyananda has given us an illuminating article *The concept of the Absolute in Vedānta*.

Similarly Swami Swahananda has written on *Vedānta and Democratic Spirit*. The author is of the opinion that Indian culture down the ages has been influenced so much by Vedāntic ideas that it has become synonymous with Vedānta. The author has dealt with different aspects of Democracy with its relation to Vedānta. The paper unfolds some of the new avenues in Vedāntic studies. Swamiji's presentation is highly erudite.

Another Swamiji of great repute, Swami Ganeswara-nanda has written on *the Dynamic power of Vedānta* and the paper explores the new horizons of Vedic thoughts which create a dynamic power in the mind of a man when he understands the true essence of being as promulgated by Vedāntic philosophers of India.

Here is paper from the A.V. Subramania Aiyar—*George Santayana and Vedānta*. This will be interesting for the students of comparative philosophy. The author has given us a short account of the life and the philosophy of George Santayana and has shown that in a few of its basic elements it has affinity with Indian Vedāntic thought.

M.P. Pandit has enricheed this volume by contributing a valuable article—*The Nātha Tradition*. He has dealt with the concept of Śiva-Śakti, evolution of universe, individual formations and Man and the Nātha-yoga, its goal and Method.

The last article, *Approach to God* explicates the methods of approaching God, the highest being. The author also makes it very clear why the approach of God is necessary in human life. He has quoted authoritative texts of the scriptures to prove his view points.

The Editor of this volume expresses his heart-felt thanks to the contributors of this volume, the well-known Saints and scholars who have tried to spread the Vedāntic ideas and ideals all over the world throughout the ages.

The Editor also expresses his sincere thanks to the Publisher C.P. Gautam, the Proprietor, the Bharatiya Kala Prakashan for publishing this work in time.

5th March 2002 **Dr. R.K. Panda**
Vadodara

CONTENTS

1
INTRODUCTION TO VEDĀNTISM

R.K. Panda

The philosophy of Vedānta, like all other systems of Indian thought, is an attempt to clearly understand and offer an explanation of the world as it appears to us in our knowledge. It is an attempt to determine the nature of the ultimate Reality and to understand how it presents before us a world of manifoldness, in order to make out clearly the place and destiny of man in the world system. In fact, we have two important questions before us, viz.: (1) the theoretical determination of the nature of substance or reality underlying experience and of the origin of knowledge, and (2) the ethical problem of duty and the ultimate ideal of human life. These questions have been thoroughly answered in Vedānta and their solutions have been offered by the Vedāntic teachers. Truely speaking, Vedāntism is not to be taken as a philosophy based solely upon revelation or faith that has no rational justification. It has got a strong hold upon the children of the soil; to some of them, it is an established principle which cannot be questioned, and this is not due to the Vedāntic thought always appealing to the *Śruti* as the aultimate source of knowledge, but to its offering a promise full of inspiring hope to humanity aspiring for eternal verities. Needless to say, Vedāntism has a strong claim to its general acceptance, as it is based upon the profoundest form of thinking and argument; in it a deep conception of life and experience has been wrought, not upon mere dogmatism, but upon a logical form of philosophy developed upon a dialectic and logical basis. The first problem which the Vedānta seeks to solve is the ontological problem of Reality, the second, the problem of cosmology, the third, the problem of psychology, while the fourth is the last problem of striving after the ideal and its attainment—the final liberation.

To my mind, the Vedānta systems are the most important ones among the Indian philosophical systems, because they are the result of well-disciplined philosophical thought and mark also the culmination of philosophical reflection in India. This accounts for their triumph over the other philosophical systems and for the respect with which they are held throughout India. The whole Hindu nation today is in some way or other influenced by the one or the other Vedānta system. Indian religions show in some form or other a clear influence of Vedāntic thought on them.

The term '*Vedānta*' is a compound of '*veda*' and '*anta*' (end). It means, in its primary signification, the latter part of the Veda or Vedas. The Vedic literature is divided into two main *kāṇḍas* (sections), the first portion being called the *karmakāṇḍa*, the section treating of *karma*, actions or duties; and the second, *anta* or *uttara* portion, the *Jñānakāṇḍa*, the section on knowledge. The division is not clearly repre-sented by the distinct books or even chapters of the Vedas; but roughly speaking, the *mantras* and the sacrificial portions of the *Brāhmaṇas* represent the *karmakāṇḍa*, and the treatises called Upaniṣads, attached mainly to the Brāhmaṇas, represent the *jñānakāṇḍa*. This *jñānakāṇḍa* of the Vedas is the *Vedānta* in the original sense of the word. As a part of the Veda, the *Vedānta* is *Śruti* or scripture. As *Śruti* or scripture, therefore, the Vedānta is identical with the Upaniṣads. The use of the term *Vedānta* in this sense will be found in the Upaniṣads themselves, for instance, in the *Muṇḍakopaniṣad* III.2.6. and the *Svetāsvatara Upaniṣad* vi.22. Śaṅkarācārya, the greatest authority on the Vedānta, uses the word in this sense everywhere in his writings. However, the word '*anta*' in '*vedānta*,' from meaning 'end' or 'latter part,' came gradually to mean 'conclusion,' 'gist' or 'purport'. The composers of the Upaniṣads claimed that they had discovered the gist or purport of all Vedic teaching in the knowledge of the Absolute, of whom the gods worshipped by the authors of the *mantras*, as well as all objects in creation were, they taught, names, forms or relative manifestations. The final end of all Vedic disciplines were, they thought, union with Brahman, the Absolute Being. In this latter sense, therefore, in the sense of the gist or purport of the Vedas, it was the Upaniṣads, again, which were called the '*Vedānta*' or '*Vedāntas*'. But the term came gradually to mean something quite different from, though closely related to, the Upaniṣads. As the Upaniṣads treated of a large variety of subjects, both essential and non-essential to the spiritual life, and as the teachings of the different treatises were apparently, if not really conflicting, it became necessary to have systematic statements of the main doctrines taught in them backed by reasonings where necessary, and reconciling apparent discrepancies in the original teaching. Thus arose what is called the Vedānta philosophy, that is the philosophy based on the Vedānta or Upaniṣads. This philosophy or the body of aphorisms which is its chief exponent, oftener goes by the name of 'Vedānta' than the Upaniṣads, the original Vedāntas and the basis of all later Vedāntic teaching. The distinction, however, between the Vedānta as *sruti* or scripture, and the Vedānta as *Darśana* or philosophy, must never be lost sight of.

The word may, however, be more appropriately understood as the end of all knowledge. However, the term Vedānta has the following meanings.

(1) Vedānta is the real heart of the Vedic teaching. As the Upaniṣads contain the essence of the Vedic teaching they are called Vedānta.

(2) The thought that systematises the Upaniṣadic teaching is also called Vedānta. (3) Again, that which decides the true meaning of the Vedic teaching as a whole is Vedānta; the system that decides the true meaning of the Veda is called Vedānta. The fact that the Veda is valid as a whole implies that it stands for a definite teaching and the system by which that central teaching was explored after a serious examination of the apparent meanings, is called Vedānta. So the *Brahma-sūtras* are also called Vedānta. Reflecting on the early history of Vedānta one feels that there were several attempts to systematise the teaching of the Vedas even before Bādarāyaṇa. But it is generally accepted that Bādarāyaṇa's work is the last and the most complete one. In his *Brahmasūtras* he has systematised the thoughts of the Veda. The *Sūtras* consist of pithy statements that are very comprehensive in their outlook. They are called *Vedāntasūtras* because they embody the systematisation of the Vedic thoughts. They are also called *Brahmasūtras* because they reveal the nature of the aultimte reality, *Brahman*. *Śārīraka-sūtras* is another name for them, because they determine the real nature of *Ātman* that appears to us in a body. They are also called the *mīmāṁsāsūtras* for their reflective character and they are specially called the *Uttara-Mīmāṁsāsūtras*. The Sanskrit term *uttara* means both latter and better. The *sūtras* are regarded as *uttara* in both these senses. They are *uttara* because they come after the Pūrva-Mīmāṁsā. They are also called *uttara* because of the fact that they deal with the knowledge, *jñāna* of the ultimate reality which is better than action (*karma*), and is the subject-matter of the pūrva-mīmāṁsā. As we know, knowledge is the direct means of spiritual advancement, and not action (*karma*). Therefore knowledge is better than *karma*. The *Brahma-sūtras* are chiefly concerned with the Upaniṣads, and with them they emphasise the importance of knowledge and make *karma* only subservient to it. Hence they are called the *Uttra-Mīmāṁsāsūtras*. The *Brahmasūtras* are 564 in

number. Not only the *Brahmasūtras* but the other two basic texts of Vedānta are the Upaniṣads and the Bhagavadgītā, Together they are referred to as the *Prasthāna-traya*, (triple canon) of Vedānta. The Upaniṣads constitute the revealed texts (*Śruti-prasthāna*); they mark the summits of the Veda which is *Śruti*. They are the pristine springs of Vedāntic metaphysics. The Bhagavadgītā comes next only to the Upaniṣads. It is given a status which is almost equal to tht of the Upaniṣads. As this text forms a part of the *Mahābhārata* which is *Smṛti* it is called *Smṛti-prasthāna*. The third of the canonical texts is the *Brahma-sūtra* which is regarded as *Nyāya-prasthāna*, because it sets forth the teachings of Vedānta in a logical order. Sometimes between 500 to 300 B.C., Bādarāyaṇa in his *Brahmasūtra* tried to work out a coherent theory from the upaniṣads, reconciling what he believed to be the apparent contradictions in them. About the same time was composed the Bhagavadgītā, which, while disparaging the view that the Veda is the all sufficient source of truth, yet claims to teach a doctrine, which is as old as the world, and is at the same time the essence of the Veda. Vedāntic schools of philosophy are based on these three *prasthānas*.

In the Upaniṣads, and even in some Ṛgvedic passages, is to be found in embryonic form the doctrine of Advaita. Bādarāyaṇa mentions a philosopher Kāsakṛtsna, who held that God himself is the individual soul; and another Bādari, who thought that the worship of 'conditioned Brahman,' can only lead to the impermanent world of Brahman. Śaṅkara's school claims Bādarāyaṇa as the teacher par excellence of Advaita.

The *Brahma-sūtras* are held in such a high esteem that any propounder of an original philosophical thought takes care to see that his views are based on the Upaniṣads and are in thorough agreement with what Bādarāyaṇa has said in the

Brahma-sūtras. The views of the different commentators have been accepted by some sections of the people, and these followers look upon their own Ācārya as infallible and his teaching as above doubt and dispute. Some of these great Ācāryas of well-established repute who commented on the *Brahma-sūtras* are :

1.	Śaṅkarācārya	788-820 A.D.	*Kevalādvaita*
2.	Bhaskarācārya	1000 A.D.	*Bhedābheda* (*anupādhikabheda svābhāvika abheda*)
3.	Rāmānujācārya	1140 A.D.	*Viśiṣṭādvaita*
4.	Madhvācārya	1238A.D.	*Dvaita*
5.	Nimbārkācārya	later half of 13th ce. A.D.	*Svābhāvika bhedābheda*
6.	Śrīkaṇṭhācārya	13th cent.	*Śaiva-Viśiṣṭādvaita*
7.	Śripati	later half of 14th c. A.D.	*Bhedābhedātmaka viśiṣṭādvaita*
8.	Vallabhācārya	1481-1533 A.D.	*Śuddhādvaita*
9.	Vijñānabhikṣu	1600 A.D.	*Avibhāgādvaita*
10.	Baladeva	1725 A.D.	*Acintyabhedābheda*

On each of these commentaries there are sub-commentaries, glosses, etc. It is well-known that in India we have got a large number of philosophical systems. Of these, besides quite a few less-known systems, the six *Āstika* (Orthodox) schools viz. Sāṁkhya, Yoga, Nyāya, Vaiśeṣika, Mīmāṁsā and Vedānta, and the three *Nāstika* (Heterodox). schools viz. Cārvāka, Jainism, Buddhism are well-known. But of these again, the Vedānta system is by far the most important and well-known. Of these Vedāntic systems the Advaita-Vedānta school of Śaṅkara is by far, the most profound and celebrated one, marking as it does, the culmination of all Vedāntic insight and inspiration of all ages. Śaṅkara's Advaita system is the first developed and complete Vedānta system. Later Vedānta systems developed more or less as counter-systems trying to disprove Śaṅkara's pure monism by different kinds of Qualified Monism or Dualistic Non-Dualism.As a result, we have got the celebrated ten schools of the Vedānta viz. Śaṅkara's *Kevalādvaita-vāda,* Rāmānuja's *Viśiṣṭādvaita-vāda,* Nimbārka's *Svābhāvika-Dvaitādvaita-vāda,* Madhva's *Bhedābheda-vāda,* Vallabha's *Śuddhādvaita-vāda,* Bhāskara's *Aupādhika-bhedābheda-vāda*, Viṣṇu Svāmini's *Śuddhādvaita-vāda,* Śrīkaṇṭha's *Viśiṣṭādvaita-vāda, Śivādvaita-vāda, Śripati's Viśeṣādvaita-vāda* and Baladeva's *Acintya-bhedābheda-vāda*, and Vijñānabhikṣu's *Avibhāgādvaita*.

The gradual development of a philosophical thought in India is linked with the gradual unfolding of the intellectual and sentimental life of a human being. It may be said to represent the theoretical aspect of human existence while the practical side is represented by the actual experiencing of it. If, therefore, a system of thought does not correspond to the actual functioning of human life on correct lines, it would have neither any practical value nor general appeal. There being people of divergent taste, it is but natural that we should have various schools of thought in accordance with their different needs. It needs no explanation when it is said that Absolute Monism of Śaṅkara, or the Qualified Monism of Rāmānuja, or the Unqualified or pure Monism of Vallabha could not satisfy every class of people. Proceeding on the assumption that everybody is not qualified for every kind of teaching and that the various schools of thought are only to represent the different stages in the growth of the intellectual and spiritual life of such people, it requires no apology to evolve any consistent school of thought to satisfy the longing of a particular group of people.

These systems represent the different stages of the growth of the same Vedānta thought. Advaita represents the first stage, Viśiṣṭādvaita the second and Dvaita Vedānta the third. Certain difficulties in the position of Advaita made a reconsideration of the whole of Vedānta thought necessary and as a result there appeard Viśiṣṭādvaita. But this system also was not without difficulties, and by way of removing them there appeared Dvaita. Further, Advaita and Viśiṣṭādvaita stand like two poles, southern and northern; Dvaita maintains a balance between the two. A full knowledge of Vedānta thought presupposes a careful study of the three systems in their historic order. The knowledge of the later two systems is necessary to understand the scope of Advaita. The knowledge of Advaita and Dvaita is necessary to appreciate the significance of Viśiṣṭādvaita and the knowledge of Advaita and Viśiṣṭādvaita is necessary to recognise the importance of Dvaita Vedānta.

It is in the detailed interpretation of the fundamental principles enumerated above that the Vedānta philosophy branches out into schools. Of these, four have the largest following, those of Śaṅkara, Rāmānuja, Madhva, and Vallabha, the followers of the first, again, outnumbering by far those of the other two. We may add the school of Baladeva Vidyabhuṣaṇa, to which the followers of Chaitanya belong, and that of Raja Rammohan Roy, the founder of the Brahma Samāj, who is faithful to the instincts of a true Indian reformer and wrote commentaries on the Prasthānatraya, and whose school, though not sticking to traditional methods in all matters, is yet important as representing a fusion of ancient Indian thought with the thought of the West.

Śaṅkarācārya's doctrine, which is usually known by the name of *kevalādvaita* (Absolute monism), maybe summed up in the four Sanskrit words: *Brahma saytam jaganmithyā*. The following are the main points of Śaṅkara's monism. All plurality is false or unreal, and superimposed upon one pure and eternal Brahman which is all-pervading and it is *Māyā* which makes us see plurality where there is unity and which itself has no independent existence.

The Individual soul is really nothing but *Brahman*.

Knowledge of the identity of these two is the only means of *mokṣa*. Actions must be performed only to purify the mind so as to make it fit to acquire the knowledge of this identity of *Brahman* and *Jīva* but afterwards they must be all given up, since without a complete abandonment of all actions *mokṣa* is impossible, for, *Karma* and *jñāna* are opposed to each other like darkness and light.

The greatest merit of Śaṅkara's system is his most successful attempt to reconcile the mutually contradictory texts of the Upaniṣads, in other words, to reconcile bold idealism, which is the result of introspection, with the realism which ruthlessly insists on forcing itself upon us from outside. This he does by the introduction of *Māyā* in his system; or his doctrine has always two aspects, esoteric and exoteric, be it in reference to theology or cosmology or psychology.

Esoterically the Brahman is knowledge or realisation itself, without qualification and without possibility of change; exoterically it is qualified, possessed of an infinite number of auspicious attributes, capable of producing this world from itself and reabsorbing it in itself—in brief it is *Īśvara*.

The exoteric cosmology considers the world as real and can express its entire dependence on *Brahman* only by the adoption of a myth, viz. creation of the world by Brahman, implying thereby a temporal character before this creation. The esoteric cosmology, however, says that all this is a mere appearance of truth. The manifold world is only an illusion, Māyā, and the reality is to be attained not by reasoning but by introspective realisation. According to the esoteric psychology the *jīva* is *Brahman* itself in full and total possession of eternity, omnipresence, omniscience, etc., but these godly qualities lie concealed within it as the fire in the wood and will appear only after the final deliverance.

Exoterically, this concealment of the divine nature is due to the external adjuncts—the mind, the sense organs and the vital airs which form the subtle body. The whole psychological apparatus together with *karman* accompanies the soul in all his migrations, without essentially infecting his godly nature.

Śaṅkara's system maintains the *Vivarta* doctrine, according to which all effects are only superimposed upon the cause, which alone is real.

According to Rāmānuja, the individual souls and the inanimate world, essentially different in themselves, form at the same time the body and mode or attribute of the supreme spirit; and, as such, they are incapable of an existence independent of the supreme spirit. This is what gives the doctrine its name of Viśiṣṭādvaita. Thus what the ordinary body is to the individual soul, so are the intelligent and non-intelligent worlds to the supreme soul; and just as the body can never be essentially the same as the Brahman. The Brahman is the cause, both material and efficient, of the universe, intelligent and non-intelligent; it is possessed of an infinite number of auspicious attributes; of which omniscience, omnipresence, omnipotence and bliss are the most essential. Brahman, having for its body and mode the *cit* and *acit* in their subtle condition, is the cause, while the same Brahman having for its body or mode the *cit* and *acit* in a gross form is the effect. The individual soul is the subject of consciousness or knower and not mere consciousness itself. Consciousness is its essential attribute. Bliss is also another essential attribute of the individual soul. Being atomic in size the individual souls are infinite in number and different for different bodies. Owing to ignorance, the individual souls are conjoined to matter and thus in spite of their original resemblance to Brahman, suffer in this mundane world. The inanimate world is also as real as the Brahman. According to Rāmānuja, Brahman, *cit* and *acit* are three entities, individually distinct from each other, all equally real, at the same time all forming a unity, in the sense in which the self and its body form a unity.

Rāmānuja admits the *Pariṇāma* doctrine or *Satkārya-vāda*, which maintains that the effect is nothing but a modification of the cause, in which it is already present.

The devotion of Vāsudeva is the only means of obtaining the highest goal of life. This *bhakti* is the initiation or immediate presentation arising from a steady remembrance (*dhruvā smṛtiḥ*) which arises from meditation. Actions are necessary only for the origination of knowledge.

According to Nimbārka, there are only three principles or entities, *cit, acit* and *Īśvara* also called by the significant names of *bhoktṛ*, *bhogya* and *Niyantṛ*. The *cit* or individual soul is of the nature of knowledge and knower also just as the sun is both light and the source of light. The *jīva* is also Ego (*ahamarthaḥ*). This Ego continues to persist not only in the state of deep sleep but also in the state of liberation. It even belongs to the *parabrahman*. The *Jīva* is also essentially active and enjoyer essentially in all its conditions. It is atomic in size, at the same time his attribute, knowledge is omnipresent, which makes it possible that he can experience pleasure and pain in any part of the body. The Jīvas are different in different bodies, and so are infinite in number.

The *acit* or non-intelligent world is of three kinds: (i) *aprākṛta* (ii) *prākṛta* and (iii) *Kāla*. The three categories in their subtle form are as eternal as the *cit* or the individual soul.

The third principle is the Highest-self, the Brahman, or Kṛṣṇa. This Kṛṣṇa is naturally free from all faults, is the store of all beneficent attributes, is adorable by all, has four forms or *vyūhas* (Vāsudeva, Saṅkarṣaṇa, Pradyumna and Aniruddha) and appears under various incarnations such as

Matsya, Kūrma etc. This *Brahman* is both the *Upādāna* and the *Nimitta* of the universe. The creation of the universe is nothing but a manifestation in a grass form of what was subtle before and is thus a sort of modification or *pariṇāma*.

To attain deliverance, the *jīva* has to commence with a complete submission to the Paramātman, or *prapatti*, whose six constituents are:— a resolution to yield, the avoidance of opposition, a faith that God will protect, acceptance of him as saviour, throwing one's whole soul upon him and a sense of helplessness. For a devotee, the knowledge of the following five things is quite necessary:— (i) the nature of the supreme soul (ii) the nature of the individual soul (iii) the fruit of God's grace or Mokṣa (iv) the feeling of enjoyment consequent on Bhakti and (v) the nature of the obstacles in the way of the attainment of God.

The doctrine of Madhva, purely dualistic in character, insists on the absolute and eternal difference between Brahman, Jīva and Jaḍa. Madhva propounds the five eternal distinctions, the clear understanding of which leads to Mokṣa. God, according to Madhva, possesses an infinite number of qualities. His chief functions are eight: creation, protection, dissolution, controlling all things, giving knowledge, manifestation of himself, involving the individual soul in the knowledge of the world and deliverance. His form is made up of knowledge and joy, he is independent of everything and remains one in the midst of different forms.

The individual souls are all distinct from God and distinct from each other individually, innumerable, going through a succession of existences and characterised by ignorance or other defects.

The world is created from Prākṛti, which is ever distinct from the supreme soul, who is thus only the efficient cause but not the material cause of the universe; for, it is against reason to suppose that the non-intelligent world can be produced from a being that is intelligent.

Mokṣa is attained by the direct knowledge or perception of Hari. Some of the means necessary for this direct knowledge are : Vairāgya, sama, sarṇāgati, Paramātmabhakti etc.

The doctrine of Vallabha is called Śuddhādvaita (Pure-monism) i.e. the unity of Brahman which is pure or free from Māyā. Thus the individual soul and the inanimate world are essentially the same as Brahman, without involving any idea of Māyā.

The *Jiva* is non-different from Brahman, atomic in size and a part of Brahman. It is produced from Brahman in the sense in which sparks are produced from fire; the *jiva* is a manifestation of Brahman itself, with the attribute of bliss obscured. Thus it is as eternal and real as Brahman and production in its case means only a manifestation. The *jīva* is either *śuddha* (pure), when its qualities such as greatness are not obscured by contact with the *avidyā* or *saṁsārin*, when it is in the bondage of *avid*yā and experiences birth, death etc., owing to its connection with the subtle and gross bodies, or *mukta*, when it becomes free from bondage, by means of *vid*yā. The *jīva*, though atomic can pervade the whole body by virtue of its quality of intelligence just as sandal-wood can by its fregrance make its existence known everywhere it does not exist.

The inanimate world is also essentially Brahman with the qualities of intelligence and bliss obscured and thus possessing the one quality of existence. It is at the same time created from Brahman in the sense that Brahman itself is manifested in the form of the gross world.

The Brahman is one, eternal, omniscient, omnipotent, possessed of an infinite number of attributes, and essentially of the nature of *sat*, *cit* and *ānanda*. It is *śuddha*, i.e. never contaminated by connection with *Māy*ā. It is possessed of *aiśvarya* which makes everything possible for it and even things mutually opposed can co-exist in its case. The Brahman is both the material and the efficient cause of the universe. The Brahman has three forms, (i) the highest divine form (*ādhidaivika*) as Kṛṣṇa or Puruṣottama (ii) the *akṣara* form (*ādhyātmika*) and (iii) the *antaryāmin* form. The relation between Brahman, the *jīva* and the *jaḍa* is one of pure identity, one that exists between a part and the whole. For Vallabha, it is non-difference alone that is real, while all difference is simply for the sake of his sport.

The *mokṣa* consists in the absolute cessation of all misery and the experiencing of the bliss. It can be attained by two means, *bhakti* and *jñāna*.

Nārāyaṇa Guru is one of the modern interpretors of Vedānta. He has presented the Vedānta philosophy in a fresh and original sūtra form. The Vedānta-sūtras of Nārāyaṇa Guru thus have a unique place in Indian philosophy as the first sūtra expression of Vedānta since Bādarāyaṇa. He has undertaken the task of revaluating and restating the Vedānta as appropriate to a modern age of science and technology. Although essentially an Advaitin, he did not solely subscribe to and support the Śaṅkara school, and he did not oppose the teachings of other schools. Like the river of Gaṅgā, the philosophy of Vedānta is flowing and will also flow for ever.

❑❑❑

2

THE SPIRITUAL HERITAGE OF INDIA

Swami Satswarupananda

"*Kasminnu bhagavo vijñāte sarvamidaṁ vijñātaṁ bhavati*—What is that by knowing which everything in this universe is known?"

—*Muṇḍaka Upaniṣad*, I.1.3.

"*Ātmano vā are darśanena śravaṇena matyā vijñānenedaṁ sarvaṁ viditam*—By the realization of the Self, my dear, through hearing, reflection, and meditation, all this is known."

—*Bṛhadāraṇyaka Upaniṣad,* II. 4.5.

I

Religion is the pivot around which the Indian life rotates. Age after age, in almost every century and generation, a succession of spiritually keen minds have appeared on the Indian soil and sought an answer to the timeless question: What is that by knowing which everything in this universe is known? This has been the paramount question of the soul of India through the ages. And in the course of her long history, this search for the ultimate Truth has found expression in various forms of religious attitude and devotional feeling that are characteristic of the soul of India.

The several systems of philosophic thought that are developed in this land; the various religious schools, sects, and cults that are prevalent all over the country; the growth of its vast and varied devotional literature; its music, art, and architecture, all aimed at depicting the devotional fervour of the human soul; and, indeed, all the religious and spiritual values which the Indian mind cherishes and holds as sacred—all these are but different expressions of this eternal quest of the soul of India at different stages of its emotional, intellectual, and intuitive development. In other words, spiritual striving has been the keynote of Indian life, and in this realm, its insight has been astounding, and its achievement almost unparalleled. Witness what the distinguished orientalist Max Muller says in this respect: 'If one would ask me under what sky the human mind has most fully developed its precious gifts, has scrutinized most profoundly the greatest problems of life, and has, at least for some, provided solutions which deserve to be admired even by those who have studied Plato and Kant, I would indicate India. And if one would ask me which literature would give us back (us, Europeans, who have been exclusively fed on Greek and Roman thought, and on that of a Semitic race) the necessary equilibrium in order to make our inner life more perfect, more comprehensive, more universal, in short, more human, a life not only for this life, but for a transformed and eternal life, once again I would indicate India.' That is the rich heritage which our forbears have left for posterity, of which we are proud, and to preserve it intact and to enrich it by our own contributions is our sacred duty.

The spiritual heritage of India is like a mighty stream, to which several tributaries, big and small, have contributed their own quota. In our study here, we shall focus our attention only on the major tributaries, leaving out of consideration minor brooks and rivulets which have no doubt contributed in no insignificant measure to the enrichment of the variegated culture of the Indian people.

Let us begin our story from the very beginning, namely, from the dim ages of Vedic antiquity, into which history cannot penetrate. Even in those distant ages, the spiritual quest of the Indian mind had greatly advanced and was pursued in all earnestness and fervour. The *Ṛg-Veda Saṁhitā*, which is considered to be the oldest religious literature extant in the world, records in excellent poetry the achievements and experiences of the human soul in its search after the ultimate Reality behind the world. A keen observer that the Vedic *ṛṣi* was, the beauty of nature and the perfect order in the universe did not escape his curious but ever watchful eyes. He began to inquire into the mystery behind the natural phenomena and arrived at certain conceptions regarding them. We are introduced to certain pre-Vedic gods who continue to be adored and praised; then we have the Vedic gods themselves who are looked upon as presiding over the various forces and functions of nature. Gods like Mitra and Varuṇa not only bring about *ṛta* or nature's recurring rhythm or ordered course, but also maintain moral order in the universe. (Some of the most important gods and goddesses mentioned in the Vedas are: Aditi, Agni, Brahmā, Bṛhaspati, Indra, Marut, Mitra, Prajāpati, Rudra, Sarasvatī, Savitṛ (Sūrya), Soma, Uṣas, Varuṇa, Vāyu, and Viṣṇu.) But the mind of the *ṛṣi,* which was out to seek the god of gods or the god above all gods, was not satisfied with this plurality of gods. There are even attempts in the Vedic hymns to bring the various gods under one conception. We have there the conception of Viśvedevas (All-gods) in which all the gods are put together. The next step is to declare that the great divinity of the gods is one. A well-known passage of the *Ṛg-Veda* reads : 'To what is one, sages give many a name: They call Him Agni, Yama, and Mātariśvan.' Thus by gradual stages, by discovering the underlying unity of the different conceptions of godhead, the Vedic seer arrived at the idea of one God.

The evolution of the conception of God—from the multiplicity of gods to the idea of one God, and later on in the Upaniṣads to the concept of the unity of Being, which is spiritual, one, eternal, and all-pervading—is the most arresting subject of the Vedic literature. From pluralism to monism was a very high step, which the Vedic seer scaled, and later he successfully reached the summit, when he arrived at the absolute non-dualism of the Upaniṣads.

In the Saṁhitās, we have not only hymns which are meant for the glorification of the Vedic gods and goddesses, but also hymns which have the characteristic of speculative thought. The well-known *Nāsadīya-sūkta,* for instance, is one among the latter group, and such hymns have been termed as 'philosophical hymns'. It is hymns of this category that point to the speculative aspect of the introspective mind of the Vedic seer. They form, as it were, the foundation and the inspiration for the grand philosophy and mysticism of the Upaniṣads, whose teachings, we may add, sustain the spiritual life of India even today, despite the wide gulf of scores of centuries that intervenes between their time and ours.

Intervening the Saṁhitās and the Upaniṣads, we have a class of literature in the Vedas, called the Brāhmaṇas, which contains chiefly sacrificial songs and litanies that are meant for definite ritualistic purposes. These sacrifices are performed in order to propitiate the gods, so that they, in return, may confer on man's health, wealth, and happiness. Not until we come to the pinnacle of Vedic thought, Vedānta—the Upaniṣads—where human insight and intuition penetrate deep into the core of Reality, is the mystery of the universe untravelled. Before the keen intelligence and the searching and pure mind of the Upaniṣadic sage, the ultimate

Truth, which is Existence-Knowledge-Bliss Absolute, stands revealed in all its native splendour and essential nature.

II

In the Upaniṣads, the seer in his quest reaches the spiritual summit, beyond which there is nothing higher to be attained. The grandest teachings of the Upaniṣads are expressed in wonderfully simple words. The unity of Being, ultimate and absolute, is proclaimed in no uncertain terms; this Being or *Sat* is the spiritual essence and basis of the entire universe. All visible forms are only appearances, and their basic reality is only that Being. In truth, apart from that Being, there is no other existence.

In charming poetry and figurative language, through dialogues and dicussions, through stories and narratives, presenting characters of men and women who were themselves the exemplars of their teachings, the Upaniṣads describe in many ways their chief theme, namely, the essential unity of Being, which is spiritual and universal, and the fundamental purity, divinity, and perfection of the human soul, which is nothing but a reflection, a spark of the absolute Being, *Brahman*. The *Ātman,* the Self in man, is, in reality, nothing but *Brahman*. Its embodied state is only apparent, relative, and temporal. With the dawn of true understanding regarding its real nature, engendered by spiritual practices, the Self in man pierces through the vile of ignorance that hides its vision and becomes aware of its unity and identity with the all-pervading, eternal, and infinite *Brahman*. The *Ātman,* indeed, is *Brahman,* which alone is real. All else is an appearance. To aid the human soul in its search after its essential spiritual nature is, then, the end and aim of the Upaniṣads.

The Upaniṣads affirm that behind all diversity, behind all this manifold manifestation, there is only one basic Reality, which is divine. Divinity is the basis of this world, its very soul, its very essence. The appearance of multiplicity is relative, not absolute. Diversity appears because of our non-perception of its spiritual basis, which is one and not many. Once the spirit is perceived,the outer crust of name and form will disappear. To the spiritually awakened, the world does not have any mundane atraction. He sees *Brahman* only everywhere and in everything. *Brahman* is all, and pervades everything. The *Kaṭha Upaniṣad* says: 'Just as fire, though one, having entered the world, assumes separate forms in respect of different shapes, similarly,the Self inside all beings, though one, assumes a form in respect of each shape; and yet It is outside.' 'He is hidden in all beings. ... By the seers of subtle things, He is seen through a pointed and fine intellect.'

The central theme of the Vedāntic thought is beautifully expressed in the very first verse of the *Īśāvāsya Upaniṣad,* which is traditionally enumerated as the first of the ten major Upaniṣads. Its opening statement *'Īśāvāsyamidaṁ sarvam'* proclaims the fundamental unity of all existence and says that it is divine. Everything is enveloped by God; everything is divine. Matter is not; only spirit is. Break through the outer form and enter into the spiritual core. Perception of the spirit is the goal of life. This is the whole scope of religion, the aim of all spiritual endeavour, according to the Indian thought at its best. Regarding this passage of the *Īśāvāsya Upaniṣad,* Gandhiji says: 'If all the Upaniṣads and all other scriptures happened all of a sudden to be reduced to ashes, and if only the first verse in the *Īśa Upaniṣad* were left intact in the memory of the Hindus, Hinduism would live for ever.'

When the spiritual oneness is perceived everywhere, there is no cause for sorrow or misery, which are caused by the notion of duality and separateness. The *Īśa Upaniṣad* says: 'He who sees all beings in the very Self, and the Self in all beings, feels no hatred by virtue of that realization. When to the man of realization all beings become the very Self, then what delusion and what sorrow can there be for that seer of oneness?' The *Kena Upaniṣad* in a grand style shows that the ultimate Reality is the origin, ground, and goal of all our sense perceptions. It says that '*Brahman* alone is really known, when It is known with each state of consciousness'. The *Taittirīya Upaniṣad* asks us to 'seek to know that from which all these beings take birth, that by which they live after being born, that towards which they move and into which they merge', and finally says that It is *Brahman*. *Brahman* is both the cause and the effect of this world. The effect, which is only a spatio-temporal appearance, is not different from the cause. By knowing *Brahman,* the universe is known. The *Chāndogya Upaniṣad* illustrates this idea thus: By knowing *Brahman,* the universe is known. The *Chāndogya Upaniṣad* illustrates this idea thus: 'By knowing one lump of clay, all that is made of clay is known; for the modification is but an effort of speech, a name, and the only reality in it is clay.'

The *Kaṭha Upaniṣad*, through the medium of a simple dialogue couched in sweet poetry and metaphorical language, presents a clear and unified exposition of the Vedāntic thought. Starting with the question of the mystery of death, we are gradually led on to profound spiritual truths. The innate purity of the Self and the unity of Being amidst apparent diversity are brought home to us again and again. This *Upaniṣad* exhorts man to wake up to his spiritual consciousness and asks him not to stop till the goal is reached, though the path leading to the goal is said to be difficult to tread on, like walking on the edge of a sharp razor. It asserts that there is no diversity whatsoever and adds further, 'He who sees as though there is difference here travels from death to death'.

The *Bṛhadāraṇyaka Upaniṣad,* the biggest of all the Upaniṣads, says that the Self is the most beloved of all, for that is the nearest to us and the very essence of our being. A familiar passage of this *Upaniṣad* says: 'It is not for the sake of all, my dear, that all is loved, but for the sake of the Self that it is loved. The Self, my dear Maitreyī, should be realized —should be heard of, reflected on, and meditated upon.' And this passage concludes by offering, as it were, the final answer to the spiritual quest of man: 'By the realization of the Self, my dear, through hearing, reflection, and meditation, all this is known.'

The celebrated *mahāvākyas* (sacred dicta) of the Upaniṣads all unmistakably point to the unity of Being and the identity of the *Ātman* and the *Brahman,* denying all duality or multiplicity in manifestation. The chief concern of the Upaniṣads is the discovery of the eternal and fundamental spiritual reality behind man and nature, and to provide the human soul with inspiration for taking to the spiritual path which would lead to Self-realization. Self-realization brings self-fulfilment; it leads to desirelessness. There is no seeking thereafter, for one's own Self is the repository of all truth, goodness, and beauty. And such is the acme of spiritual perfection.

III

The Vedas and the Upaniṣads are the fountain-head of all later philosophic thought and religious life in India. The yearning of the human soul to realize the Infinite, which permeates the Upaniṣadic atmosphere, continues throughout and expresses itself in diverse ways and forms in later times.

The orthodox philosophies, which grew into definite systems of thought, all without exception swear by the Vedas and the Upaniṣads. The three Vedāntic schools, systematically formulated by the three great Ācāryas—Śaṅkara, Rāmānuja, and Madhva—build their entire superstructure on the foundation of the Upaniṣads. The several religious schools that flourish on the soil of India, and come under the general name of Hinduism, trace their origin to the Vedic religion itself. The Vedic gods later apper in our mythological literature, much more magnified and with greater splendour. The Itihāsas and the Purāṇas, which have contributed so much to the growth of popular Hinduism, all draw their inspiration from the Vedas and the Upaniṣads. The latter-day minor sects and cults, which are but offshoots of the principal religions of India, and which came into being to meet the spiritual and religious needs of the different sections for her population, all look up to the same common source of our spiritual heritage. Even Jainism and Buddhism, which developed outside the pale of orthodox tradition, and did not recognize the authority of the Vedas, could not remain completely free from the influence of certain doctrines which are fundamental to the Vedic religion and philosophy.

In the course of the gradual evolution of the religio-philosophic thought of India, the *bhakti* element, which is noticeable in rudimentary form in the Saṁhitas, becomes its dominant feature. With *bhakti* becoming predominant in the religious life of the nation, there was an efflorescence of the human spirit, which gave expression to its emotional and spiritual cravings in several forms—in devotional literature, of hymns, songs, and lyrics, in art, and in architecture. Through the centuries, a huge volume of religious literature has accumulated in the different parts of the country, both in Sanskrit and in regional languages, which is noted for its deep devoitonal fervour, spiritual insight, and charming poetry. The songs of the classical music of India, both in its southern and northern variations, to put it in one word, are nothing but devotional. The poets and poetesses who composed these songs were themselves great saints, and sang the beauty of the divine vision they had as the crowning glory of their spiritual struggle. Saturated as they are with the deep devotional fervour of the saints who composed them, these songs even today stir the souls of those that listen to them, when they are sung in proper mood and atmosphere. As to the monuments of religious art and architecture, there is hardly any other country in the world which has so many of them sprinkled all over the length and breadth of the land as in India. The temples of India are not only 'the houses of gods and goddesses', but they are also our national art galleries. The masterpieces of sculpture in these temples depict the entire mythology and the deeds of gods. Several of these temples have even anecdotes connected with our Itihāsas and Purāṇas.

Thus, through all these avenues, the devotional feeling of the human soul is sought to be expressed. Whether it is in the hymns of the Vedic sage who praised the deities presiding over the natural phenomena; whether it is in the flashes of spiritual insight of the Upaniṣadic seer which penetrated into the core of Reality; whether it is in the depiction of mythological personalities who were the embodiments of great moral principles and spiritual truths; whether it is in the devotional fervour that became the dominant feature of the latter-day religious schools, sects and mystics; whether it is in devotional songs, hymns, or lyrics; whether it is in sculpture, painting, or architecture—in all these, we notice that the mind of India is ever a thirst for understanding and expressing the ultimate Truth that underlies everything in this universe. And that is the spiritual heritage of India.

The spiritual tradition is a living one in India. Through the corridor of time, this precious heritage has been handed down from generation to generation in an unbroken succession. Right from the beginning, the essential principles of spiritual life were exemplified in the lives of sages, seers, and saints who guided the general masses of our people on the path of righteousness and divine life.

The sanctity that the Indian mind attaches to every object, animate or inanimate, springs from the Vedāntic idea that all is divine. This distinctive attitutde of the Indian mind is reflected in its adoration of every object that is there in heaven or earth—the sun, moon, and stars; oceans and mountains; rivers and pools; animals and reptiles; trees and shrubs; men of extraordinary qualities, every one of these comes in for a share of divine honour and devout worship.

To the Indian, human life is sacred. It is a spiritual sojourn on earth. Its purpose is to help the soul to seek its own divine nature and to get back to its source. Every act we do, every word we utter, every thought we think should become conducive to the gradual unfoldment of our inner spiritual being. Religion provides all kinds of aid in this process of the manifestation of the divine within. To outgrow the animal passions lurking in us, to sublimate all our human aspirations, and to become veritable divinities on earth is the message of the spiritual heritage of India. That mighty stream is flowing by. It is for us to have a dip in it and get refreshed, so that its sacred waters may cleanse us of all dross and make us the worthy inheritors of this invaluable spiritual heritage.

❑❑❑

3

ON THE PEACE INVOCATIONS OF THE VEDAS

Swami Vimalananda

ॐ वाङ्मे मनसि प्रतिष्ठिता मनो मे वाचि प्रतिष्ठितमाविराविर्म एधि वेदस्य म आणीस्थः श्रुतं मे मा प्रहासीरनेनाधीतेनाहोरात्रासन्दधामि ऋतं वदिष्यामि सत्यं वदिष्यामि तन्मामवतु तद्वक्तारमवतु अवतु मां अवतु वक्तारम्। ॐ शान्तिः शान्तिः शान्तिः।

Knowledge can be imparted and assimilated only in an atmosphere of peace and security. Therefore the Vedic study commences with a peace invocation in order to secure this necessary condition. Though this chant is pronounced by the disciple, it is meant for the preceptor as well. The four Vedas to which all the Upaniṣads are but parts have their respective peace invocations. The *mantra* we have recited now is chanted before the study of Upaniṣads.

May my speech be firmly fixed in my mind. May my mind be unswervingly directed towards my speech. O, wisdom! contained in the Vedas, reveal thyself more and more in me. O, thought and speech, you usher into me the knowledge of the Vedas. May not the revealed knowledge depart from me. Day and night continuously let me engage myself in the study of the Veda and I shall declare the right thought therein; I shall declare the Truth revealed by the Vedas. May the Truth protect me; May the Truth protect the Preceptor. Let there be peace in our mind and body and world around.

According to the Vedic seers speech starts from the mind. Speech is again conceived as *laukikī* and *vaidīkī;* the former denoting the discourses of this world and the latter denoting Divine Knowledge or spiritual wisdom beginning with intellectual understanding and ending in Realization. In this *Mantra,* the term *vāk* refers to the religious lore of the Veda. A student of Vedic knowledge is enjoined to think and express in perfect harmony. His mind must be in complete unison with the speech and his speech must be absolutely sincere to his mind. Again the *Mantra* embodies a prayer to the Supreme Spirit for revealing Himself more and more in the aspirant. Through Divine grace alone complete realization of the Truth taught in the Vedas in accomplished. Mind and speech are here spoken of as the ushers *(āṇī)* of Veda or God-knowledge. It was the greatest concern of the Vedic student that knowledge once gained should never slip away from the mind. Not only they prayed for it but also took the strong resolve to live continually, day and night, in remembrance of what they had learnt. In the Vedas, *Ṛtaṁ* and *Satyaṁ* are two pregnant terms denoting the attributes of the Divine Reality. The first term *Ṛtaṁ* translated as 'Right' denotes the unerring laws that govern the universe and the moral principles that rule in the heart of man. The second term *satyaṁ* denotes God as existence. The aspirant after Divine Knowledge engaged in the study of the Vedas declares that these words will be employed in proclaiming to the world the glory of Truth. The *Mantra* concludes with the longing expressed for divine protection. Only when the teacher is strengthened with the necessary competence, enthusiasm and selfless application, and the disciple is vouchsafed with the clear intelligence capable of comprehending, recalling and assimilating the knowledge imparted, success in their endeavour is possible. Hence there is the appropriateness of the last wish. The term peace is repeated three times implying the need of security, for study, in body, mind and environments where learning is conducted.

> ॐ पूर्णमदः पूर्णमिदं पूर्णात्पूर्णमुदोच्यते
> पूर्णस्य पूर्णमादाय पूर्णमेवावशिष्यते।
> ॐ शान्तिः शान्तिः शन्तिः।

This *Mantra* occurs as the first verse of the 5th chapter of the *Bṛhadāraṇyaka Upaniṣad* and is repeated as the peace chant while commencing the study of the Upaniṣads belonging to the *Yajurveda* of one particular recension, (called *Śukla Yajurveda).* According to Śrī Śaṅkarācārya, this verse contains an epitome of the essential teachings of the Vedas. The verse may be freely rendered into English as follows : *Para Brahman* or the Divine Reality transcending the phenomenal world is in itself complete and full. This world is also full because it is filled by that Reality. When the seeker of Truth realizes that Transcendent Reality through this phenomenal reality, as its substance and background, he establishes himself in that all comprehensive Truth, which is the all in all of this world and what is beyond it.

From this paraphrase we can see that four points are made clear in the verse.

1. The Divine Reality which is the goal of the seeker of liberation is beyond the world of *samsāra* and that it remains for ever full and complete without being in anyway limited or tainted by the world. Such a Reality alone constitutes *Mokṣa* or liberation. It is ever perfect, eternal and is of the nature of Intelligence and Bliss. When one realizes It, one is liberated from *samsāra,* without the possibility of ever returning to *samsāra* again. If the Supreme Reality is conceived partly penomenal and partly transcendental there is no security for the liberated soul who has become or who

has discovered his identity with such a Reality. Hence the primary doctrine of Advaita Vedānta is that the Highest Truth is perfection itself and absolutely free from any association with the changing universe. The *Mantra* here sets out reality of this description to be the Highest Truth which is identified with *Mokṣa,* or the goal of every transmigrating soul.

2. In the second word the *Mantra* declares that this world is also *pūrṇa* or complete. Superficially it is a paradox to assert two realities full and perfect. The world is not complete or perfect either as an infinite reality or as the highest of values to be sought by a religious seeker. So, Śrī Śaṅkarācārya points out here that the world is real and complete because the same transcendent Divine reality permeates and sustains the phenomenal world as its core. The world has no existence apart from the background of the Divine Reality. Just as a toy elephant made of wood is not apart from the source out of which it is made, so also world is not apart from its Divine Background. It follows therefore that this world also is *pūrṇa* or full, because its reality is the same *niṣprapañca brahman* (Transcendental Reality).

3. In the third word we are told of the method of *sādhanā* or practice required for the realization of the Supreme Truth. Here the first term *pūrṇāt* refers to the phenomenal world as we see and the second *pūrṇa* refers to the Divine as its background. It is then stated that the Divine is distinguished and worshipped in the phenomenal world. The passive verb *udacyate* is from the root which gives the sense of separating as well as valuing and worshipping. The scripture is for the purpose of showing the way to one who is bound by *saṁsāra.* The bound soul has to see in the world an occasion to get a glimpse of the Divine. Therefore he has to see the perfect in the imperfect world, the perfect Reality of which it is an

appearance and pursue the Reality in and through the world till he attains to this goal.

4. The last line states that when a person attains to realization of the truth,he knows and remains as the perfect whole. This is the description of *Jñāna*. *Jñāna* can arise only when ignorance is dispelled. Ignorance consists of understanding *Brahman* and the world as two opposite realities. As long as a man is engrossed with and sees only the world, he knows not *Brahman*. When he realizes *Brahman*, he sees *Brahman* alone, not the world. Therefore it is stressed that when the seeker of liberation is illumined he grasps *Brahman* and rejects the world and remains as *Brahman*.

The four points hinted by this *mantra* thus bring home to us the outstanding principles of Advaita Vedānta.

ॐ सहनाववतु सहनौ भुनक्तु सहवीर्यं करवावहै
तेजस्विनावधीतमस्तु मा विद्विषावहे ॐ शान्तिः शान्तिः शान्तिः॥

This is the *Śanti Mantra* recited at the beginning of the study of the Upaniṣads in the *Kṛṣṇa Yajurveda* and it appears as a part of the *Taittirīya Upaniṣad*. This again is a prayer expressing the conditions necessary for an effective study of the subject on hand. The prayer is pronounced by the disciple on behalf of himself and the preceptor: 'may *Brahman*, taught in the Vedas, protect us (the preceptor and the diciple) together by granting us knowledge. May we engage ourselves in the pursuit of imparting and receiving knowledge with continued energy. May the learning acquired be efficient and fruitful. May not the disciple's inability to grasp, inadvertance or incorrect procedure bring about hostility between the disciple and the preceptor; may we not be hostile to any one'.

The *Mantra* besides invoking the favour of God for

rendering the process of learning effective through energetic, active and efficient study in an atmosphere of Divine protection and peace, stresses also the need of mutual love and freedom from all feelings of hatred or dislike towards anyone. Knowledge can be communicated and assimilated only in an atmosphere of love.

ॐ आप्यायन्तु ममाङ्गानि वाक्प्राणश्चक्षुश्श्रोत्रमथो बलमिन्द्रियाणि च सर्वाणि सर्वं ब्रह्मोपनिषदं माहं ब्रह्म निराकरोत् अनिराकरणमस्तु अनिराकरणं मेऽस्तु तदात्मनि निरते य उपनिषत्सु धर्माः ते मयि सन्तु ते मयि सन्तु॥

ॐ शान्तिः शान्तिः शान्तिः॥

Let my limbs wax strong. Let my speech, my breath, my eyes, my ears and all my senses become powerful. All is *Brahman* taught in the Upaniṣads. May I not deny that *Brahman*. May not *Brahman* deny me. Emphatically may I never doubt or reject *Brahman*. Those principles and those laws taught in the Upaniṣads, ever devoted to *Ātman,* may those truths be present in me and ever remain in me.

This *Mantra* is the peace chant repeated before the study of the Sāmavedic Upaniṣads. The first condition required in respect of a student is a healthy body, unflagging energy, senses that suffer no defect and strength born of self-confidence. Secondly, an aspirant after spiritual Truth has to start with an active faith in the reality of his quest. Truths that are beyond the experience of the senses cannot be demonstrated at the outset. That all is *Brahman* is an axiom that has to be accepted first on the statement of Śruti alone. That the central subject matter of all the Vedas is *Ātman* or *Brahman* is again a declaration of the Śruti itself. On the acceptance of these two teachings depend the illumination and realization spoken about in Vedānta. He who denies this has nothing to do with religion and spirituality. Threfore it is the constant wish and heartfelt prayer of the student engaged in Vedic study and practice that he may not at any time become an agnostic and deny God or *Brahman*. According to the doctrine of *Bhakti* hinted in the Veda, this is also evident that knowledge of God can arise only through His grace. That is to say God or *Brahman* should not deny Himself to the devotee. This doctrine is of such great importance that the *Mantra* repeats the statement twice in order to emphasize it. The *Mantra* concludes with the entreaty of the aspirant to enable him to possess within himself the qualities and virtues that are taught in the Upaniṣads and which are essential for the attainment of his goal. We can find from this that the Upaniṣads are not meant to be learnt merely as a part of literary education, but as a guiding authority for the practice and accomplishment of spiritual and ethical conduct and realization.

ॐ भद्रं कर्णेभिः शृणुयामदेवा भद्रं पश्येमाक्षभिर्यजत्राः स्थिरैरङ्गैस्तुष्टु-वांसस्तनूभिः व्यशेमदेवहितं यदायुः।।

स्वस्ति न इन्द्रो वृद्धश्रवाः स्वस्ति नः पूषा विश्ववेदाः स्वस्ति नस्तार्क्ष्यो अरिष्टनेमिः स्वस्ति नो बृहस्पतिर्दधातु। ॐ शान्तिः शान्तिः शान्तिः।।

ॐ नमो ब्रह्मादिभ्यो ब्रह्मविद्यासंप्रदायकर्तृभ्यो वंश ऋषिभ्यो महद्भ्यो नमो गुरुभ्यः।।

These two *Mantras* are originally found in the Ṛgveda Saṁhitā 1st maṇḍala 89th Sūkta and are repeated as Śānti *Mantras* before the study of the Atharvaveda Upaniṣads. They are in the form of supplications addressed to various Vedic Gods. Originally these *Mantras* along with some others, which occur in the Ṛgvedic context, were recited at the completion of a *yajña* by the performer of the *yajña* standing in the *yajñavedi*. The sense of the *Mantra* is this: Oh! Devas, may we listen to what is auspicious and good; may we have the strength and capacity to worship you and also may our eyes perceive what is auspicious and beneficial. May we, who sing your praise and pray, live our allotted span of life in perfect health and strength.

May Indra extolled in the Vedas, Pūṣan who knows all, Tārkṣya who saves us from all harm and Bṛhaspati, who protects our spiritual lustre give us progress in the study of the scriptures and practice of the truth taught therein. We offer our salutation to the propounders of the lineage of *Brahmavidyā,* by way of succession from preceptor to disciple beginning with *Brahma* and also to the great *Ṛṣis* who have established *Vidyā Vaṁśa* or the lineage of teaching and learning the Vedic lore and also to the great Gurus who have handed down from generation to generation the knowledge of the Vedas.

The first *Mantra* refers to the aspirant's wish to see and hear only what is good and auspicious. In a mixed world the seeker of spirituality must resolve himself and pray for listening to what is beneficial and seeing what is good. The senses are the gateways of the mind and they are to be guarded properly by refusing admission for evil speech and sight. The next point to be noted : The span of one's life on earth was believed to depend upon the grace of God. Life being a divine gift is best used in the worship and service of God. These can be discharged with efficiency and satisfaction when there is the necessary strength and hence the seers of the Vedas were never tired of praying for strength. Weakness is the contrary of virtue and right strength alone makes life worthwhile. The second *Mantra* is addressed to Indra, Pūṣan, Tārkṣya and Bṛhaspati who were the various Vedic Gods. These names however, need not be taken to imply a plurality of Gods. They are personifications of the different powers and attributes of the Divine reality conceived differently by the devotees for the purpose of worship and supplication of their individual needs. Thus, Indra is the regent of strength, Pūṣan of knowledge, Tārkṣya of protection from harm and Bṛhaspati of religious wisdom. When the welfare of the seeker is secured, he makes progress in his religious path. The last passage is a salutation to all ancient teachers and preceptors through whom knowledge devolves on successvie generations of disciples. This is repeated as a remembrance of one's reverence, gratitude and humility towards the source of knowledge beginning from Brahmā, the first teacher, down to the last one in the link, namely one's own preceptor, without which knowledge cannot dawn or continue in its efficacy.

❑❑❑

4

THE VEDIC CONCEPT OF THE KARMA DOCTRINE

Prakash Dubey

The doctrine of *Karma* may be called the essential element, not only of all moral theories in India, but also of popular belief. (*Encyclopaedia of Religion and Ethics,* Vol. VII, p. 675) With the exception of the Cārvākas, all other systems accord recognition to the doctrine. The Vedic seers have built the temple of wisdom, the tower of which is spiritual fulfilment, on the firm foundation of the *Karma* doctrine. Here we will have a glance over the concept of *Karma* as found in the Vedic literature.

The Meaning of the Concept

Broadly speaking, the meaning of the *Karma* doctrine as accepted in the different Indian systems is as follows: Whatever action is done by the individual leaves behind an impression, which has the power to ordain for him joy and sorrow in the future, according as it is good or bad. When the fruits of actions cannot be enjoyed in the present life, one has to take another birth in order to enjoy them. The act passes away as soon as it is done, but its moral effect is treasured in a potential form, which fructifies in the future. Every single thought, word, or deed enters into the living chain of cause and effect, which makes us what we are.

The Vedic belief was that the *mantras* uttered in the

correct form at the sacrifices with exact observance of ritualistic details, without the slightest error, had a magical virtue to automatically produce the desired object. This was probably the earliest form of the *Karma* doctrine. It implies the faith that certain mystical actions can produce, at a distant time, certain effects without the natural sequence of causal relation. When the sacrifice is performed, the action leaves an unseen *(adṛṣṭa)* new *(apūrva)* magical virtue by which the desired object is achieved. The *modus operandi* of the sequence of act and its result is *adṛṣṭa*. (S.N. Dasgupta : *A History of Indian Philosophy,* Vol. I, p. 71)

The concept of *Karma* is associated with the Vedic conception of *ṛta,* the inviolable order of things. Sin results from the violation of this order in moral sphere. Virtue results from the obedience of this order. In the unalterable law of good and bad effects, flowing from good and bad conduct, are to be found the first germs of the *Karma* doctrine. The unvarying regularity of natural phenomena suggested to the mind of the Vedic seers the idea of unchanging order in nature. The same order was discovered in the moral realm also. Varuṇa was the preserver of this order—*ṛta.* Like the physical order, moral order also produces results in the moral sphere. This moral order is mentioned in the Upaniṣads, where the word *ṛta* is actually used in the sense of *Karma.* (*Kaṭha,* I. iii. 1; also see *Maitrī,* II. vi. 6)

The word *'karma'* is derived from the Sanskrit root *'kṛ'.* Etymologically, *karma* means deed, act, or work. But besides the primary meaning, it has a special meaning. It stands for the sum total of the results produed on the agent by his activity. It stands for the aggregate of the effects wrought on the character and constitution of the agent by his work.

The law of *Karma* emphasizes the importance of

conduct. Man is continually shaping his destiny. Each action has a definite consequence. The universe is ethically sound. The world will be a moral chaos without the moral law of *Karma*. The law of *Karma* is not a blind necessity nor a mechanical rule. It not only implies an extension of the principle of causality to the sphere of morality, but also involves the application of the principle of conservation of energy. The cosmic energy is never destroyed, it only changes its form. The *Karma* theory that all actions must have their inevitable result is due to the principle of conservation of energy. This principle is stated in the Upaniṣadic language thus: 'As you do and behave,so you become.' *(Bṛhadāraṇyaka Upaniṣad,* IV, iv. 5) It is nothing but the extension of the scientific language: 'Action and reaction are equal.'

The law of *Karma* holds that not only an equal physical reaction will take place, but that the wrong will be righted, the sufferer will get his recompense, and the offender his just punishment. This theory satisfies both the demands of human nature, by insisting that an adequate reaction will take place not only in the physical plane, but on the moral plane also. Sri Aurobindo rightly remarks: '*karma* is not merely a mechanical law of antecedent and consequence. *Karma* is action, there is a thing done, and a doer and an active consequence, these three are the three joints, the three locks, the three '*sandhis*' of the connexus of *Karma*.' *(Problems of Rebirth,* p. 118) To these three shall be added, by absolutistic, theistic systems, a fourth also, namely, the giver of the fruits of *karma,* the spirit which constitutes the indwelling reality of the doer. This law is not merely in the vague sense that on the whole good will be rewarded and evil punished. It is a clear and distinct law that every act works out its retribution. Every part of the material universe—man, woman, insect, or tree—is the dweling of an eternal spirit that is working out its destiny. In receiving reward and punishment for the past, it is only laying up for the future. This view of existence as an endless and concomitant sowing and reaping is accepted by the learned and the unlearned alike as accounting for those inequalities in human life which might otherwise lead men to doubt the justice of God.

Traces of the Doctrine in the Saṁhitās

The origin of the *Karma* doctrine may be traced in the Vedas. Though it is not very clearly named as in the later literature, it is not post-Vedic. The idea was fully developed in the form of rebirth and transmigration. Really speaking, it is rebirth and transmigration which have given rise to the doctrine of *Karma*. This doctrine is found in the Saṁhitās, which are the earliest works found. In the *Ṛg-Veda* (IV. xxvi. 1), we find the sage Vāmadeva referring to his former birth: 'I was afore time, Manu, I the sun.'' In another verse, he sets forth the doctrine of transmigration. *(ibid.,* X. lxxxviii. 15) In this verse, the path of the fathers and the path of Gods are described, on which everything meets which moves between father and mother. The dead body either goes through *pitṛyāna* or through *devayāna,* and when all its merits are exhausted, it returns back to be born on earth. Those who die in the bright half of the month of the *Uttarāyaṇa* go through *devayāna* and enjoy heaven. Those who die in the other half go through *pitṛyāna,* and suffer in hell. In a still further verse, Vāmadeva is said to have learnt all the births of the gods lying in the womb. *(ibid.,* IV. xxvii. 1) At one place, Vasiṣṭha refers to his previous births. *(ibid.,* VI. 33) How the particular organs transmigrate to different elements is very clerly described in the Saṁhitās. At death the eye of man goes to sun, the breath to wind, etc. *(ibid.,* X. xvi., 3) The deaths and births, transmigration and suffering in the world, indicate the *Karma* doctrine. Without accepting *Karma,* how can we explain rebirth and transmigration? Rebirth and transmigration prove the law of *Karma*. A clear and direct reference to the *Karma* doctrine is available in a well-known *mantra* of the *Ṛgveda*. God and soul are both in the same phenomenal world, but the former is only the witness of *karma* and the latter enjoys the fruits of *karma*. This has been explained by an analogy: Two birds with fair wings, knit with bonds of friendship in the same sheltering tree have found a refuge. One of them eats the sweet fruitage, the other does not eat, sees only.' (*ibid.*, I. clxiv. 20)

In the Brāhmaṇas

In the Brāhmaṇas also, germs of the *Karma* doctrine are to be found. *Aitareya* and *Śatapatha* are the two most important Brāhmaṇas. The *Śatapatha Brāhmaṇa* (I. vi. 3) says that the consequence of the incorrect performance of rites was to be borne by the sacrificer. 'The deeds pass betwen two fires which lead the good man go safely but burn the evil doer.' Every one is weighed in the balance. Everyone takes birth after death and receives reward or punishment according to past good deeds or bad deeds. This limited idea of *karma* developed into the moral concept that good or evil conduct produced a better or worse character. The *Śatapatha* speaks of repeated births and deaths in the next world, even for the man who has correct knowledge and performs a certain sacrifice, resulting in his attaining immortality. In the Saṁhitās, *Karma* is identified with *ṛta;* here, in the Brāhmaṇas, it is identified with *yajña*. It is *yajña* that gives proper reward and punishment. The ignorant defaulter ultimately becomes the prey of death. The *Aitareya Brāhmaṇa* (XI. 5) refers to a third birth after death, beside that from the father and by initiation.

Prof. A.B. Keith, an eminent orientalist, says that the origination of the transmigration and rebirth is one of the most difficult problems of Indian philosophy. *(Religion and Philosophy of the Vedas and Upaniṣads,* p. 570) He says that the references to transmigration which have been traced in the *Ṛgveda Saṁhitās* are all of the most improbable character. He further says that the Brāhmaṇas contain on the whole no acceptance of the doctrine of transmigration. But his view does not seem sound. If we study the Saṁhitās and the Brāhmaṇas closely, we will find that they contain the doctrine of transmigration and *Karma*. It was to the task of the Brāhmaṇas, the prose treatises which exhaustively describe the ceremonies and explain the significance of the rituals, to develop the idea of *Karma* in association with the introduction of the theory of transmigration.

In the Upaniṣads

The doctrine of *Karma* which was implicit in the Saṁhitās and the Brāhmaṇas is developed in the Upaniṣads fully. The ethical doctrine of *Karma,* connected with the doctrine of transmigration, is developed in *Bṛhadāraṇyaka Upaniṣad*. It is a poetic beauty, unsurpassed, perhaps, in the literature of the world. It is the earliest and clearest description found in the Vedic literature. It tells us about the fortunes of the souls and incidentally develops the doctrine of the transmigration of souls and, in close connection with it, the ethical doctrine of *Karma*. *Karma,* with the infallibility of the law of nature, must produce its consequences and regulate the new births. New birth depends on man's own deeds and makes man truly 'an architect of his own fate'. This is the germ of the Buddhist doctrine, which, while denying the existence of soul altogether, allows *karma* to continue after death and determine the next birth. With pointed examples, the *Bṛhadāraṇyaka Upaniṣad* (IV. iv. 4, 5) sets forth the doctrine thus : Just as a goldsmith takes a piece of gold, and out of it creates a different, a newer, and more beautiful design, so does the self throw this body away, or make it senseless, and make another—a newer and more beautiful one, that of the manes, or *gandharva,* of a god, or Prajāpati, or man, or that of some other being. As he has acted, as he has lived, so he becomes; he who has done good is born again as good one, he who has done evil is born again as evil one. He becomes good through good action, bad through bad action. Therefore it is said: 'Man here is formed entirely out of his desire, and according to his desire he has his resolve, and according to his resolve, he performs action, and according to the performance of the action is his destiny.

The *Karma* doctrine was, however, not accepted without the influence of its ethical element, viz reward and punishment for merit and demerit. The same word *karma,* which meant ritual act in the Saṁhitās and Brāhmaṇas, means in the Upaniṣads moral act and the result of action. This appears in the clearest form in the mouth of Yājñavalkya, who has been its originator. Man suffers dissolution at death, but his *karma* is the cause of a new birth which inherits the good or bad deeds of the former life. This doctrine gives place to a compromise in the theory of five fires mentioned in the *Chāndogya Upaniṣad* (V. 10). In the *Chāndogya* (VIII. i. 6), we find the temporal nature of *karma.* The *karmas* meant for either here or hereafter are of temporal existence. Those who die without knowing the true nature of the Self do not get their fulfilment. Those who go to the other world with the knowledge of the Self and all its true wishes get proper place in all the worlds. Here are the seeds of absolutistic interpretation of the *Karma* doctrine interpreted by great Śaṅkarācārya, which will be the subject matter of the fifth chapter. The *Chāndogya* view is an advance towards the absolutistic trend.

It must be noted that the Upaniṣads teach a twofold retribution, once in the other world and again in this world. This has led to a good deal of misunderstanding. Professor Deussen failed to grasp the true character of the Upaniṣadic doctrine (see *The System of the Vedānta*). When all extraneous circumstances disappear at death, the soul is left with nothing but a configuration of the subtle body, and the kārmic traces of the causal body as the result of his past deeds. This configuration determines the place of the life of man and his character in the next world. (*Bṛhadāraṇyaka Upaniṣad,* IV. iv. 5) Again, as a result of the life lived in the other world, there arise further traces in the causal body, leading to its final configuration, and when the subtle body is destroyed in the other world, the soul is left with nothing but this configuration of the causal body called *'Karma'. (ibid.,* III. ii. 13) It is this *karma* which causes reincarnation on earth. This is the law of *Karma*. Thus, the Upaniṣadic theory of a twofold retribution is not a self-contradictory theory as Deussen thinks, but a natural consequence of the complex constitution of man.

Next teaching of the Upaniṣadic doctrine of *Karma* is that the quality of our life in this and in the other world is determined by the quality of our actions performed in this and the next world. (*ibid.,* III. ii. 13; also *Kaṭha,* II. ii. 7; *Praśna,* III. 7) This doctrine, if rightly understood, should provide the strongest incentive to moral efforts, for, by throwing all responsibility on the individual, it saves him from supernaturalism, and puts him on his guard against vices which yield the harvest of evil here and hereafter.

It was generally believed that it required some time before the *adṛṣṭa karma* could fructify and give the doer the reward or punishment. Only the imprints of those actions which are extremely wicked or particularly good could be reaped in this life. The nature of the next birth is determined according to the maturing acts of this life. Duration of this life is determined by the acts of the past life. Once a certain action becomes fit for giving certain experiences, these cannot be avoided. But those actions which have not matured are uprooted once for all, if right knowledge of the Self or *Brahman* is attained.

There are four kinds of *karma* advocated in the Upaniṣadic or Vedic literature: (1) *śukla-karmas,* 'bright' or meritorious acts; (2) *kṛṣna-karmas,* 'dark' or vicious acts, which result in demerit; (3) *śukla-kṛṣa-karmas,* where merit and demerit are combined together, and (4) *aśuklā-kṛṣṇa-karmas,* acts which are neither meritorious nor vicious. It is the last kind of *karma* which the *Gītā* expounds. Only this kind of *karma* gives liberation, because it does not produce virtue or sin, being desireless and passionless. It is the act of self-renunciation or meditation which is not associated with any desire for fruit. (S.N. Das Gupta : *A History of Indian Philosophy*, Vol. I, p. 72)

An Objection to the Doctrine of Karma

An objection is raised by some against the doctrine of *Karma,* because many self-contradictory and inconsistent ideas regarding the doctrine are found in later literature. (See Hopkins : *Journal of the Royal Asiatic Society,* July 1906, pp. 581 ff.) Transmigration of souls and transfer of *karma* from father to son, or from guest to host, or from husband to wife, or from king to subject, for example are found in the laws of Manu, the *Mahābhārata* and the *Bhāgavata*. Not only good *karmas* but bad *karmas* are also shared by the inmates. The main obstacle to a right understanding of the *Karma* doctrine is man's tendency to use his personal ideas of fairness, rightness, and justice, all of which are significant and applicable only within the limited sphere of human relations. The reward-punishement ideology is also a great obstacle to the right understanding of the doctrine. Many believe that what is pleasant or unpleasant is the exact reward or punishment for past good or evil done by the same man. But no individual is wholly a separate person, for he is intimately interrelated with others around him. We are all interlocked in *karma* (action) and its consequences on others.

The law wholly fulfils itself. Each man's action in thought, word, or deed works out and bears fruit in unison with his whole environment. In fact, the whole dynamic world process is one of continuous actions. This process, which includes nature, man, and the workings of the Divine, is the kārmic process.

The kārmic process, in so far as it involves the operation of natural law and human law, is indispensable. Suffering, expiation, etc. cannot be written off arbitrarily. 'Man has always to wash his sin stained feet in the blood of his heart.' In fact, the truly repentant will gladly accept the suffering consequent upon wrong-doing as testimony of sincere repentance. Thus, man can rise to purify and absolute selflessness and unite with the ultimate reality.

Karma and Spirituality

Karma is not mere physical law of conservation of energy or causality. It is not a mere blind force that operates impersonally and aimlessly. It is not insentient will that blindly unfolds into the world of diversity constituting and contributing to the diverse experiences of living beings. The law of *Karma* is a spiritual law. It relates to the process underlying spiritual evolution and adjustment upon the higher planes. It is a spiritual law of cause and effect, which ensures the yield of just and right results, so that throughout evolution perfect balance is maintained.

The law of *Karma* must not be confused with hedonistic or juridical theory of reward and punishment. The reward for merit is not a life of pleasure, nor is punishment for sin animal pain. (S. Radhakrishnan : *An Idealistic View of Life,* p. 275) Pleasure and pain may govern the lower or animal nature of man, but man is not a mere animal. Through suffering and sorrow is brought about a chastening of the soul, its evolution in a spiritual sense. It is this goal that the law of *Karma* aims at. Moral purity is a necessary pre-condition for the advent of spiritual life. *Karma,* when sublimated and transformed, becomes the life of the spirit. The *Muṇḍaka Upaniṣad* (I. ii. 1) says that the intelligent seers directly intuited the true significance of *karma.* By doing them with the proper perspective, one may get the best out of them. The *Bṛhadāraṇyaka Upaniṣad* (IV. iv. 6) also has described the spiritual nature of *karma.* The man who desires *karma* gets the specific result. He goes to the other world to enjoy the results, and after exhaustion of *karmas,* he again returns back to this world. Only a man who has desire for results does so. The man who is desireless, whose desires are self-fulfilled, attains Brahmanhood by being *Brahman.* What is implied here is the sequence between desire for result of the *karma* and desirelessness, the former being a schooling for the latter. In this sense, *Karma* is a spiritual law.

Karma is the bond that binds the soul to *saṁsāra* and also a preparation and schooling for transcending *saṁsāra.* This is why the different philosophical systems of India in quest of realizing the highest value of spiritual freedom *(mokṣa)* accord a central place to the discussion of this doctrine. Spiritual freedom is conceived more or less uniformly in all of them as implying, among other things, freedom from the law of *Karma*. And this freedom, again, is conceived in some sense or other to depend upon the understanding of the inner dynamics of the law of *Karma*. A true knowledge of *karma* and its operation is among the means for achieving freedom from *karma*.

❑❑❑

5

THE GRANDEST DISCOVERY OF THE UPANIṢADS

M.K. Venkatarama Iyer

From very early times the main concern of philosophy has been the quest after Ultimate Reality. This quest is the outcome of man's intense desire to ascertain what is permanent and unchanging behind and beneath the passing shows of the external world and the everchanging states of the interal self. It takes two forms, objective and subjective. The former consists in making a thoroughgoing analysis of the phenomena of nature, while the latter proceeds by studying the internal states through which an individual passes in the course of a single day. Since the Upaniṣadic view seems to be that reality, external or internal, is thickly laid over with incrustations, it is the method of analysis and elimination that is found most suitable. Under favourable conditions provided by nature, it is possible to discover what remains as the hard, inner core, when all else that is in the nature of superimpo-sition has been removed one by one. In western logic this method is known as 'Natural Experiment'.

Bernard Bosanquet has said in one of his Gifford Lectures that if we carry out a systematic and dispassionate analysis of the experiences of a normal human being running through a single day, we will be able to establish the philosophical creed known as Absolute Idealism which believes in the ultimacy of spirit. But by and large western thinkers do not bestow much thought on this line of approach. Their studies are confined to the waking experience of man and the objective world which is presented to it. If they study the phenomena of dreams at all, they do so purely from the psychological and not from the metaphysical point of view. Needless to say that they give little or no thought to the phenomenon of dreamless sleep. As for mystical experiences, they are dismissed as apocryphal. Poets may indulge in them but philosophers can have no concern with them.

In refreshing contrast to this one-sided view, we find Indian thinkers bestowing equal attention on both lines of approach to reality. The Nyāya-Vaiśeṣika and the Sāṁkhya systems of thought have made systematic attempts to arrive at Ultimate Reality by the analysis of the external world. In the view of the Nyāya-Vaiśeṣika the whole world is reducive to matter which, in its turn, lends itself to further analysis. It is found that the tiniest particle of matter is the atom *(aṇu)*. The analysis does not stop here. It proceeds to break up the atom into two dyads *(dvaṇuka)* and again each dyad into three ultimate particles known as *paramāṇu*. The objects of the world take shape by the combination of these ultimate particle of which, however, there are many kinds.

Withou entering into a detailed examination of the *paramāṇu-vāda,* we may only note that the atoms, being insentient, cannot come together of their own accord. It is necessary, therefore, to recognize another entity endowed with sentience. This is what the Sāṁkhya calls *Puruṣa*. It also shows that since there can be no variety or difference in the so-called ultimate particles, we may stop with matter *(Prakṛti)* and not proceed further with the analysis. *Prakṛti* and *Puruṣa* are the two ultimate entitites to which, according to the Sāṁkhya, the whole world is reducible. *Prakṛti* is composed of three *guṇas, sattva, rajas* and *tamas*. These are not its attributes but its very constituents. The mere presence of *Puruṣa* is enough to disturb the equilibrium of the three *guṇas* and set *Prakṛti* in motion. This is called evolution or *sarga*. It is needless to go into the details of the process of evolution.

The Vedāntic criticism is that since *Prakṛti* cannot move except in the presence of *Puruṣa,* it must be treated as insentient *(jaḍa)*. It can neither move of its own accord nor reveal itself. It exists but does not know that it exists. It has being *(sat)* and no knowing *(chit)*. It follows that *Prakṛti* does not have the same ontological status as *Puruṣa*. It must be held to be subordinate to the latter. And again, *Puruṣa,* being pure sentience, can admit of no plurality. There is no warrant to believe in a multiplicity of *Puruṣas*. If the unessential elements in them are eliminated, only pure sentience will remain which obviously cannot be more than one.

Thus we arrive at the conception of spirit which has matter for its adjunct. This is the *Īśvara* of the Vedānta. The Upaniṣad[1] speaks of 'spirit hidden in the *guṇas*'. Further analysis of *Īśvara* leads to the conception of *Saguṇa Brahman* which is a complex of spirit and matter. The latter is shown to be a superimposition on Pure Spirit owing to foundational ignorance. When this ignorance is dispelled by the advent of right knowledge, matter automatically disappears and *Brahman* emerges as the sole reality. It is strictly 'the one without a second'. All this is beautifully set forth in Uddālaka's instruction to his son Śvetaketu. This section of the Chāndogya Upaniṣad is a good example of reaching the highest reality through the objective method. He shows in the first instance that the whole world is reducible to matter and mind. Then he points out that the latter is only a transformation of the former in one of its varieties known as *anna* the other two being water and fire. Through permutation and combination *(trivṛt karaṇa)* these three become gross elements. In their subtle form they are mere projections of *Brahman* who is spoken of as *sat*. It must also be a sentient entity *(chit)* since it is said to have thought *(aikṣat)* before projecting itself. As we have already shown, sentience is always homogeneous. There being no variety or difference in it, there can be no discord or tension. It must therefor be full of bliss *(ānanda)*. Putting the three notions together we get the conception of *Brahman* as *Saccidānanda*. That the finite self *(Jīva)* is identical with *Brahman* is first boldly declared by means of the *mahāvākya 'Tat Tvam Asi'* and then demonstrated by means of a number of analogies such as rivers losing their individuality when they discharge their waters into the sea, and honey collected by bees from different sources becoming one and homogeneous when once it is put into the pool. Thus by adopting the objective method of study Uddālaka establishes the supremacy of *Brahman* as the sole reality.

The Upaniṣadic thinkers proceed to reinforce this conclusion by analysing the states through which an individual passes in the course of a day. This is not the same as the anaysis of the experiences of man such as ethical, aesthetic, religious and mystical.[2] These experiences relate only to the waking state. They therefore admit of being studied in an objective manner. But our concern just now is with the states of man other than his waking condition. These are the dream and dreamless-sleep states. A few gifted souls who have successfully gone through the discipline of the eight fold *yoga* have a fourth state known as *Turiya*. This also will have to be studied with a view to discover the inmost reality of man. Prajapati's instruction to Indra,[3] Yājñavalakya's instruction to Emperor Janaka[4] and Ajātaśatru's instruction to Balāki[5] are based on the analysis of the three states. The *Māṇḍūkya Kārikā.* The identification of the three states with the three letters, *a, u* and *m* which constitute the mystic syllable *'Aum'* and the further identification of the fourth syllable known as *'amātra'* with the fourth syllable known as *'amātra'* with the fourth *pāda* called *Turiya* have contributed to the great esteem in which this Upaniṣad is held. The *Muktikopaniṣad*[6] maintains that the proper study of this one Upaniṣad is by itself sufficient to carry a man to his highest goal. In some other Upaniṣads[7] also there are stray references to the analysis of the three states.

In the waking state the mind as well as the organs of sense are fully active and through the latter the former gets into touch with the objects of the external world. This impact gives rise to sensation which are vague and indeterminate. They are worked up into judgments by the mind which interprets them in terms of categories like *jāti, guṇa, karma* and so forth. These judgments are next referred to the intellect *(buddhi)* which decides on the course of action that is found necessary. The circuit then becomes complete. The bulk of our knowledge arises in this way and it is known as *pratyakṣa jñāna.*

In sleep our sense-organs are quiescent. They cease to function and consequently the mind loses touch with the external world. But all the same, we have perceptions. As the Upaniṣad[8] puts it: 'There are no chariots, nor animals to be yoked to them, nor roads there, but the mind creates the chariots, animals and roads.' This statement is typical of all dream experiences. All that we see, hear, taste, smell and touch in the waking state is reproduced in sleep. But dream perceptions do not look like old memories recalled for the moment. They are clear, vivid and have the same feeling of 'presentess' as the waking perceptions. The mind is active in that state and making use of the impressions of the waking state, it constructs curious and fanciful judgments. The Upaniṣad[9] speaks of the mind as the agent of dream perceptions. 'When he sleeps he takes way a little of the impressions of this all-embracing world, viz., the waking state,' and constructs the perceptions that we see in dreams.

These are so many states of the mind called *Vṛttis*. Since they are insentient and cannot reveal themselves, we must suppose that they are rendered luminous by some innerlight. In the waking state we have the light of the sun and moon and we may think that the states of mind are revealed by their light, but in sleep they are absent. Light therefore must come from some other source. In his instruction to Emperor Janak, Yājñavalkya points out that when the sun, moon,fire and the human voice have all failed, it is the light of the innerself that serves our purpose. This light is unfailing. Even in the waking state it is this inner light that renders the *vṛttis* luminous and not the light of the sun or moon. That in the state of dream, though the sun and the moon are absent, we still have perceptions proves conclusively that the light which renders them luminous comes from the self.[10] In this state (dream) the man himself becomes the light (Bṛ. Up. IV. iii. 10).

The next state is dreamless sleep. This is defined as the state wherein the sleeper has no desires and consequently perceives nothing. This definition seems to anticipate the modern Freudian theory that dreams are wishfulfilling in nature. Unfulfilled desires, according to Freud, find satisfaction in dream constructions. But if there are no desires at all there can be no dreams either. Since the mind is the seat of desire, the absence of the latter implies the quiescence of the former. In dreamless sleep, therefore, even the mind does not function. In absence of perceptions, this state may look like a blank, a mere void and total annihilation. That is how it strikes Indra and he expresses his dissatisfaction to Prajapati.[11]

But it is wrong to think that when there are no particular perceptions, the inner light that illumines them also gets extinguished. In the waking and dream states there are the *vṛttis* and the inner light serves to illumine them. In the state of dreamless sleep, since even the mind ceases to function, there is nothing to illumine and the inner light shows that it is a void or blank. The author of *Pancadaśī* gives the example of the light which continues to burn on the stage even after the dancer and the spectators have retired. The light then shows that there is nothing in that place. Even this is a judgment and it presupposes a light which illumines the void. The inner light is sentience all-compact and it can never suffer extinction.[12]

We recall that experience the next morning and exclaim 'I slept well, I did not know anything'. We recall only those experiences which we have actually perceived previously. Recall also presupposes the presence of an entity common to both past and present. Some entity which was the witness of the void of the previous state of dreamless sleep must be present in the waking state also. In the absence of such a connecting link we can never remember the past experience of happy, dreamless sleep. The sentient element which lights up the perceptions of the waking and sleep states is also the entity which shows that there is nothing to be perceived in the state of dreamless sleep and which enables one to recall that experience the next morning. It follows that the sentient element is the constant factor involved in all the three states. It is called the witness consciousness *(sākṣi jñāna)*. The states may come and go, but this goes on for ever. It is the light of all our seeing and hearing, it is the light which illumines all our dream-perceptions and finally, it is the light which burns by itself even when there is nothing to illumine.

Even if we confine our attention to the experiences of the waking state alone we reach the same conclusion. It is well-known that in the waking state we have a succession of *vṛttis*. It is a series. One state is different from another. And yet we have knowledge of these different states as constituting a series. In a cinema show a number of pictures is projected on the canvas in quick succession. Supposing there is no one to witness the whole show, can the snaps be aware of themselves as constituting a series? No. In the same way, there are our mental states, each differing from the others and each making place for another. If we have knowledge of the series as a while and as meaning something, it presupposes a witness consciousness. Knowledge of change and difference is possible only if there is a knowing entity which is changeless and always identical with itself. A *sākṣin* is therefore implicit in our knowledge of change and difference. 'A series', as T.H. Green as well said, 'cannot be aware of itself as a series.' If, as the Buddhists maintain, there is nothing constant either in the external or in the internal world and everything is reduced to a series, we cannot explain how any knowledge can arise at all. The knowledge of change presupposes something unchanging; knowledge of difference presupposes something that remains identical with itself. Change and difference may pertain to the object of knowledge but not to the knowing subject.[13]

Freed from its adventitious association with the sense-organs, mind and intellect, the Self is then said to rest in itself and be united with the Real.[14] It emerges from its limitations and rises to its full stature. 'The serene light, rising out of the body, and having reached the highest light, appears in its own form.'[15] The nature of this transcendence has been elucidated by Śrī Śaṅkara by the examples of stars beginning to shine at night when the sun is no longer there to overpower them, a white crystal appearing in its real colour when the red flower is removed from its proximity. In its true state the self is known as the *Atman*.

The fourth state is known as *Turiya*. It is a shortened form of *Caturiya*. Since it passes beyond the subject-object relation, it does not admit of a positive description. Hence it is named the fourth state. In this state consciousness of the Absolute is transformed into Absolute Consciousness *(akhaṇḍa caitanya)*. There is no perceiver and perceived, no knower and known. It is impartite consciousness which nullifies all distinctions including that between subject and object.[16] In one of his minor poems known as *Swarūpānusandhānāṣṭakaṁ* (5) Śrī Śaṅkara gives some account of the Yogin's experience in this fourth state : 'The *Poorṇa (Brahman)* which is beyond the three states, which is non-dual and one, makes itself manifest to the mind of the yogin who is in deep *samādhi*. He realizes that it is identical with his inmost Self.'[17]

The *Poorṇa* is realized at this stage to be identical with the inmost Self of the Yogin. The two lines of approach to reality converge here. It is like two astronomers observing a planet or star from two different parts of the world and ultimately discovering that both of them have been studying the same heavenly body. This equation *'Ātmā ca Brahma'* is the grandest contribution which the Upaniṣads have made to philosophic thought. It will stand unchallenged for all time.

REFERENCES

1. देवात्मशक्तिं स्वगुणैर्निगूढाम्। Svet. Up. I.3.
2. This is a different subject for study. If it is carried out in full it will lend additional support to the main conclusion of the Upanisads.
3. Chāndogya VIII. vii to xi.
4. Br. Up. IV. iii.
5. Br. Up. II. i. 15-19.
6. माण्डूक्यमेवालं मुमुक्षूणां विमुक्तये। Muktikopaniṣad, 26.
7. Kaṭha, IV. 4; Praśṇa, IV; VI. 8; Kaivalya, 13; Kausitakī, III. 3.
8. Br. Up., IV. iii. 10.
9. Br. Up., Iv. iii. 10.
10. Sri Sankara writes :
    अपि च जागरिते विषयेन्द्रियसंयोगात् आदित्यादि व्यतिरेकाच्च आत्मनः स्वयं ज्योतिष्टवं दुर्विवेचनमिति तद्विवेचनाय स्वप्न उपन्यस्तः।
    Vol. III. p. 566. (Memorial Edition, Sri Vani Vilas Press).
11. Ch. Up., VIII. xi. 1. विनाशमेव अपीतो भवतिA
12. Br. Up., IV. iii. 30.
    नहि विज्ञातुः विज्ञातेः विपरिलोपो विद्यते अविनाशित्वात्।
13. In his *Atma Vidya Vilasa,* Sri Sadasiva Brahmendra writes:
    भेदोऽपि साच्यगत एव न साक्षिणीमे भेदस्य साक्षिणि कथं प्रभवेत्स भेदः।
14. Ch. Up., VI. viii. 1.
13. Ch. Up., VIII. xii. 3.
16. Compare Haristuti : 4
    ज्ञातृ ज्ञान ज्ञेय विहीनोऽपि सदा ज्ञः।
17. निषेधे कृते नेति नेतीति वाक्यैः समाधिस्थितानां यदाभति पूर्णम्।
    अवस्थात्रयातीतमद्वैतमेकं परं ब्रह्मनित्यं तदेव ह्यस्मि।।

❑❑❑

6

THE CONCEPT OF MĀYĀ IN THE UPANIṢADS

M.K. Venkatarama Iyer

This is a highly controverted question. The critics of Śrī Śaṅkara maintain that the concept of *Māyā,* which is the keystone of his edifice of Advaita, finds no support in the classical Upaniṣads, of which that system purports to be a systematic formulation. They contend that the concept is wholly extraneous to those ancient treatises and that it is a pure invention of his. Some critics suggest that he has imported it from Buddhism, since it is powerfully reminiscent of the Mādhyamika *Śūnya Vāda (sarvam śūnyam),* especially of the statement of Nāgārjuna, in his *Mula Madhyamika Karika,* that when we begin to reflect on things they give way and dissolve. Hence Śri Śaṅkara is charged by some of his uncharitable critics with being a Buddhist in disguise *(Praccanna-bauddha).*[1] The attack against the concept is directed as much from the historical as from the doctrinal side. The critics are of the opinion that if they succeed in pulling it down the whole structure of Advaita will collapse like a house of cards.

Since our concern in this paper is with its historical aspect alone, we have to enter into a somewhat detailed and close examination of the essential teachings of the Upaniṣads. Paul Deussen who has made a careful study states, in his *Religion and Philosophy of the Upaniṣads,* that though the concept of *Māyā* is not explicitly discussed in them, it is certainly implicit in their teachings and that it is the necessary, logical complement of the doctrine of the sole reality of *Brahman* taught in several texts. George Thibaut lends indirect support to this view in his own way. He thinks that though Śrī Śaṅkara's doctrines of *Nirguṇa Brahman* and *Māyā* are not found in the *Vedānta Sūtras* they are certainly taught in the Upaniṣads which form the basis of the *Sūtras*. We may or may not agree with him in thinking that there is a rift between the Upaniṣads and the *Vedānta Sūtras*; we are only to note that in his view Śri Śaṅkara's philosophy is fully in accordance with the teachings of the Upaniṣads.

Before entering into an analysis of their main teachings, we may state that direct references to the term Māyā are not altogether absent in them. In the *'Madhu Vidyā'* we read: 'Indra (the Lord) appears in manifold forms by the powers of His Māyā'[2] (notions superimposed by ignorance). In the *Śvetāśvatara,* which though not a classical Upaniṣad is not a very late one, it is stated that *Māyā* is *Prakṛti* and its wielder is *Īśvara*.[3] The term *avidyā* occurs in many contexts[4] in the Upaniṣads. Its connotation is the same as that of *Māyā*. The only difference is in respect of its incidence. *Avidyā* is the adjunct of the finite self *(Jīva)* while *Māyā* is the adjunct of the Cosmic Self *(Īśvara)*. By whatever name it is called, its function is the same. It conceals the true nature of an object and projects something totally different in its place. These two functions of concealing and projecting arise from its two powers known as *āvaraṇa śakti* and *vikṣepa śakti*. The statement, in the *Chāndogya*[5] that true desires are hidden by the untrue and that though people daily go to the region of *Brahman,* they know it not as they are carried away by the untrue contains a reference to *Māyā* though this term does not explicitly occur in it. True desires being hidden by untrue ones can only mean that the former are concealed by the power of *Māyā*. The finite self is in essence identical with *Brahman* but being deluded by primeval *avidyā* it is unable to realize this. This is the import of that passage.

We may now take up for consideration the important and most purportful passages and see what they imply, what has necessarily to be assumed to make them intelligible. Among them the pride of place must be given to the statement which declares unequivocally that reality is one without a second.[6] This passage is not content with saying that reality is one; it goes on to add that there is no second. This additional declaration is significant. It is meant to deny any kind of difference. A cow, for example, is different from a horse, different from other animals of the same species and there are also different limbs in its bodily organism. These differences must be kept in mind to know a particular cow properly. These differences may be termed external *(vijātīya)*, internal *(sajātīya)* and organic *(svagata)*. These differences must be kept in view to arrive at a clear knowledge of any object. We must know how it differs from objects belonging to another species, how, again, it differs from similar objects belonging to the same species and how it is diversified within itself. The point of the additional declaration in the passage quoted above is to deny these kinds of difference with regard to *Brahman*. These denials add emphasis to the first part of the passsage. We are to understand, therfore, that *Brahman* is supreme, transcendent, indefinable, unclssifiable and beyond all relations.

It follows that only negative definitions are possible. Generally we define any object by reference to the higher genus to which it belongs and by stating the peculiar qualities which distinguishes it from the other similar objects comprehended under the same genus *(per genus et differen-*

tia). But such a positive definition is out of the question so far as *Brahman* is concerned. We can therefore only say what it is not, and not what it is. Such negative definitions are found in the Upaniṣads in many contexts. There is first of all, Yājñavalkya's famous declaration, 'Not this, not this' *(neti neti)*.[7] This clearly means that no quality that can think of, can possibly be predicated of *Brahman*. Nothing on this side of human experience, however refined or exalted, can be affirmed of it. There is no use of lacing a forced interpetation on this text. It neither means 'not only this, not only this' nor 'not that it is no'. Its plain meaning is that it is beyond thought and speech.[8] The eye goes not there, nor speech nor mind.[9] Since it is attributeless it can only be described as neither gross nor subtle, neither short nor long, neither red nor any other colour, neither shadow nor darkness neither air nor ether[10] and so forth.

As if to reinforce the statement that *Brahman* is the sole reality, the Upaniṣads proceed to declare that if this is known everything else is known. In two contexts[11] the question is asked about the Supreme Reality by knowing which one could claim to know everything else. The answer to these questions is found in Yājñavalkya's discourse to his wife: 'The *Ātman*, O Maitreyi, should be realized—should be heard of, reflected on and meditated upon. By the realization of the *Ātman,* through hearing, reflection and meditation, all this is known.'[12] What exactly does this declaration mean? How can one who has realized the *Ātman* claim knowledge of everything else? Broadly speaking we may say that in addition to the *Ātman* there are two other realities of which we are aware in our everyday experience, the world of inanimate things and a plurality of finite selves. We may assume that these two are either created by the *Ātman* or are its manifestations. Even so it is not easy to understand how by ralizing the *Ātman* one can claim to know all things created by it or all the forms of finite through which it has manifested itself. There are no examples in support of such a contention. The potter creates pots with the help of clay, but since he is only the efficient cause, he remains outside the articles he creates. By knowing him we cannot claim to know all about the earthenware he creates. Clay enters into the pots and jugs and the latter may be said to be the forms in which the former has manifested itself. But these are not the only manifestations of clay. It may take many other forms. And further, clay by itself is incapable of undergoing modifications. By knowing clay, therefore one cannot claim to know all its manifestations. It follows that neither the knowledge of the efficient cause by itself nor of the material cause by itself enables one to know all things that follow from them. We may combine the two causes in *Īśvara* so far as the world and the finite selves are concerend. Even so it does not follow that by knowing *Īśvara* will cease to be an independent reality only if the realizes his identity with the latter. The identity can be realized only by removing all the adventitious adjuncts from both. After this removal only the spark of the spirit will remain. Both the sparks will merge in the Universal Spirit which is their source. Both *Jīva* and *Īśvara* merge in *Brahman*. Nothing else then remains to be known.

This is the import of the *Mahāvākyas* found in the Upaniṣads. 'There are four of them, 'That thou art', 'I am *Brahman*', 'This *Ātman* is *Brahman*' and 'Consciousness is *Brahman*'. These are found in the *Chāndogya, Bṛhadāraṇyaka, Māṇḍūkya* and *Aitareya Upaniṣads* respectively. A full discussion of the import of these great sayings is outside the scope of this paper. It is enough if we add that they affirm the identity in essence between the finite self *(Jīva)* and the Supreme Self *(Brahman)*. The identity is realized by the proces of analysis and elimination. The spiritual element in both is stripped bare of all its material appurtenances. When the latter fall away, the spiritual element in both merge in their source, even as the reflected images of the sun merge in the latter when the water in the pools gets dried up.

So far we have shown that the finite souls do not stand over against *Brahman* as an independent reality, but are only mere appearances arising from an adventitious circumstance. There still remains the world of nature with all its manifold diversity. This is a given fact of experience. It is the scene of all our labours. We live and move and have our being in it. We are so closely bound up with it that its denial appears unimaginable. And yet the Upaniṣads proclaim : 'There is no diversity here.' This statement occurs in two contexts.[13] To reinforce this declaration the Upaniṣad goes on to add that the man who sees diversity goes from death to death. It means that only by realizing the sole reality of *Brahman* a man qualifies himself for release from the cycle of transmigration. Knowledge of the sole reality of *Brahman* makes for release while knowledge of diversity makes for bondage. To elucidate this point, the Upaniṣad adds that if a man sees even a second reality, fear arises for him.[14] Fear makes for bondage while utter fearlessnss is the same as the state of *Mokṣa*.[13]

How can the world of diversity be conjured away? The Upaniṣads are clear in their declaration that so long as we carry the world with us, in its unmanifest or manifest form, there is no release from bondage. It must fall away and it will do so when we realize that it is a mere appearance arising from adventitious circumstances. We cannot get rid of it by trying to integrate it somehow with Brahman. It is the method of analysis and elimination that will avail and not the method of synthesiṣ and reconciliation. In the rope-serpenṭ illusion for example, we get to know the truth not by somehow connecting the latter with the former but by firmly rejecting it. A higher level of knowledge always results in the total rejection of the notions which we previously held. When we come to the waking state the lion that was pursuing us in dream simply disappears. We do not believe that it has taken shelter in some cave in the neighbourhood.

The same thing takes place with regard to our knowledge in the waking state itself. Fresh discoveries in the field of science lead to the total rejection of the older theories. The old Ptolemaic Astronomy was simply put on the shelf when the fresh theory of Galileo and Copernicus took the field. There was no way of reconciling the two. Newton's laws of motion were given the go-by in the light of Einstein's theory of relativity. The theory of Evolution propounded by Darwin has been completely superseded by recent theories of emergent evolution. It is needless to add more examples.

The same law of replacement of old notions by new knowledge obtains in the field of spiritual experience also. The world with all the knowledge that has gathered round it in the shape of the sciences gets sublated when we rise to the unitary experience of the ground which underlies it. With the dawn of *Brahman*-realization, the world with all its variety ceases to be real. The realization of the One precludes the possibility of the 'Many' also being equally real. But since the latter is an experienced fact, it cannot be dismissed as totally unreal like the hare's horn. Anything that is experienced even for a brief moment must be admitted to be so far real. But it has to be assigned a lower status when a higher level of knowledge with regard to the same subject arises in the same individual. Thus arises the theory of grades of reality and levels of experience. Śrī Śaṅkara recognises three grades and three levels, the phenomenal *(prātibhāsika)*, empirical *(vyāvahārika)* and transcendental *(pāramārthika)*.

Illusions and dream experiences come under the first head, our waking experiences and all the knowledge that we acquire in that state come under the second. Our highest experience, *Brahman*-realization, comes under the last.

It is wrong to imagine that these three are three independent realities. Rather it is one and the same reality that appears differently under different conditions. Without undergoing the least change Brahman appears as the world of diversity at one level and as illusions and dream-experiences at a still lower level. The adventitious circumstance which is responsible for hiding the true nature of *Brahman* and showing it as something wholly different is called *Māyā*. The conception is inherent in the essential teachings of the classical Upaniṣads. Without resorting to it, it is impossible to explain how one and the same reality can appear as the world of nature and as a multitude of finite selves. This is the only way by which we can reconcile our perceptual knowledge with the statements of the Upaniṣads that 'reality is one wihtout a second' and that 'there is no diversity whatsoever'. In making use of this concept Śrī Śaṅkara has neither introduced something of his own nor has he imported anything from Buddhistic sources. He has only brought to clear and explicit consciousness a concept that is germane to those sacred texts.

These texts are the utterances of renowned saints and sages. The eternal verities which flashed on their highly purified minds have been recorded exactly as they occurred to them. They did not reach them by processes of laborious reasoning. They took long jumps and assume many things for granted. They are content to leave them as they are and do not feel any obligation to indicate all the steps in the reasoning. This is the case with regard to all mystical experiences. They are a law unto themselves. They belong to a plane which far outstrips our usual mental processes. They are the eternal truths which are reflected in pure and immaculate minds like the human face in a clear mirror or trees in the limpid and still waters of a lake.

It is the task of the interpreter to supply the missing links and bring the teachings into a coherent whole. In doing this he must not start with pre-conceived notions. If his mind is already wedded to a theory he cannot resist the temptation to find support for it somehow from the texts. This may sometimes lead to a twisting and torturing of the texts. To avoid this danger he must keep aside all his predilections, read and re-read the texts in a spirit of reverence, allow the teachings to soak his mind and shape it into tune with their spirit. The interpreter, so fashioned, will simply act as their mouth-piece. The texts will, in reality, be speaking for themselves.

The interpretation of the texts in terms of the concept of *Māyā* is not, as we have seen, foreign to them. Under its influence *Brahman,* the only reality, appears as knower and known, as subject and object, as so many finite selves and the world of diversity lower down the same reality appears as illusions. The doctrines of grades of reality is a natural corollary of the concept of *Māyā*. In the Upaniṣads there is reference to higher and lower knowledge. The four Vedas and the six Vedāṅgas are comprised under the latter while the knowledge relating to the Imperishable which is beyond thought and word comes under the former.[16] Sanatkumara makes a sharp distinction between the various sciences which Narada had already mastered and the *'Bhūma Vidyā'* which he is going to impart. Sciences like Mathematics, Astronomy, Economics, Ethics, Politics do not avail since they do not help a man to overcome sorrow. *Brahman*-knowledge takes man beyond the reach of sorrow. That makes all the difference. The former, therefore, belongs to a lower grade. *Brahma-vidyā* takes the pride of place.[17]

Closely allied to the doctrine of grades of reality is the concept of grades among the eligibles. *Adhikarins* are of three types, superior *(uttama)*, middling *(madhyama)* and less than average *(manda)*. It is an accepted principle of education that the instruction must be suited to the intellectual and moral attainments of the pupils and it must therefore be gradual. It is no use discoursing on the doctrine of the acosmic Absolute to students who are not qualified to grasp and profit by it. Such instruction will simply pass over the heads of the pupils. To the *adhikārins* of the lowest grade, *Brahman* must be taught as assuming a personal form and invested with several attributes such as punishing the wicked and rewarding the virtuous. To the *adhikārins* of he next higher grade *Brahman* appears as the Cosmic Absolute *(Saguṇa Brahman)* who creates the world, sustains it and ultimately reabsorbs it into Himself. Only to the highest *adhikārins* like Śanaka, Sanandana, Sanātana and Sanatkumara the doctrine of acosmic Absolute can be taught. Thus all passages are accommodated. For this doctrine of *adhikāribheda* Śrī Śaṅkara takes the clues again from the Upaniṣads themselves. We find it stated in several places that the teacher did not impart the highest instruction without first satisfying himself about the fitness of his pupils.[18] Yama makes a sharp distinction between the man whose eyes are turned inwards and the rest who are outward-looking. The former is characterised as a *dhīra*. He is intent on working for his abiding good *(śreyas)* and does not run after the momentary pleasures *(preyas)*.[19] Yājñavalkya classifies people under two heads, those who are under the sway of desires and those who have risen to the state of utter desirelessness. The majority of the people are smitten by sundry desires and long for the good things of earth and heaven. The few who have transcended desires are those who have realized that the *Ātman* is the supreme object of desire.[20]

It is needless to multiply examples. Enough has been said to show that the concept of *Māyā* is by no means extraneous to the teachings of the classical Upaniṣads but quite native to their soil. Apart from the concept being a necessary and logical complement to them, the term itself finds explicit mention in the *Bṛhadāraṇyaka* and *Śvetāśvatara* Upaniṣads. Its equivalent *'avidyā'* is freely mentioned in several places. We may go further and say that there is an implicit reference to the concept of *Māyā* in some *mantras* of the Ṛgveda. In the *Nāsadīya Śūkta,* for example, the question is raised about the origin of the world: 'Did it spring from existence or non-existence? Who can tell the truth about it? The gods had not then been born and hence it is no use looking to them for light in regard to this matter. Can even the Lord in Heaven enlighten us on this profound mystery?'

We may conclude by saying that any attempt to explain the teachings of the Upaniṣads without reference to the concept of *Māyā* will mean either ignoring several important passages or placing a most unnatural interpretation on them.

REFERENCES

1. Compare the saying :
मायावादं असच्छास्त्रं प्रछन्नं बौद्धमेव च।
2. *Br. Up.*, II. v. 19.
3. IV. 10.
4. *Īśa.*, 9; *Kaṭha.*, I. ii. 4; *Muṇḍaka*, I, ii. 9 and *Br.* IV. iv. 10.
5. VIII. iii. 2.
6. *Chāndogya,* VI. ii. 1.
7. *Br. Up.*, IV. ii. 4.
8. *Taitt. Up.*, II.9.
9. *Kena.*, I. i. 3.

10. *Br.Up.*, III. viii. 8. For similar negative descriptions see *Kaṭha*, I. iii. 15; *Māṇḍūkya*, 7; *Taitt.*, II. 7; and *Śveta*, IV. 19.
11. *Muṇḍ.*, I. i. 3 and *Ch.*, VI. 3.5.
12. *Br. Up.*, II. iv. 5.
13. *Kaṭha*, II. i. 11 and *Br.*, IV. iv. 19.
14. *Taitt.*, II. 7 and *Br.*, I. iv. 2.
15. *Br.*, Iv. ii. 4 and IV. iv. 25.
16. *Muṇḍaka.*, I, i. 4-5.
17. *Chāndogya*, VII. i. 2.4.
18. *Kaṭha.*, I. i. 21-29; *Praśṇa*, I. 2; *Taitt.*, III. 1-6; *Chāndogya*, VIII. viii-xi.
19. *Kaṭha.*, II. i. 1-2.
20. *Br. Up.*, IV. iv. 5-6.

❑❑❑

7

THE METHODOLOGY OF THE UPANIṢADS

M.K. Venkatarama Iyer

The quintessence of Upaniṣadic wisdom is contained in the four great utterances *(Mahāvākyas)*, 'That Thou Art' *(Tat Tvaṁ Asi*[1]*)*, 'I am indeed Brahman' *(Ahaṁ Brahmā Asmi*[2]*)*, 'This Ātman is Brahman' *(Ayaṁ Ātmā Brahma*[3]*)* and 'Brahman is consciousness all compact' *(Prajñānaṁ Brahma*[4]*)*. Of these, the first three affirm the essential identity of the finite self *(Jīva)* with the Supreme Being *(Brahman)*, while the last states the nature of the identical element between them. In their ultimate essence both are nothing but Pure Consciousness. The finite self, rid of its adventitious adjuncts through analysis and elimination, comes to its own and shines as infinite consciousness. This is the transcendence *(abhi-niṣpatti)* spoken of in the Upaniṣad.[5] Pure Consciousness is homogeneous. There is no place in it for diversity of any kind *(ekarasa)*. It is consequently one without a second in the literal sense of the term *(ekameva advitīyaṁ)*. In the absence of any tension arising from lack of fulfilment, it is bliss-all-compact. It is therefore characterized as *sat, cit* and *ānanda*.

There are several other statements in the Upaniṣads conveying the same ideas. '*Brahman* is real, *Brahman* is knowledge, *Brahman* is infinite' *(satyaṁ jñānaṁ anantaṁ Brahma*[6]*)*. Knowledge here does not stand for particular knowledge *(vṛtti jñāna)* but for consciousness which illumines all the modes of the mind *(vṛttis)*. What is real and infinite may yet be insentient. That is the Sāṁkhya conception of *Pradhāna*. In the statement given above what is real and infinite is said to be a conscious entity. It cannot therefore be the *Pradhāna* of the Sāṁkhya. It is the *Brahman* of the Vedānta. *'Kaṁ Brahma Khaṁ Brahma'*.[7] *Brahman* is not the oridinary pleasure arising from sense-objects but infinite, unlimited pleasure which is the same as bliss. 'The Infinite is pleasure' *(yo vai bhūmā tat sukhaṁ*[8]*)*. This carries the same sense as the previous statement. 'Who is the *Ātman* and what is *Brahman*' *(ko nu ātmā kiṁ brahma*[9]*)*. The two words qualify each other. *Ātman* qualified by *Brahman* ceases to be the mere finite self and *Brahman* qualified by *Ātman* ceases to be an object of worship external to us. The two words taken together stand for the non-difference between the *Ātman* and *Brahman*. 'He who knows *Brahman* becomes *Brahman*' *(sa yo ha vai tat paramaṁ brahma veda brahmaiva bhavati*[10]*)*. The knower of *Brahman* can become *Brahman* only if in his essential nature he is already *Brahman*. The statement that by knowing *Brahman* one becomes *Brahman* is intelligible only on the assumption that the knower is *Brahman* though he is not aware of it. The statement therefore must be taken as calling our attention to what we are already, 'Whatever here the same there; whatever there, the same here' *(yadeveha tadamutra yadamutra tadeviha*[11]*)*. This statement, according to Śrī Śaṅkara, means that we should consider ourselves as identical with *Brahman* which is all sentience and which is infinite like space.[12] These six additional statements convey the same ideas as those crystallized in the *Mahāvākyas* and serve to reinforce them.

In the Upaniṣads there is no indication to show that the truths set forth above were reached by a process of elaborate reasoning. They are not put forward as conclusions that follow inevitably from given premises. We have therefore to take them as intuitions *(Mantras)* which dawned on the minds that were fit to receive them. They are the eternal verities which come in a flash to saints and sages whose minds are refined and purified by strenuous discipline. What prevents the oridinary mind from receiving these timeless truths is the impurity that has accumulated on it from a dateless past. From their manner of operation these impurities are classified as desire *(kāma)*, anger *(krodha)*, greed *(lobha)*, delusion *(moha)*, arrogance *(mada)* and conceit *(mātsarya)*. These are spoken of as the six insidious enemies of man *(ariṣaḍ-vaga)*. In the last analysis they are the outcome of the feeling of 'I' *(ahaṁkāra)* and 'mine' *(mamakāra)*. A mirror on which much dirt has accumulated reflects the objects in front of it only very indistinctly and sometimes in a distorted manner. If it is cleansed, it reflects the objects properly. The same is the case with the mind. Any knowledge, including that of *Brahman*, has to appear as a state of the mind *(vṛtti)*. A mind which is pre-occupied, which is therefore not free to receive new ideas or a mind which is not sufficiently alert, will fail to grasp the truth of even the objects that are external to it and which are consequently open to observation and experiment.

The difficulty is considerably enhanced when the reality that is to be known is inside of us and hence not open to the ordinary scientific methods of study. 'To the man whose mind is subject to the passion of desire and aversion', writes Śrī Śaṅkara, 'there cannot arise a knowledge of things as they are even of the external world; and it goes without saying, that if his intellect is overpowered by passion, the knowledge of the internal self can never arise as it is beset with many difficulties.'[13] The mind refined by the subjugation of the passions *(śama)* and the body *(dama)* and equipped with the teachings of the scripture and the teacher forms the sense by which the self may be seen.'[14] In another place he writes that 'divine visions relating to the *Ātman* occur to him who is free from sundry desires and aspires to know *Brahman* and for this purpose is engaged in the performance of the obligatory works enjoined in Śruti and Smṛti'.[15] The Upaniṣad says :

> 'Where Agni from the chips of wood
> Darts forth, where Vāyu too appears,
> Where Soma also flows freely
> There is the Manas developed.'[16]

The idea is that where *dharma* and ritual are practised, there inspiration is born.

Heavenly bodies which are very far away in space can be brought near to our eyes by means of a powerful telescope; hings which are exceedingly minute can be magnified with the help of the microscope. These and other mechanical aids will prove useful when we are studying the external world but they will be of no avail when we want to discover the highest spiritual reality. This is not to be found anywhere outside of us, but has to be sought within the depths of the heart;[17] we have to turn our eyes within, practise meditation and get into communion with the Spirit in us. Very few are capable of taking to this line of investigation. Our attention, which has long been accustomed to look outwards, has to be turned inwards. This costs much effort. The process is as difficult as seeking to divert the course of a mighty river in the direction exactly opposite to that in which it has been flowing for a long time. The Upaniṣad therefore characterizes the man who can accomplish this task as a *'dhīra'*.[18]

It follows that we have to cultivate introspection, self-analysis and deep meditation by slow degrees. Only by long discipline in this direction we can hope to raise our moral and spiritual stature and knowledge relating to the intensity of our moral endeavour. By steady and well-directed *Tapas,* a man is transformed into a seer. The ego-sense will completely disappear from him and his mind will acquire the purity for the dawn of the highest truths. In that state he will feel himself more a passive recipient than an active participant. He will become unselfconscious and will simply listen to the whisper in the inmost depths of his heart. Truths, received in this manner are known by the name of *Śruti*. The sages do not therefore claim to be authors of those discoveries. Their work is merely to record for posterity what the 'still small voice' whispers from within. This is the most rational way of explaining the *apauruṣeyic* character of the Vedas. Since these truths are given to the sages in their moments of exalted imagination, there can be no dross in them, nothing that is purely local, contingent, accidental or adventitious. They will therefore be the eternal verities, true for all times and places. The march of time and the consequent changes in the conditions and modes of our living will not affect them. The progress of scientific knowledge will leave them untouched. They belong to the highest spiritual plane.

What occurs under high inspiration from above is a law unto itself. It comes when it comes and there can be no prognostications or predictions about it. Even para-psychology has not been able to throw light on the conditions under which it will come or the mode and shape which it will assume. It has therefore been the custom to attribute it to the grace of God. There is no theological bias in doing so. The Upaniṣad affirms that the sage is able to perceive the truth owing to his contemplation and the grace of God.[19] Inspiration, according to this statement, is the joint product of man's contemplation and God's revelation. Scientists like

Einstein have admitted that they owe their suprerior intuitions to the grace of God.

The nearest analogue to what we have said above relating to the rise of the timeless truths in the minds of sages is to be found in the sphere of artistic production. It is said of great poets that they were beside themselves when they composed their masterpieces. Sage Vālmīki sat on Kuśa grass and went into deep meditation before he composed the *Śrīmad Rāmāyaṇa.* Brahmā's visit and His blessing carry a deep inner meaning. It means that on the poet, who had purified himself by *Tapas,* the grace of God descended in full measure. Since the great Epic was written to dictation as it were from above, it has stood the test of ages and has become popular not only in this vast sub-continent but also in other lands. Brahmā said: 'The story of Rāma will remain current in all the worlds as long as the hills and the rivers last'. This has proved literally true.

Milton has said in his prose writings that 'a great work is not to be raised from the heat of youth or the vapours of wind or the trencher fury of a rhyming parasite, nor to be obtained by the invocation of Dame Memory but by devout prayer to that Eternal Spirit who can enrich with all utterance and knowledge and send out His Seraphim with the hallowed fire of His altar to touch and purify the lips of whom He pleases'.

> '................................ I thence
> Invoke thy aid to my adventurous song
> That with no middle flight intends to soar
> Above the Aonian Mount, while it pursues
> Things unattempted yet in prose or rhyme.
> And chiefly Thou, O Spirit, that dost prefer
> Before all temples the upright heart and pure
> Instruct me, for Thou knowest ....

..... what in me is dark
Illumine, what is low raise and support;
That to the height of this great argument
I may assert External Providence
And justify the ways of God to man.'[20]

Speaking of some of the best lyrics of Wordswoth and Byron, Matthew Arnold observes that it looks as if Nature took the pen from the hands of these poets and wrote these pieces for them.[21] It can only mean that these poets composed their best pieces in their unself-conscious mood. They had forgotten themselves for the time being.

So far we have given some account of the psychology of intuitions. We have shown that they are not reached by any clear-cut method but by a process of intellectual, moral and spiritual preparation. It is akin to clearing the ground of all weds and noxious growths before the soil becomes fit for cultivation. The seed however is to be sown from above. The essential condition is the utter passivity of the mind and laying itself open to be impressed by the eternal verities. This presupposes the elimination of one's links, prejudices, preoccupations and obsessions. Only one aspiration is permissible and that is the earnest desire to know and realize the highest Truth.

We may now proceed to give some account of the devices adopted by the seers to put their findings across. This task is beset with many difficulties. The truths which have dawned on their minds go beyond speech and mind.[22] Not within the range of sight is this form nor by the eye does any one see it. It is realized only when it is reached by the mind, i.e., in the heart which can exercise self-control. They who know this become immortal'.[23] It is transcendent and bears no relation to anything that we know *(asaṁspṛṣṭa)*. It is therefore indefinable. 'There is no likeness of Him whole name is great glory.'[24] It rises above all distinctions including that of subject and object and hence it cannot be known in the way in which we usually know the things around us. It is not therefore the known in relation to a knower. 'He who says that he has known *Brahman* really does not know.'[25] It is the prius and presupposition of all proof and consequently incapable of being proved in the ordinary way. The light which ilumines all the modes of our minds and all the states of our experience cannot be known by any other light. 'How can we know the ulltimate knower?'[26] Exposition in an intelligible manner is therefore a practical impossibility.

The next difficulty consists in trying to bring deeply felt experiences to the lower plane of rational understanding. There is always a difficulty when we attempt to translate the experiences of a higher level into the language current at a lower level. Just as a logical proposition is an inadequate representation of a judgment, even so a judgement is an inadequate representation of an intuition. Thought rises superior to language, and communion, by the same token, rises superior to thought. The identity between the finite self *(jīva)* and the Supreme Being *(Brahman)* is felt in depths which thought cannot plumb. The difficulty in trying to put this experience across is obvious. To seek to rationalize it would mean doing great violence to it. Syllogistic proof is out of the question as no middle term is available. The Mīmāṁsakas and the Naiyāyikas put forward plausible arguments but they do not realize that the middle term which they employ is not of their coining, not supplied by experience, but by Śruti. Śrī Śaṅkara has drawn pointed attention to this fact in the introduction to his commentary on the *Bṛhadāraṇyaka Upaniṣad*.[27]

Nor is our language adequate for such high experiences. It is pedestrian, having come into being to serve the humdrum business of everyday life. If it is applied beyond its proper sphere it will break down. Similes and other figures of speech provide partial glimpses but, as George Eliot has said, 'Words are but broken light on the depths of the unspoken'. The Upaniṣadic seers are therefore said to have adopted the method of silence to expound the doctrine of *Brahman*. Śrī Śaṅkara quotes from an Upaniṣad which is no longer extant: 'A student by name Baskali requested his teacher, Badhava, to instruct him. The teacher remained silent. The student repeated the request a second and a third time. The teacher observed : 'I am teaching you all the time, only you do not understand it. This *Brahman* is silence'.[28] The same attitude was adopted by Śrī Dakṣiṇāmūrti when he gave instruction to Sanat, Sanandana, Sanātana and Sanatkumāra. It is said, that His exposition of the doctrine of *Nirguṇa Brahman* by the method of silence dispelled all doubts from the minds of students.[29]

This method may be all right with regard to very advanced pupils like the mind-born sons of Brahmā, but it will not do with others who are *adhikārins* of a lower grade. Some exposition in terms of language has necessarily to be given for their benefit. To make up for the deficiencies of language, the seer frequently resorts to parables, parallel cases and similes. It is well known that Śri Ramakrishna used to elucidate many of his spiritual experiences by means of apt parables. In the Upaniṣad the parable of the blind-folded man, left in a lonely place by robbers, finding his way home by seeking the guidance of people at various points, is given to illustrate the ignorant man finding his way to enlightenment with the help of a competent *guru*.[30] A man becoming oblivious to everything inside or outside of him when he is embraced by his beloved is given as the nearest parallel to the deep communion with the Infinite which the finite self experiences in *samādhi*.[31] Rivers losing themselves in the ocean and honeys collected from different flowers losing their distinctive taste when they are put in the common pool are given as the nearest similes to illustrate the merger of the *jīva* in *Brahman*.[32] The salt crystal, completely dissolving in water leaving no substance behind, is given to elucidate the notion that consciousness is not an attribute of the *Ātman* but its very stuff.[33]

Now we come to the methods adopted to give instruction. Gradualness is an accepted educational method. The student has to be led step by step, from what he knows to what he does not know, from what he is familiar with to what is unfamiliar to him. Varuṇa's instruction to Bhṛgu is an excellent instance in point.[34] From the notion that matter is *Brahman* the student is led on to the notion of 'Bliss is *Brahman*' through easy stages. From matter to vital force, from vital force to consciousness and from consciousness to self-consciousness and lastly to bliss. The student is asked to dig deeper and still deeper till he lights on the rock-bottom truth. It is like pulling out the inner mind which is deep down in the reeds.[35]

Ṣage Sanatkumara's instruction to Narada is yet another instance of the same method.[36] Though the latter had mastered all the branches of learning that were extant at the time, he had not attained peace of mind. He had learnt from teachers that only the knowledge of the Ātman will take a man beyond the sphere of sorrow. To receive this instruction, he approach-ed Sanatkumara. The latter characterized all the vast learning that Narada had acquired as '*mantra*' or name. This characterization created the desire in Narada to know what was superior to '*mantra*' or name. That provided the occasion for the sage to start with speech and proceed by stages to the *Bhuman* which is of the nature of bliss and therefore beyond all sorrow. In between the two there are twenty intermediate steps. Each succeeding one is superior, from the moral and spiritual standpoint, to what precedes it. Thus till the end Narada's curiosity is kept on edge. At each stage he feels a strong urge to know what is higher. Broadly speaking we may say that the instruction proceeds from what is exterior to what is interior, from what is gross to what is subtle, from what is caught in the realm of distinctions to what rises above all distinctions.

Another method is to get some one to state a number of inadequate definitions of *Brahman,* examine them, bring out their deficiencies and thus prepare the way for a fuller and more adequate definition. The final definition comes as the logical culmination of the notions already examined and found wanting. It does not look like one imposed from without and wholly unrelated to all that has gone before. The continuity is kept up in a skilful manner. King Aśvapati's examination of the definition of *Ātman* Vaiśvānara advanced by the six Brahmin pupils who approached him,[37] king Ajātaśatru's analysis of the twenty odd definitions of *Brahman* mentioned by proud Bālāko[38] and Yājñavalkya's critique of the six notions regarding the Supreme Being that Emperor Janaka had gathered from various scholars[39] are good examples of this method of procedure. The important point to note is that the inadequate definitions are not dismissed outright but given their due place. They are shown to be based on certain attributes of *Brahman,* which are undoubtedly useful as supports for meditation. They therefore point only to the *Brahman* with attributes *(Saguṇa Brahman)* and not the *Brahman* without attributes *(Nirguṇa Brahman).* Meditation on *Saguṇa Brahman* however will gradually prepare the way for the realization of the *Nirguṇa Brahman.*[40]

To ascertain the circumstance which is most essential for the occurrence of a phenomenon, analysis and elimination are necessary. If we had full control over the situation we could employ experiment under laboratory conditions, effectively eliminate all the unessential circumstances and demonstrate beyond a shadow of doubt which particular one is causally connected with the phenomenon. Where we do not have full control over the situation we have to wait for favourable conditions to turn up in the course of nature. It is well known that students of Astronomy undertake journeys to distant places to observe the skies under a total eclipse of the sun. Such a method of observation is known as 'Natural Experiment'. The seers of the Upaniṣads fall back on this method to demonstrate their findings. That the vital Force *(Prāṇa)* is the most essential condition for the substenance of life is shown in a somewhat picturesque manner in what is known as the *Prāṇasaṁvāda*.[41] The other competing factors such as the eye, ear and so forth are made to leave the body one by one and it is shown that nothing serious happens. But when the *Mukhya Prāṇa* just makes an attempt to quit, everything is thrown into disarray and it becomes quite clear that it is th *sine qua non* of life.

Another important instance of the same method of study is provided by the analysis of the three states to show that it is the light of the *Ātman* which illumines every experience including the perceptual. Many factors are present when we perceive an object in our waking moments, the light of the sun, the functioning of the sense of sight, the activity of the mind and the self behind them all. When however we pass from the waking state to the state of sleep, the sense of sight does not function and consequently we lose contact with the light of the sun and the objects of the external world. But we perceive objects in dreams. Though there are no chariots, horses or roads in that state,[42] we perceive them all the same. This is due to the activity of the mind.[43] When we pass to the state of dreamless sleep, we have no particular experiences. We have to conclude that even the mind ceases to function here. But though there are no particular experiences in this state, it is not a mere blank. There is an experience of happiness. This becomes clear from the recollection of the next morning. An experience presupposes an experiment. In the absence of the mind, we have necessarily to suppose that the light of the Self, which is the only residuary circumstance left, must illumine that state. In fact, it is this light which streams out through the mind and the sense organs and illumines the objects that we see even in the waking state. The light of the sun is an adventitious aid. It may go out, but perceptions will still be possible. The *Ātman* is the only unfailing light.[44]

The final method—if method—it can be called as the mere assertion of a deep heart-felt experience *(anubhava)*. This admits of no questioning as it is an authentic and genuine experience. It is self-certifying and stands in no need of external proof. 'The subtle, extensive, ancient way has been realized by me' says the sage.[45] Śrī Śaṅkara affirms a similar experience of his in his *Sūtra Bhāṣya*.[46] Such an affirmation gives the quietus to all doubts and objections.[47] Such experiences are open to verification. They are within the reach of all who go through the required discipline.

REFERENCES

1. *Ch. Up.*, VI. viii. 7
2. *Bṛ. Up.*, I. iv. 10.
3. *Māṇḍ. Up.*, 2.
4. *Ait. Up.*, V. 2.
5. *Ch. Up.*, VIII. xii. 3.
6. *Taitti. Up.*, II. i. 1.
7. *Ch. Up.*, IV. x. 5.
8. *Ch. Up.*, VII. xxiii. 1.

9. *Ch. Up.*, V. xi. 1.
10. *Muṇḍ. Up.*, III. ii. 9.
11. *Kaṭha Up.*, II. i. 10.
12. विज्ञानैकरसं नैरन्तर्येणाकाशवत्परिपूर्णं ब्रह्मास्मीति पश्येदिति वाक्यार्थः।
13. Memorial Edition of Sri Sankara's Works, Vol. XI, p. 228.
14. *Ibid.*, Vol. XI, p. 37.
15. *Ibid.*, Vol. VI, p. 40
16. *Śvetā. Up.*, II. 6.
17. *Kaṭha Up.*, II. 12.
18. *Ibid.*, IV. i.
19. *Śvetā. Up.*, VI. 21.
20. Paradise Lost, Book I, lines 12 to 26.
21. Essays on Criticism: Essay on Wordsworth.
22. *Taitti. Up.*, II. 9.
23. *Kaṭha Up.*, VI. 9 and *Muṇḍ. Up.*, III. i. 8.
24. *Śvetā. Up.*, IV. 19.
25. *Kena Up.*, II. 3.
26. *Bṛ. Up.*, II. iv. 14.
27. Mem. Edition, Vol. VIII, p. 5.
आगमेन त्वात्मास्तित्वेऽवगतवेदप्रदर्शितलौकिकलिंगविशेषैः तदनुसारिणो मीमांसकास्तार्किकाश्च अहंप्रत्ययलिंगानि च वैदिकान्येव खमतिप्रभवाणीति कल्पयन्तो वदन्ति प्रत्यक्षश्चानुमेयश्चात्मेति।
28. *Ibid.*, Vol. III, p. 587. उपशान्तोऽयमात्मा।
29. गुरोस्तु मौनं व्याख्यानं शिष्यास्तुच्छिन्नसंशयाः।
30. *Ch. Up.*, VI. xiv. 2.
31. *Bṛ. Up.*, IV. iii. 21.
32. *Praśna Up.*, VI. 5, *Muṇḍ. Up.*, III. ii. 8, *Ch. Up.*, VI. 9.
33. *Ch. Up.*, VI. 13 and *Br. Up.*, II. iv. 12.
34. *Taitti. Up.*, III. 1-6.
35. *Kaṭha Up.*, VI. 17.
36. *Ch. Up.*, VII.
37. *Ch. Up.*, V. xi-xviii.
38. *Bṛ. Up.*, II. i.
39. *Ibid.*, IV. i.
40. Amalananda's Kalpataru :
वशीकृते मनस्येषां सगुणब्रह्मशीलनात्।
तदेवाविर्भवेत् साक्षादपेतोपाधिकल्पनम्।।
41. *Praśna Up.*, II. 1-5; Ch. Up., V. 6-12; *B(. Up.*, VI. i. 7-13; *Kauṣitaki Up.*, II. 14.

42. *Bṛ. Up.*, IV. iii. 10
43. *Ibid.*
44. *Ibid.*, IV iii. 7.
45. *Ibid.*, IV. iv. 8.
46. *Vedānta Sūtra*, IV. i. 15.
47. अनुभवावसानत्वाद् ब्रह्मज्ञानस्य।

❑❑❑

8

AN ANALYTICAL APPROACH TO THE BHAGAVAD GĪTĀ

V. Perumal

The *Bhagavad Gītā* is the song of God as well as the song about God. It is a song of divine order which has permanent value and which has proved and continues to prove the test of time. It is the music of life which has a double capacity, of arresting the heart and holding the intellect, simultaneously. The *Gītā* is like a deep ocean. The more one controls one's breath and remains at the bottom the greater the amount of pearls can one collect from the bed of the ocean. Similarly, the more intensely one studies the *Gītā* and practises the tenets enunciated therein the greater becomes one's intellectual and spiritual achievements.

The vast majority of people think that the *Gītā* is not helpful in their day to day life since it deals with God, universe, renunciation and the like. But it is a wrong conclusion, hastily arrived at. The maxims propounded in the *Gītā* can certainly be applicable to every human being on the globe provided they are correctly comprehended. The *Gītā* does not contain dry and vague philosophy which can be divorced from human life. In a word, the *Gītā* is a spiritual reference book which contains the sum and substane of advanced thought, explained and illustrated in an easy flowing language. An ancient verse extols the *Gītā* thus: 'All Upaniṣads are the cows; the cowherd's son, Kṛṣṇa, is the one who milks; Arjuna is the calf and intelligent men are those who drink that milk, the nectar of the great *Gītā*.

The *Gītā* conveys its sublime message through the oral method, which is one of the powerful ways in imparting knowledge from the pedagogical point of view. Though the *Gītā* is a gist and synthesis of the Hindu scriptures, one will find that it has a universal appeal as it envisages a religion which comes from within.

Man has two natures, a higher and a lower. The *Bhagavad Gītā* aims at the manifestation of one's higher nature and elimination of the baser; in other words it aims at the removal of animality and manifestation of divinity of man. Let us here confine to the twelfth chapter of the Bhagavad Gītā and arrive at the religion it reveals from different points of view.

The Physical Aspect

'A sound Mind in a sound body' is a well-known proverb. The superstructure and its many-sided architectural excellence cannot exist unless the building has a firm foundation. Likewise one cannot build up a spiritual life unless one possesses a sound physique.

Human beings are classified into three main divisions according to their outstanding capacities: (1) those possessed of a great amount of physical stamina; (2) those having a preponderantly emotional nature; and (3) those possessed of intellectual brilliance. The *Gītā* makes this classification clear and then prescribes the way each class of people are to follow to reach 'the kingdom of God', or enjoy ever-lasting bliss.

People having a restless temperament can follow the *Karma Mārga* or the path of action; those that are emotionally inclined can follow the *Bhakti Mārga* or the way of devotion and those whose power of discrimination is sharp and are always on the alert can follow the *Jñāna Mārga* or the path of knowledge. Thus, the *Gītā* gives everyone ample scope to unite his soul with God. The temperamentally active persons, as said already, can by righteous deeds or action that are pleasing to God pursue their spiritual path.

> *abhyāse'pi asamartho'si matkarma paramo bhava*
> *madrthaṁ api karmaṇi kurvan siddhiṁ avāpsyasi.*
>
> —*Gītā* XII. 10.

'Cleanliness is next to godliness.' Physical cleanliness is the index of mental health and spiritual purity. If the body is healthy, the mind can be clean; if the mind is clean, thoughts arising in it will be flawless; if thought is fllawless the words will be pure; if the words are pure, the actions will be pious; if the actions are pious the results will be fruitful. So, it goes without saying that physical purity has its own value in the spiritual life also.

The *Gītā* aims at the attainment of individual's equanimity at every level—physical and mental. It expects everyone to possess a sound physical constitution. The body should not only be free from diseases and deformities but should have a resisting capacity to extreme heat and cold. Further, the body should be trained and cultivated in such a manner as to experience alike the pairs of oposites, pain and pleasure and the like. Such a type of physical neutrality is the foundation for intellectual equipoise.

> *śitoṣṇasukhaduḥkheṣu samaḥ saṅgavivarjitaḥ.*
>
> —(*Ibid.* 18)

Thus, from the physical and physiological points of view, the *Bhagavad Gītā* aims at the harmonious development of man.

The Mental Aspect

Every profession requires and demandes certain special

abilities and traits. If a person does not possess the requisite qualifications, he cannot succeed in that career. A soldier should have enormous physical verve; a technician must possess skill; a lawyer should possess the gift of speech; an author must have a good command of language; and a man who practises religion should have the right type of mental aptitude. The religion envisaged by the *Gītā* has a wide appeal because it caters to the needs of people with different mental make up. So, it stands to reason that mental propensity is an essential qualification for a person to embrace a faith.

Though there are three main paths viz., the paths of action, devotion and knowledge, the ultimate goal is one and the same. For instance, a man may travel from one place to another by bicycle, bus, train, ship or plane. The choice of the vehicle depends mainly on his financial capacity and next on his whims and fancies. Though people may travel by different kinds of vehicles, under normal conditions, it is a physical certainty that all of them will reach their destiny. Similarly the follower of each path shall certainly reach his goal, provided he has fixed his mind on God. Such a single-minded devotion is emphasizd throughout the *Gītā*.

mayī āveśya mano ye māṁ nitya yuktā upāsate
śraddhayā parayopetāḥ te me yuktatamā matāḥ.

(*Ibid.* 2)

From the spiritual point of view, the fundamental condition expected of every man is the control of his senses. The conept of Lord Kṛṣṇa serving as a charioteer conveys a great message. We can give an allegorical meaning also to it. The body is the chariot, Arjuna is the soul, the master of the chariot; intellect is the charioteer Kṛṣṇa; mind stands for the reins; and the senses are the horses. It here implies that all the senses should be under the full control of the intellect if we have to be sanely occupied. Controlling the senses does not in any way mean that one should suppress one's feelings, just like controlling the horse does not simply killing the horse. Just as the rider has to bring the horse under control with the help of reins, so also one's intellect must fully control one's senses through one's mind. There is a proverb, 'A man without religion is like a horse without a bridle'. In short, the purport of the injunctions of the *Gītā* is that man must be the supreme and unquestionable master of his senses. When man controls his senses and is guided by unprejudiced reason he certainly lifts himself from the animal plane to the spiritual plane. On the other hand, when he becomes a slave to his senses he remains on the animal plane itself. Hence man's progress and perfection is directly proportionate to the control he has obtained over his mind and senses.

It is a well-known psychological truth that more often than not man is carried away by his emotions, sentiments and feelings. He is elated at a gain and depressed at a loss. Until and unless man stabilises the emotional arena in himself, he will find it impossible to create a mental equilibrium. Mental equanimity is the mother of 'peace of mind'. Peace of mind easily paves the way for the realization of God.

Devotion and contemplation are the actions connected with the mind. And it is said that heart is the seat of the mind. When the mind is entirely free from the pairs of opposite emotions there will be no mental agitation, there will be the climate for peace of mind. And peace of mind is important not only from the spiritual point of view but in fact it is a psychological necessity for the harmonious development of man's mental health.

The *Gītā* advocates a single-minded devotion. It expects of a devotee as much onepointedness in his meditation, prayer and contemplation as a hunter does while aiming his arrow at the target.

Most people do not even move their little fingers to help another without expecting some thing in return. Many count their chickens before they are hatched. The behaviour of man corroborates beyond doubt that he is highly selfish and his mind, heart and intellect are perfectly focusses on the fruits of his action. Regarding actions and fruits, the *Gītā* has much to say. Briefly it lays down two principles: (1) that every man should do his duty with all his might and main; (2) that he must completely renounce the fruits of his actions along with his 'I'ness and 'my'ness. If these two sublime principles are adhered to, the sorrrowful aspect of human life can be minimized. By way of advocating these two maxims the *Gītā* teaches the right type of mental training which blossoms into mental culture in the long run. It says: Knowledge is better than practice (without knowledge); meditation (with knowledge) is better than mere knowledge; renunciation of fruits of actions is better than meditation bcause peace follows such a renunciation.

śreyyo hi jñānaṁ abhyāsāt jñānāt dhyānaṁ viśiṣyate
dhyānāt karmaphalatyāgas tyāgāt śāntiranantaram.

(*Ibid.* 12)

In this verse the *Gītā* has revealed the secret of human happiness. This sacred book trains its votary to live in the world without becoming worldly, as the water-drop on the lotus-leaf.

The Social Aspect

The *Gītā* appeals to the social sense and social consciousness of people to a large extent. Man is a social being. He must contribute his share towards the social harmony and prove that he is human by his actions. He should identify himself in the joys and sorrows of his brethren. One of the social duties of man as envisaged by the *Gītā* is that he should rejoice in the welfare of all beings, for unless the social horizon of man's mind expands, realization of social harmony will prove to be a utopia.

Human beings are expected to live in amity and brotherhood for that is one of the qualities that distinguishes them from animals. To err is human and to forgive is divine. One's greatness lies not in meeting out vengeance on his fellowman but in forgiveness. Thus the *Gītā* briefly, at the same time vividly, teaches:

> *adveṣṭā sarvabhūtānāṁ maitraḥ karuṇa eva ca*
> *nirmamo nirahaṅkāraḥ samaduḥkha sukhaḥ kṣamī.*
>
> (*Ibid.* 13)

The relationship between man and world has been described in the *Gītā* as follows: Man should acquire such perfection that he could live without injuring others and his mental stability should be such as would not be upset by any thing. In order to enjoy social liberty and social harmony man should be absolutely free from envy, fear and anxiety. When these and other tensions are absent, harmony and peace will certainly enter into the social atmoshpere. Thus, the teachings of the *Gītā* can be practised in society for its upliftment.

The Intellectual Aspect

It is the religion, the inquiry into the beyond, that makes the difference between man and animal,' says Swami Vivekananda. Man is a rational animal. Religion is not based on blind faith. The very purpose of *Jñānamārga* or the way of Wisdom implies the realization of God through knowledge. In order to discover our divinity through the intellectual process (discrimination) one should anchor his intellect in God. Unless one's discrimination is used to incline the intellect Godward nothing spiritual can be attained.

The second important characteristic enunciated in the

Gītā is the intellectual skill and alertness based on intellectual integrity. It is a moral certainty that one's discriminating faculty will stand him in good stead in his spiritual pursuit. To follow a faith without its knowledge is like undertaking a journey without knowing the destination.

The third significant trait is intellectual equilibrium. Just as man is expected to maintain physical equilibrium in cold and heat and mental equilibrium in enmity and friendship, similarly, he should maintain intellectual impartiality in honour and dishonour. As a matter of fact, intellectual equipoise is the mother of sanity of thought which blossoms into intellectual maturity in the long run. Such a man will not attach any importance to name and fame. Thus the *Gītā* prepares man to comprehend and digest the real philosophy of life with much ease.

The Spiritual Aspect

At the physical level there is no difference between man and animal, as sensual pleasure is common to both but at the intellectual level, there is a wide gulf between them. Man can reason logically and scientifically whereas an irrational being cannot. At a more subtle level there is the spiritual aspect. Intellectual maturity results in spiritual budding. At the gross level man enjoys physical pleasure, at the mental level he enjoys intellectual pleasure; at the refined subtle level he enjoys spiritual bliss.

One's spiritual bliss lies not only in peace but in completely identifying oneself with God. Unless a sense of oneness with God is felt, the words, spirit, spiritual bliss, peace that passeth understanding and the like will be nothing but meaningless jargons. Though the religion revealed in the *Gītā* has a wider connotation and appeals to the various faculties of man, its spiritual appeal is unique and vital. But very few people realize this.

The Moral Aspect

If wealth is lost, nothing is lost; if health is lost something is lost; if character is lost everything is lost, runs a proverb. Morality coupled with wisdom is the sum and substance of the Hindu culture. 'Desire, anger and greed, says the *Gītā,* is the way to darkness, therefore renounce them. A world of meaning is contained in this aphorism and requires a life time to unearth it fully. The *Gītā* at other places too gives practical directions regarding duty, moral behaviour, and the like. But mere knowledge of the contents of the *Gītā* does not help. One's life should also be moulded in the line of its tenets. The moral aim of the *Gītā* is to enable its votary to implement the maxims in his daily life.

God as revealed in the Gītā

There are certain characteristics attributed to God which have been accepted by almost all saints and seers. The third verse of the twelfth chapter mentions eight of these characteristics, viz. undecaying, indefinable, unmanifested, omnipresent, imponderable, unchangeable, immovable and eternal. God is undecaying. A thing which has birth, has death also. This is the law of nature. The other corollary namely that which has no birth, has no death is also true. God is not born and hence can have no death. He was, is, and will be.

God is indefinable. We can define an object if it comes under our sense perception and experience. For instance, gold can be defined as a precious yellow metal. Its uses can also be defined. But we cannot define God because, He does not come under the purview of common human perception and experience. Hence, He cannot be defined in human language.

He is unmanifest. He is visible neither to the naked eye

nor to the uncleansed mind. However, He shows Himself to a devotee who has purified his mind. Likewise, presence of god can be felt only by a spiritually advanced soul, but they are very few.

God is present eveywhere at all times. God is present in every atom and He manifests Himself indirectly, as the fragrance in flower, as the light in the moon, as fire in the fuel and so on.

God's nature cannot even be pondered over, for the thinking faculty of human being is limited. Man can think of matters of everyday experience. He can only imagine those objects which he is ignorant of.

God is immutable. Every object is liable to change. Whatever is created is mutable. Man's idea about God might change but He does not. If He is subject to the law of change He is subject to the law of perishability. Neither does God change by Himself from one stage to another nor can He be changed by any force whatever, for all forces get their strength and sustenance from God.

God is ubiquitous. Scientifically speaking an object can move from the place which it occupies to another, i.e. movement can be with reference to another object, movement is relative. Since God pervades the entire universe, the question of His moving from one place to another does not arise.

God is conditioned neither by space nor by time. He eternally exists.

Conclusion

Summing up, we come to the conclusion that religion does not make man inactive, inert and irresponsible. On the other hand, it corrects man when he goes wrong, guides him when he stumbles, puts him on the right path when he goes astray. The *Gītā* never encourages idleness. That the *Gītā* was taught on the battlefield shows how much valuable it is for all people who are fighting their individual battles on the homefront. It is a scripture which supplies the needs of all devotees and seekers.

❑❑❑

9

ŚRĪ KṚṢṆA AND THE IDEAL OF LIFE

Vidya Chaitanya

Nowadays the concept of a theistic religion hardly appears to pose any problem in philosophy and religion. But it was not so in the Upaniṣadic era. The underlying thought that runs through the esoteric portion of the Vedas is that of a reality that is devoid of any form and is beyond speech and mind. The charm, rhythm and dignity of the Upaniṣadic language were appealing but unintelligible and incomprehensible to the general people. A concrete representation of Truth, Beauty and Goodness was necessitated for a meaningful blend of the doctrine and its realization, the ideal and the real. The conception of the descent of a Godhead into our empirical world is thus neithter a myth nor a legend but a providential necessity which undertook to bridge over the gulf between the transcendent and the immanent, between the impersonal and the personal, between religion and philosophy. The advent of Śrī Kṛṣṇa, is the fulfilment of such a conception which servs a two-fold purpose:

(1) The supreme *Puruṣa* or the Upaniṣadic Reality, which exists like a pole star in its own glory unaffected by creation or dissolution, appears to assume a human form into a world of appearance and relativity, of temporal and spatial change.

(2) Secondly, in its playful mood, the eternal, infinite Spirit after accepting the limiting adjuncts of a human body becomes an object of love and devotion, of worship and contemplation to fulfil the spiritual hankering of the aspirants.

Thus, the life of this great Incarnation, who was spirit personified, is in itself an explanation of the great transition from absolutism to theism in Indian thought. It is still a wonder to see how with great love and reverence Śrī Kṛṣṇa, an embodiment of Vedāntic Reality, is being cherished in the devoted hearts of millions of the Hindus. The growth of a religious sect on the footsteps of an Incarnation is not rare, but what is noteworthy in the case of Śrī Kṛṣṇa is that even after 3,000 years of his earthly existence he is held in the highest regard by millions and millions of Indians. And it is not without justification. His statesmanship, his magnificent personality, his secular wisdom and his spiritual power have been reckoned as unparalleled in the religious history of the world. Truly, Śrī Kṛṣṇa has been described in the *Bhāgavata* as God Himself, whereas the other Incarnations are merely parts or aspects of *Īśvara*.

His life history as depicted in the *Mahābhārata* and the *Bhāgavata* is replete with legends and sometimes appears to be full of miracles. How from a prince-carming among the cow-boys who used to sport and gambol in the breezy meadows of Vrindavan, the lad developed into a mighty hero who could destroy the demoniacal might of Śiśupāla and Jarāsandha is not known. Vrindavan-Leela, as it is popularly called by the ignorant, wherin one sees him engaged in the amorous disport with the Gopis is really an allegorical representation of a highly ecstatic play on the superconscious plane of existence devoid of any mundane tint. His political mission and social policy as revealed in a great measure in the administration of his kingdom of Dwaraka and his handling of the Kuru-Pāṇḍava affairs prove that the secular wisdom and spiritual vision can be blended in the life of a single personality.

Amidst the pageants embedded in the past in the anecdotes of Śrī Kṛṣṇa's life we find that therein the ideal has become the real. For could a prophet incarnate without any special mission? And that special mission is to steer the boat of life across the turbulent and rough sea of sensuality and desire and harbour it safely in the haven of spiritual bliss. Life without such a directive and control is like a ship without a sail. Not destined for any goal, it is wrecked and destroyed.

On the field of Kurukshetra the mighty hordes of the Kauravas and the Pāṇḍavas stood in battle array. At his critical hour Śrī Kṛṣṇa delivered his ambrosial message—the *Gītā*. The attitude of the Kaurava princes towards the Pāṇḍavas was full of hatred, rancour and jealousy of the worst type. Their plans and programmes reveal the workings of evil minds at its vilest. What they give vent to are the lowest tendencies of human mind—lust for power, jealousy, hatred and desire. The climax of the drama is reached in the game of dice as a result of which the Pāṇḍavas were exiled to a life in the forest.

The part played by Śrī Kṛṣṇa in the lives of the Pāṇḍavas is remarkably significant. Before the war began he plays the role of a great ambassador and a counsellor with a peace mission. His utmost effort was to avoid war. In reply to Vidura's question why he tried to negotiate for truce with the cruel king Duryodhana, Śrī Kṛṣṇa feelingly told, 'I will sincerely endeavour to bring out peace between the Kurus and the Pāṇḍavas. Great is the merit earned by him who liberates the earth from the mess of destruction. Lest the inimical persons blame me of not exercising my good offices,

I have come hither. If without sacrificing the interests of the Pāṇḍavas I can being about peace among the parties, my conduct will be regarded as highly meritorious'. Śrī Kṛṣṇa's honest counsel did not bear fruit because (a) the Kurus were adamant in their resolve to fight and refused to hear anything in the interest of the Pāṇḍavas, (b) they grew into fanatical war-mongers and were determined to come out victorious against the seemingly less powerful Pāṇḍavas and, (c) the destruction of the Kurus seemed to be providential.

In the war, Śrī Kṛṣṇa asked his powerful Vrishni army to fight for the Kurus but he himself sided with the Pāṇḍavas. In the critical hours of the war, he devoted his whole attention to one cause viz. to bring victory to the Pāṇḍavas. None but Śrī Kṛṣṇa was acquainted with the weak points of the enemies and with this knowledge he could easily bring about their downfall. The war saw the strategic display of many weapons dangerous in action. It was Śrī Kṛṣṇa's ingenuity which rescued the Pāṇḍavas from their destruction.

In between these periods, before and during the war, humanity was blessed with the celestial song—the *Gītā,* sung by Śrī Kṛṣṇa to his dearest friend and disciple Arjuna. One is to ponder a little over the possibility of such a highly metaphysical discourse on philosophy being delivered on the eve of a grim war. Moreover, should we think that fightings and killings are the only teaching one is to learn from the *Gītā* since it was immediately followed by a fierce war?

What is taught in the *Gītā* has its own immortal and independent bearing irrespective of Kuru-Pāṇḍava story. The *Gītā* is a philosophy of life—a message eternal—the *mokṣa sāstra* par excellence which is revered and held in high esteem by posterity. It teaches man's duties in his thorny course through life. Its import is fraught with the reconciliation of the ideal and the real, the eternal and the temporal, the secular and the spiritual. Nowhere Śrī Kṛṣṇa is seen so much effective in his approach to the aspirations of people at large as he is in the *Gītā*. In it we find both the concrete example of the prophet and the abstract ideal of his message being united in a harmonious blending, bestowing peace and beautific vision. And what came out from his lips are, by virtue of their deep spiritual import, benedictions to the future generations.

To analyze this point further we should carefully observe with what conviction and boldness Śrī Kṛṣṇa dealt with the foremost problems of life. In the *Gītā* he delivers a message which resolves a critical moral problem. In it a message of peace and solace is accompanied by a message of manliness and strength, not by passivity and timidity. It exhorts man to be inspired with the ideal of faith and fearlessness, with self-reliance and indepnedence. In a typical moment of despair and desolation which cast a dark shadow on Arjuna's mind Śrī Kṛṣṇa admonished him for yielding to the spell of unmanly weakness which is unfit even for an ordinary *kṣatriya,* what to speak of a hero like him. He inspired him to rise to the occasion, viewed the situation from the standpoint of *Dharma* and fight for the promotion of universal good.

While advising Arjuna in his way Śrī Kṛṣṇa was mindful of a higher ideal of life which was spiritual *(Mokṣa)* to the core. The world and the *jīva,* both movable and immovable are permeated in and through by the Spirit. The reality is immanent but also transcendent. The being of the world depends upon that of reality but not the reverse. While *jīva* is essentially of the nature of Brahman, *jīvahood* is a creation of *avidyā*. Hence *jīva* is product of both *cit* and *acit,* spirit and matter apparently—really he is only existence, knowledge and bliss absolute. In this latter state, the state of *sthitaprajña,* he is without affection for any side, he does neither rejoice nor loathe when he obtains good or suffers evil.

Thus two ideals of life, one subordinate to the other, have been propounded in the *Gītā*. One may be called the ideal for the ordinary man, by virtue of its socio-political status and association, the other, the spiritual ideal because it is concerned with the supreme goal. The scope of the latter is all-comprehensive because it is concerned with the *summum bonum* of life. The four-fold division of caste that is seen among men in society is not due to limitations imposed by man but due to the innate difference in human tendencies and temperaments. Being endowed with respective duties enjoined in the different stations of life one may pursue the ideal fit for his nature with utmost zeal and earnestness for the fulfilment of his aspirations.

Two distinct attitudes towards the world coupled with two kinds of fruits of action have been put forth in this connection. One may devote oneself to obligatory duties with an uneven mind, conjoined with the possibility of success or failure. Even if duty is done in this attitude, one need not shirk one's responsibility. Śrī Kṛṣṇa encourages Arjuna to plunge into the fierce fight which will give him the fruit of action either way.

hato vā prāpsyasi svargaṁ jitvā vā bhokṣyase mahīṁ.

Dying thou gainest heaven; conquering thou enjoyest the earth. *(Gītā,* II. 37)

But Śrī Kṛṣṇa really prefers duties to be accomplished in a disinterested way—in a spirit of worship to the omnipotent Lord. For it is the only way to transcend the fetters of mind and matter and to attain to highest perfection. Herein lies the fulfilment of *Dharma* ideal. It ultimately leads to *Jñāna* in which alone lies liberation, due to purification of the mind.

sukhaduḥkhe same kṛtvā lābhālābhau jayājayau
tato yuddhāya yujyasva naivaṁ pāpamavāpsyasi.

Having made pain and pleasure, gain and loss, conquest

and defeat, the same, engage thou then in the battle. Thus shalt thou incur no sin. *(Ibid.,* II. 38)

tasmāt asaktaḥ satataṁ kāryaṁ karma samācara
asakto hyācaran karma paramāpnoti pūruṣaḥ.

Therefore do thou always perform actions which are obligatory, without attachment;—by performing action without attachment one attains to the highest. *(Ibid.,* III. 19)

naiṣkarmya siddhiṁ paramāṁ sannyāsendhigacchati.

He attains by renunciation to the supreme perfection consisting of freedom from action. (Ibid., XVIII. 49)

In this ideal the world is viewed from the transcendental standpoint and so is negated as transitory and illusory. God alone is held to be real. So He becomes the sole refuge and sheet-anchor.

anityaṁ asukahṁ lokaṁ imaṁ prāpya bhajasva māṁ.

Having attained this human birth in this transitory and unhappy world, worship Me. *(Ibid.,* IX. 33)

Having mentioned the supreme ideal, Śrī Kṛṣṇa lucidates in various ways how the ideal is to be reached. He enunciates the different *yogas,* the *yogas* of work, of devotion, of knowledge and of psychic conrol. Looking down upon one's own duties and giving preference to those of others is considered not only to be derogatory but sinful. Duties in themselves do not differ from one another qualitatively since they originate from the difference of aptitude and are not based on merit. All actions are the product of ignorance and hence are mixed up with evil. He alone crosses the veil of delusion who sees inaction in duties, by strictly adhering to ethical and religious disciplines in a spirit of detachment. Such a person attains to *Brāhmī-sthiti.*

A new horizon of spiritual ideal opens when one hears the benedictory words of Śrī Kṛṣṇa in his message of hope and promise in the *Gītā*.

sarvadharmān parityajya māmekaṁ śaraṇaṁ vraja
ahaṁ tvām sarvapāpebhyo mokṣayiṣyāmi mā suca.

Relinquishing all *dharmas,* take refuge in Me alone; I will liberate thee from all sins; grieve not. (*Ibid.,* XVIII. 66)

In the *Gītā,* Śrī Kṛṣṇa gives a correct interpretation of the Upaniṣadic thought. The *Gītā* is a concretised Upaniṣad and Śrī Kṛṣṇa is the embodiment of the Upaniṣadic ideal.

❑❑❑

10

ON THE ADVENT OF ŚRĪ KṚṢṆA

M.V. Sridatta Sarma

I

"Yo rāmaḥ kṛṣṇatāmetya sārvātmyam prāpya līlayā.
Atoṣayaddaivamounipātalam tam natosmyaham."

(Kṛṣṇopaniṣad)

"I offer my salutations to that Rama who assumed the form of Kṛṣṇa in sport and manifested Himself in all beings and gladdened the multitude of denizens of the celestial zones as also the ascetics."

Various derivations have been given by scholars to the term Kṛṣṇa in literary works. According to Amarasiṁha, the word signifies one who is capable of accomplishing every thing *(sarvam karotīti kṛṣṇaḥ)*. Another interpretation assigned by him is one who causes injury to the fiends *(daityān karṣatīti kṛṣṇaḥ)*. A third meaning suggested is *kṛṣṇa-varnatvāt kṛṣṇaḥ* i.e., because of His dark hue, He is styled *kṛṣṇa.*[1] Yāska in his *Nirukta* also adopts the same interpretation. In the *Śāntiparva* of the *Mahābhārata* Kṛṣṇa says to Arjuna, 'Because of my dark complexion, I am called Kṛṣṇa, Oh Arjuna.' कृष्णो वर्णस्य मे यस्मात् तस्मात् कृष्णोऽहमर्जुन।। Ch. 352, Sl. 14.

In the *Brahmavaivarta Purāṇa,* there are some more elucidations : *kṛṣṇa* means the Universal Spirit. *kṛṣi* denotes a generic term, while *na* conveys the idea of the self, thus bringing for the meaning viz. : Omniscient Spirit. *(kṛṣiśca sarva vacano nakāraścātmavācakaḥ prakīrtitaḥ*). A second explanation offfered is: one who commands the esteem and respect of all, so much so that they devote or dedicate their lives in his service (*Dāsya*). (*Kṛṣi sad bhaktivacano naśca tad dāsya kārakaḥ, dāsyapradātā yaḥ sa kṛṣṇaḥ parikīrtitaḥ*.) He is the Lord, who confers servitude. In the *Bhāgavata, dāsyavṛtti* is held to be one of the modes of *Upāsanā*. A third meaning adopted is in the sense of causation, in view of the Absolute being, the source or cause (seed bed) of creation. *(kṛṣiśca sarvavacano nakāro bījavācakaḥ, sarva-bījaṁ paraṁ brahma kṛṣṇa ityabhidīyate.)*

In the term *kṛṣṇa,* the syllable *ṛ* is derivative of *Brahma*. *Sa* denotes *Śiva* and *ṇa* is indicative of *dharma*. The letter **a** is suggestive of Viṣṇu, who has for his abode the *Śveta Dvīpa*. The *Visarga* conveys the sense of *Naranārāyaṇa* and the accumulation of all *tejas*. He is a mass of all brilliance and splendour and is the one support, as also the seed or cause of everything. *(Sarveṣām tejasām rāśiḥ sarvamūrti svarūpa-kaḥ.)* He manifests Himself in different forms.

According to another interpretation *kṛṣi* signifies the eradication of *Karma* (residuary operative). *Na* is *dāsya-vācaka,* while *a* is *dātṛvācaka* (in the sense of conferer of beatitude in response to the supplications offered). He is the One who cuts asunder all the knots of action and in returrn confers on the aspirant *Haridāsya*. From this, He is remem-bered as *kṛṣṇa*. *Kṛṣ* denotes the unmoving or static force. *(kṛṣi niśceṣṭavacano nakāro bhaktivācakaḥ. Akāraḥ prāptiva-canaḥ tena kṛṣṇaḥ prakīrtitaḥ). "Kṛṣṇajanmakhaṇḍa"* Ch. 13. sl. 60-61.

There is one more derivation given which brings forth the idea of deliverance or the conferment of beatitude (the summum bonum). *(kṛṣir nirvāṇa vacano nakāro mokṣavāca-kaḥ) Kṛṣṇa* is the granter of the highest bliss. His name is charming and instils reverence.

Kṛṣṇeti sundaraṁ nāmaṁ maṅgalam baktidāyakaṁ
kakāroccāraṇādbhaktaḥ kaivalyaṁ mṛtyujanmahaṁ.
—*Op. cit.* 65.

By the very repetition of the syllable *Ka,* the neophyte will obtain immunity from the cycle of births and deaths. By the repetition of *r,* the aspirant will become His devoted servant and by *na* he begets the divine communion. The deity is assimilated in the *bhakta.* A likeness or resemblance will be noticed *(Sārūpya),*[2] by the utterance of the *Visarga.*

tatsārūpyaṁ visargādeva labhante nātra saṁśayaḥ.
kakāroccāraṇādeva vepante yama-kiṅkarāḥ.
—*Op. cit.* 67.

By the repetition of the syllable *ka,* the attendants of *Yama* will flee away and stand at a league's distance. By the utterenace of *ṣa* all evils are wiped off. *Na* is a curer of diseases. While repeating *a,* one conquers death.

ṛkārokter na tiṣṭanti ṣakarāt pātakāni ca.
nakāroccāraṇād rogā akārānmṛtyureva ca.
dhruvam sarve palāyante nāmoccāraṇa bhīravaḥ
smṛtyukti śravaṇodyogāt kṛṣṇanāmno vrajeśvaraḥ
—*Op. cit.* 68-69.

(The fiends can neither hear nor pronounce the name of the Lord.)

Another etymological derivation is given in the *Mahābhārata* (Udyogaparva : Ch. LXX-5) according to which *kṛṣiḥ* denotes existence *(kṛṣiḥ sattāvacanaḥ)* while *ṇa* is expressive of intelligence and bliss *(nakāro nirvṛtivacanaḥ).* The union of these two words is called *Kṛṣṇa* or the Eternal *Brahman.*

कृषिर्भूवाचकः शब्दो णश्च निर्वृतिवाचकः।
विष्णुस्तद्भावयोगाच्च कृष्णो भवति शास्वतः॥

Śrī Rāma's personality was so fascinating that it produced an everlasting effect (impression) in the minds of the forest-dwelling sages. It was stupefying even for men *(puṃsām mohanarūpāya)*. Hanuman describes Rama thus: 'That Rama with the eyes resembling the lotus petals captivates the minds of all beings. *(Rāmaḥ kamalapatrākṣaḥ sarvabhūtamanoharaḥ.)*' Even the friend Mārica praises Rāma's handsome form. He says: 'This scion of the Raghu's race is really handsome, with the bow and arrows held in his lotus shaped hands.' *(Raghunandana eṣa sundaraḥ karapadmārpita bāṇa kārmukaḥ.)*

The *Bhaktas* could not afford to part with Rāma at the end of his mission, being filled with ecstasy. These great souls striving after spiritual knowledge and concentrating their minds in perfect absorption into the one object of their meditation dedicated their souls to him and even thought of clasping him. No obstacles could deviate these masters of their selves while in the pursuance of their ends (in that state of superconsciousness). They were assured by the Lord that in his next incarnation, he would afford them full oppportunities to clasp him. This forms the subject matter of the *Kṛṣṇa Upaniṣad* (the eighth incarnation of Viṣṇu), while the sages were reborn as Gopis, who sported with Him. The anecdote serves as a hint or forecast to the full-fledged *Avatāra* of Viṣṇu in the form of Kṛṣṇa. The forest dwellers fest satisfied for having accomplished their ends and they remained in a state of bliss.

The Upaniṣad discusses at full length the import or the part played by the different characters who came in contact with Kṛṣṇa. In short, this is an allegorical or metaphorical account. The three *guṇas* or constitutents are assigned thus: the *sattva* or the quality of goodness to Rudra; the *rājasic* (passion) trait to *Brahma* and the devotees; and the *tāmasic* aspect (state of inertia) to the fiends. Nanda stands for the Supreme Spirit, while Yaśodā lays the role of the mistress in the house of liberation. Vāsudeva symbolizes the Vedic Texts, while the quintessence of the holy knowledge is centred round Balarāma and Kṛṣṇa, who as a sequel to the prayers whispered silently by the *Bhaktas* descended down on the earth. Kṛṣṇa rallied round and played in sport with the cowherds, maids and the denizens of the celestial zone at Brindavan.

The 16,100 gopis and cows were associated with Kṛṣṇa are mere personifications of the hymns of the Vedas or what all they uttered and sang before Him were revelations of divine knowledge (the mystical writings attached to the *Brāhmaṇas* i.e. *Upaniṣads)*. The staff held by the cowherds stands for the lotus-seated Brahmā, who witnessed the scene. The bamboo flute and the horn which served as musical instruments represent Śiva and Mahendra respectively. (While Śiva's body is made up of Nāda, Mahendra strikes it with the thunderbolt). The villages and groves surrounding Gokula, which form the background for the divine recreation is interpreted as Vaikuṇṭha, the abode of Nārāyaṇa. The trees around indicate the sages, who, as it were, remained motionless, transfixed into that state of *Nirvikalpa Samādhi* and eschewing all those knots rising from illusion, misapprehension and irresolution.

ātmārāmāvihitaratayo nirvikalpe samādhau
jñānotsekāt vighṭitatamogranthayaḥ satvaniṣṭhāḥ.
(*Veṇīsaṁhāra* : I-23).

They were like those wise men, who have realized the higher truths of religion with a view to reunite with the Absolute, cutting asunder the effects of *Karma* and warding off all doubts.[3] Avarice and anger represent the demoniacal forms which disturb the seeker after Truth.

Lord Hari in the form of the cowherd waged war against these forces (evil spirits) and suppressed them. These were in other words suggestive of the *dānavas,* who disturbed the eternal order of righteousness and moral virtues. As if by illusion, the entire world was stupefied by His *Līlās* (unfathomable sport). The result was that the earth became unconquerable by evil forces, while the sages and the twice-born became bold enough to continue their austerities. Like a wizard, Kṛṣṇa transformed Rudra into a flute. In an instant, the prowess and knowledge of the *devas* was captured. Their minds were turned down from all speech. Their associations with Him rendered them fearless, remaining in that state of bliss.[4] The serpent Śeṣa assumed the form of Balarāma, while the eternal Lord descended down to earth as Kṛṣṇa.

The wrestler Chāṇūra stands for malignity, while the pugilistic encounterer Muṣṭika (with his fisticuff) is a byeword for envy. The elephant demon *Kuvalayāpīda* is an epithet for arrogance (insolence). Agha, the serpent demon, is a synonym of dreadful diseases like black leprosy. Baka, the bird demon is always remembered for his pride. The ruler Kaṁsa is none other than Kali himself—the very personification of wickedness.

Mother Rohiṇī serves as the asylum for compassion, while Satyabhāmā remains as an attribute for Mother Earth, who silently bears with perseverance and tolerance the misdeeds of mortals. Sudāmā, the next neighbour of Kṛṣṇa in the days of His childhood is the very embodiment of mental quietness (equipoise), being free from all passions. Akrūra as his very name connotes is an example of sincerity and genuineness. The noble Uddhava serves as a model for all to follow in the tendency of drawing the mind from evil propensities.

Viṣṇu establishes himself as Lakṣmī in the conch-shell. The ocean of milk springs up and the thundering clouds shower rains. Assuming the form of a child Kṛṣṇa sports as before in the great ocean. With a view to suppress the evil forces at work and to defend the meek, the Lord came down to earth. He devised the disc *(Sudarśana),* which is indicative of the composite part of the Supreme Spirit. His splendour is shown by the glittering sword (representing *Rudra* or *Maheśvara Śakti).* The mortar and the cord with which Kṛṣṇa was fastened symbolize the Sage Kaśyapa and Aditi, the parents of all living beings (worldly existence). The discus and the conch denote absolution and final beatitude attained by constant action and effort *(Cakraṁ śaṅkhaṁ ca saṁsiddhiṁ binduṁ ca sarvamūrdhani).* The *bindu* is indicative of the highest centre—the thousand petalled lotus *(Sahasrāra)* situated in the head. The bow Śārṅga is Kṛṣṇa's own artifice.

The lotus stem held by Kṛṣṇa for amusement indicates the seed of the universe. Garuḍa, the celestial eagle signifies the fig tree *(Vatabhānda).* The basil or Rādhikā is suggestive of *Bhakti* (devotion), as also *Kriyā* (comprehension or intellect) that is manifest in all beings.

In *Gopālatāpinyupaniṣad (Uttara),* we find a continuation of the metaphorical description of Kṛṣṇa. The three constituents together with the conceit or conception of individuality (ego sense) serve as His four hands. The conch held by Him is representative of the five elements, while the discus is signified by the wavering mind *(calasvarūpaṁ atyantamanascakraṁ nigadyate).* Primordial *Māyā* is the horny bow *Śārṅga (ādya māyā bhavecchārṅgaḥ).* The *Padma* or lotus is expressive of the Universe *(padmaṁ viśvaṁ kare sthitaṁ).* The mace held by Him is indicative of the first science (knowledge). The bracelet worn by Him, comprise duty, wealth and desire (three of the ends in life). His neck is formed of what is beyond properties or qualities and it is decorated with the garland of eternity. The Supreme *Sattva* quality (which is immovable, unchangeable and remains perpetually the same) serves Him as the crown. The imperishable existences which spread far and wide decorate

Him as ear-rings. The person, who meditates on Him will attain salvation.

'To him, who is engrossed in meditation, will be revealed the nature of the Self. In this state, the devotee will realize that he is identical with the Infinite. To him, I will grant the knowledge of the Self.'

"dhyāyen, mama priyo nityaṁ sa mokṣaṁ adhigacchati.
sa mukto bhavati, tasmai ca ātmānaṁ dadāmī."
—Gopālottaratāpinyupaniṣad.

The Supreme Lord represents that mighty force or form which remains neither split nor unsplit. He serves as a sign of the collective unit or the Universal Spirit. From the point of view of the collective unit or the aggregate of all parts, He serves the purpose of a single whole or integral part (Unitarian or *Samaṣṭi*). Each part in turn *(Vyaṣṭi)* remains consubstantially the same with the whole. *(tasmānnābhinnam nābhirbhinnamābhirbhinno na vai vibhuḥ.—Kṛṣṇopaniṣad)*

By virtue of the knowledge of the identity of the whole *(Hiraṇyagarbha)* with the part, the conception of the totality remains. In the absence of that knowledge on the part of the *Jīva*, the question of individuality will arise.

"samaṣṭirīśaḥ sarveṣām svātma tādātmya vedanāt.
tadabhāvāt tadanye ca jñāyante vyaṣṭisaṁjñayā."
(Pañcadaśī).

REFERENCES

1. It is stated that Viṣṇu is white in *Satya Yuga*, red in *Tretā Yuga*, yellow in *Dvāpara* and dark in the *Kali* Age. That which is most perfect is known as Kṛṣṇa, which is a bye-word for the Infinite.
2. There are four stages for realisation. *(a)* attainment of the vicinity of the Divine Form *(Sāmipya)*. *(b)* Remaining in the same world or sphere *(Sālokya)*. *(c)* Attaining the sameness of form *(Sārupya)*, and *(d)* Intimate union, or identification or absorption with the deity *(Sāyujya)*.

3. *bhidyate hṛdayagranthiśchidyante sarva saṁśayāḥ.*
kṣīyante cāsya karmāṇi tasmin dṛṣṭe parāvare.
—Cf. *Muṇḍaka Upaniṣad,* II-8.

4. *yato vāco nivartante aprāpya manasā saha*
ānandam brahmaṇo vidvān na bibheti kutaścana.
—*Taittirīya Upaniṣad,* II-9-1.

❑❑❑

11

KURUKSHETRA—THE LAND OF THE BHAGAVADGĪTĀ

Mallika Clare Gupta

Less than a hundred miles from Delhi, just off a modern macadamized motor road, is the ancient and historic site of the battle of Kurukshetra. Besides being the scene of the famous conflict between the Pāṇḍavas and the Kauravas, as related in the great epic of India, the *Mahābhārata,* it has other claims to glory as well.

There, in ancient times, on the banks of the River Saraswati, Ṛṣis chanted in sonorous tones the glorious Sanskriti of the Vedas; the gods themselves performed sacrifices and great sages realized the immortal Self. There were Ashramas in Kurukshetra with thousands of students. These Ashramas were like universities where the Vedic culture and philosophy as well as secular subjects were taught. Kurukshetra has existed from the earliest dawn of Aryan history in India. It was settled by one of the five original groups of Aryans who migrated into (or lived in) India thousands of years ago. Located to the northwest of modern Delhi, it comprised many villages and towns with its capital at Sthāniśvar, now known as Thāneśvar. Sthāniśvar may be translated as the place of *Īśvara,* or the land of God. For ages and ages pilgrims and devotees have cherished in their hearts its holy tradition, for Kurukshetra is the place where Śrī Kṛṣṇa taught the immortal truths of the *Bhagavad Gītā.*

An ancient text relates that King Kuru, who was an ancestor of both the Pāṇḍavas and the Kauravas and whose date may be roughly calculated by studying the names of the kings from Yudhisthira (eldest brother of the Pāṇḍavas) back to Kuru as one-thousand years before the battle of Kurukshetra, came to this land in a golden chariot and out of its gold made a plough. He borrowed Shiva's bull and Yama's buffalo and started to plough the earth. Soon Indra came and asked the king what he was doing. Kuru replied, 'I am preparing the land for the cultivation of the eight-fold virtues.' (This has reference to the disciplines of Yoga) Indra asked, 'Where is the seed?' And Kuru replied, 'Oh, it is in my possession.' Indra went on his way and Kuru returned to his ploughing. Then Viṣṇu appeared and asked of the king the same questions Indra had asked. Again, Kuru gave the same replies. But Viṣṇu said, 'Give me the seed and I will sow it for you.' Thereupon King Kuru extended his right arm and it was cut into pieces by Viṣṇu's *Cakra* (invincible, circular-shaped weapon), and the pieces were sown in the field. In the same way Kuru offered the rest of his limbs and, finally, his head. Viṣṇu was pleased with his sacrifice, blessed him, and disappeared. Then Indra, who had witnessed all this, returned and told Kuru that any boon he might ask of him would be granted. Kuru asked two boons; one,that this land would be a holy land and that it would be named after him; the other, that anyone dying here would go to heaven whether he had been a saint or a sinner. So, the land became known as the field of Kuru, or Kurukshetra, and tradition holds it to be most holy.

Kurukshetra is as hoary with history as it is with legend and tradition. In fact, these combine to give it continuity from the most remote times until today. The date of the battle of Kurukshetra, which sets it on the historical stage, has, however, often been in question. In the *Mahābārata* there is a reference, made just before the battle took place,to certain inauspicious planetary positions which, it was believed, foreshadowed unprecedented death and destruction on the battlefield. From this astronomical reference calculations have been made and some people believe that the date of the battle of Kurukshetra is about 2500 B.C., approximately 4500 years ago. Other sources date it about 1500 B.C. Whatever the date may be we find that from the time of that devastating battle down to the end of the 5th century A.D. Kurukshetra does not feature in the innumerable wars of conquest recorded in Indian history. We have to rely on tradition and the stray mention of it by writers and travellers. The invasions of the Persians (beginning of the 5th century B.C.) and of the Greeks (3rd century B.C.) as well as the incursions of other foreign forces do not appear to have affected Kurukshetra adversely to any great extent, for when Megasthenes visited it in about 300 B.C. he found it very prosperous. There was peace and plenty, and art and industry flourished under royal patronage. During the ascendancy of Buddhism it still retained its position as a great centre of Hindu culture. In fact, from about 270 B.C. to 470 A.D., throughout the eras of the Mauryan Empire and the Gupta (Golden Age) Dynasty, Kurukshetra prospered both materially and spiritually. But towards the close of the 5th century A.D. when the Huns, the fierce barbarians who came from the stepes of Central Asia, over-ran parts of upper India Kurukshetra was in the front line of defence. History tells us that the rulers of Thaneswar stand pre-eminent among the Indian kings who distinguished themselves in defending the country against the invaders. These incursions of the Huns continued during most of the 6th century until the outsiders were repelled. In the beginning of the 7th century (606 A.D.) King Harsha Vardhana of the royal house of

Thaneswar came to power. He also took over the throne of the King of Kanauj after the assassination of that monarch by conspirators. Harsha has been described as a great warrior, a scholar, a patron of learning and a connoisseur of the arts. He was the author of several plays himself and the well-known writer, Bāṇa, was one of his courtiers. Bāṇa described Thaneswar as a place of great wealth and religion, and he said that the atmosphere was full of the sound of Vedic hymns. During Harsha's rule half of the income of the State was given to the spreading of education and culture. The place was visitied by scholars, students and pilgrims from all parts of India. It was during the reign of Harsha that the Chinese traveller, Hiuen Tsiang (Yuan Chwang), visited Thaneśvar which then included the whole area of Kurukshetra. He wrote in glowing terms about the life there at that time. He found the government honestly administered and the inhabitants truthful and of pure moral principle. He said the city of Thaneśvar had one-hundred temples and that there was prosperous trade with other lands. The climate was good and the soil productive.

After the death of Harsha, without heir, there were bitter contests for the empire he had consolidated, which stretched from upper India to Bihar and Orissa. Though the civil strife recorded in history for the next fourhundred years is like a marathon chess game, which involved most of the kingdoms of India, Kurukshetra again seems to have been left to itself, probably because the capital of Harsha's empire had been removed from Thaneswar to Kanauj, and so Kurukshetra was not a political prize. We may presume that conditions remained more or less peaceful in that area, that it was not strategically important and that it was considered by all to be a holy land. However, when the Muslim invaders from the west began to pour into India from the 11th century onwards, Kurukshetra was constantly involved in the struggles with the invaders. In fact, it experienced repeated invasions, occupations, and cruel domination by the foreign rulers. The great Rajputs, the valiant Sikhs, and the heroic Maharattas fought bravely against the enemies. The famous battles of Kaithal, Karṇal, Thaneswar, and the three momentous battles of Panipet, all within the Kurukshetra area, inflicted great sufferings. This reached its height during the reign of Aurangzeb, the most bigoted of the emperors (1658-1707) and continued down to the invasion of Ahmed Shah Abdali (Durrani, 1761). The glorious and ancient temples were demolished, images were dashed to pieces, seats of learning desecrated, and cities sacked. After these repeated and devastating onslaughts most of the inhabitants of the area at last migrated towards the Himālayas.

Today, the area indeed looks like an old battlefield. Much of it is without trees and for vast expanses one sees little cultivation. Here and there are large mounds of earth overgrown with wild grass under which, one feels, trophies of the wars could easily be found if one but scratched the earth with a fingernail. There are many temples and small shrines but none of these is very old. However, they serve to remind us of the glorious past as they are built on the ruins of the old. It is to the holy men and the *Saṁnyāsīs* of ancient times that we owe what details we have today of Kurukshetra. They had no worldly goods to lose and they had gone beyond fear, so they roamed about the area throughout the awful years, lining in caves, where unmolested they could meditate in peace. These holy men marked with stones the places where shrines and temples had been and occasionally they offered their worship to these. They retained and handed down to their disciples the history, which we now call tradition, of the holy land of Kurukshetra. Today, a visitor is shown the place where Karṇa, one of the greatest heroes of the *Mahābhārata,* was killed by a powerful weapon from the mighty bow of Arjuna when one of his chariot wheels sank deep into the earth. Bhishma, the grand old man of the *Mahābhārata,* grand uncle to both the Pāṇḍavas and the Kauravas, was fatally wounded during the battle and like the true warrior that he was lay on a bed of arrows, there to expire like a hero. Bhiṣma asked Arjuna for some water with which to quench his thirst, but as Arjuna knew that he would not drink ordinary water he pierced the earth with an arrow and out gushed a spring of pure, clear water. (This is an allusion to the origin of Bhiṣma who was supposed to have been born of Gaṅgā.) This spot is about three miles from the Kurukṣetra tank and is called Bāṇ Gaṅgā. Before the battle of Kurukṣetra the five Pāṇḍava brothers, in exile, spent some time in the Kamyaka forest and this is believed to have been on the site of the present town of Kamada. About five miles from Thaneswar is the village of Amin, situated on a huge mound. There, Dronacharya, the guru in warfare of both the Pāṇḍavas and the Kauravas, used the military strategy called, Chakra-vyuha, a surrounding tactic much like the pincer movement of the last war. It was there that Abhimanyu, the son of Arjuna, lost his life. People say that the name of the village, Amin, is a corruption of his name. About one-half mile from this village is the place where Arjuna killed Jayadhratha, who was responsible for the death of his son. Near Thaneswar is a Kali temple where, it is said, the Pāṇḍavas worshipped, this form of the Deity just before the battle. This temple is one of the fifty-two most sacred temples of the Devi which are found in various parts of India.

Besides places associated with the battle of Kurukṣetra the area abounds in sites connected with other great traditional interests. One is shown the place where the ancient sages Viśvāmitra and Vasiṣṭha had their hermitages and practised austerities. There is a cave known as Vasishta's cave with a sacred well nearby where the ashes of the dead are sometimes put. It is claimed that Vāman, the Dwarf, or the fourth incarnation of Viṣṇu, was born near Amin. The immortal Parsuram, guru of Dronacharya, performed Vedic sacrifices in this area. One is told that the town of Kaithal (corrupted from Kapisthal—land of monkeys) is the birthplace of the great Hanuman, the heroic devotee of the Lord in his incarnation as Rama. These are only a few of the three-hundred and sixty tirthas (ancient and holy places) within the area of Kurukshetra. As recent as 1948 a part of the ashes of Mahatma Gandhi was immersed in the Brahmasar Tank in Kurukshetra. Kurukshetra is visited by thousands of pilgrims every year, some on their way to the Himalayan shrines of Kedarnath and Bhadri Narayan. It is said that the great Śaṅkarācārya stopped at Kurukshetra on his way to the Himalayas and this also adds holiness to it for the pilgrims of today. During solar eclipses hundreds of thousands of pilgrims from all parts of India gather at Kurukshetra.

Although the ancient glories, the shrines, the temples, the great Ashramas, the sacred forests, the holy rivers and ponds have disappeared or dried up and little trace of them is left, there is one particular spot which is claimed to be much as it was some 3500, or more, years ago. It, in fact, has always been considered as the most sacred spot in the whole of Kurukshetra. Three miles from Thaneswar under a garlanded and very ancient Banyan tree, said to be the living witness of the event, is the place where according to tradition Śrī Kṛṣṇa, who had assumed the role of the Charioteer of Arjuna, taught the immortal truths of the *Bhagavad-Gītā*. The Pāṇḍava army was approaching from Viratnagar in the west and the Kauravas from Hastinapur in the east when

Arjuna asked the Divine Charioteer to place his chariot in the middle of the field, between the two opposing forces. The war-chariot of Arjuna, banners and ensign flying and drawn by four majestic white stallions keyed up for the fray, was brought to a sudden halt. Kings from all over India with their greatest warriors and gathered together. They were all in battle dress, protected by intricate armour which slittered and shone like jewels. Their colorful costumes and turbans were beset with gems,some of fabulour value. It is believed by some that the great hero, Karṇa, wore as his turban decoration the famous diamond later known as the Koh-i-noor, which had been given to him by Śrī Kṛṣṇa. The Pāṇḍava army consisted of seven divisions, that is approximately 150,000 war-chariots and the same number of specially trained and armoured elephants, and 450,000 cavalry and 750,000 foot soldiers. The army of the Kauravas consisted of 11 divisions. As these two massive armies were advancing towards the battlefield the blare of trumpets and the blowing of horns and conch-shells pierced the air time and again, as each great warrior's challenging blast was accepted and flung back from the other side. Colourful banners and flags were flying in the wind, cymbals were clashing, horses neighing, elephants trumpting and there was loud beating of war drums. The mingling of these mighty omens of battle was deafening. War had been declared and as both sides awaited the commands of their leaders there was comparative quiet again. When Arjuna, standing in his chariot between the two armies, saw his brother, cousins, nephews, uncles, and other revered members of the two families, and all the other great warriors thus arrayed against each other he lost all interest in the forthcoming battle. He could not bring himself to take part in the awful slaughter which was imminent. It was at this point that the immortal dialogue known as the *Bhagavad-Gītā* took place.

The *Bhagavad-Gītā* is considered by Hindus to be almost an encyclopedia of spiritual counsel. Many are the commentaries written by eminent scholars down the ages, highlighting and eulogizing particular aspects of the teachings, and various are the opinions as to which path is superior to the others but Sri Ramakrishna, who could pinpoint the most abstruse philosophies and reconcile diverse and conflicting opinions, has given us in one word the essence of the teachings of the *Bhagavad-Gītā*. Sri Ramakrishna said that if you keep repeating the word, *Gītā,* it becomes *T(y)āgi*. A *Tyāgi* is a man of renunciation, one who has renounced or surrendered himself to God. Whether God be considered as the *Brhaman* of the *Jñānīs*, the *Paramātman* of the Yogis, the Lord and Doer of all actions of the *Karmis,* or the beloved Lord, God incarnate, of the *Bhaktas,* the individualized ego, the small self, must be surrendered, must be renounced. So, through the *Bhagavad-Gītā* Śrī Kṛṣṇa taught Arjuna the various ways by which one may surrender himself and all his actions to God.

As a climax to these teachings Śrī Kṛṣṇa gave Arjuna the vision of his universal form, or the visual experience that all forms, all space, all time and all causality are in the Almighty Being. It was as if Arjuna suddenly saw a blazing form which contained the whole universe. The sun, the moon, the stars and planets which embraced everything that was or had been. In wonder he gazed and saw that within that Resplendent One were myriads of faces, mouths, bodies, limbs. All the Gods, the ancient sages, the noble ancestors,—all were in that universal form. Then Arjuna saw that the great warriors of Kurukshetra, his own kith and kin, with their chariots, horses, elephants, whole armies—all things—were being mercilessly crushed in the massive jaws of the universal Being, the Doer of all actions. In one mighty moment past, present and future were telescoped into one and Arjuna stood face to face with timeless Time. The impact of his staggering experience swept Arjuna into a mental whirlpool; his senses reeled and he felt that he was being forsaken by his mind. He grasped for the memory of his beloved companion, counsellor and guide, Śrī Kṛṣṇa, and with folded palms implored the universal Being to show him again that gentle, human form to which he was so happily accustomed. The infinite Being, infinite in might and in mercy, again assumed the form of the familiar Kṛṣṇa, and Arjuna fell prostrate at his feet.

Tradition claims that this experience of Arjuna's and the teachings imparted to him by Śrī Kṛṣṇa, which are recorded in the *Bhagavad-Gītā,* took place at Kurukshetra, under the ancient Banyan tree believed to be the living witness of it all. The place is called Jyotiśwar, which means the brilliance of the Light of God. It is called so because here Arjuna had the vision of the Resplendent One. Just besides the tree is a large pool of water and devotees believe that the pool of Jyotiśwar still retains some of that splendour. True, it is unusually brilliant. The reflection of the sun on its waters is almost blinding. Perhaps science could give some reason for this phenomenon but the accepted explanation has satisfied millions and millions of people for the last 3,500 or even more, years.

Whether the *Bhagavad-Gītā* as we know it today was interpolated at some later date into the great epic, the *Mahābhārata,* as some modern scholars think, is of little importance to thsoe who love the *Gītā* for they 'have come to eat the mangoes, not to count the leaves on the tree,' to use an expression of Śrī Ramakrishna. Epics were sometimes handed down from generation to genertion, long before they were compiled and put into script. The verity or the antiquity of the actual happenings of the *Gītā* are not affected by the date of its compilation. It may even be that the teachings of Śrī Kṛṣṇa took only a few minutes of time, as we know it, somewhat like the experiences Swami Vivekananda had when touched by his Master, Sri Ramakrishna, for the teacher was God Himself and the disciple His own counterpart.

Tradition also holds to the belief that Jyotiśwar is the sacred place where the *Gītā* was enacted, because from time immemorial great scholars, renowned *sadhus* and saints, and earnest devotees from all over India have made pilgrimages to Kurukshetra for the express purpose of reading, or hearing read, the holy *Bhagavad-Gītā* at Jyotiśwar, under the ancient Banyan tree, beside the pool of the Light of God.

❑❑❑

12

THE GOAL OF HUMAN LIFE ACCORDING TO JÑĀNAYOGA

Swami Gnaneswarananda

The highest goal of human life has been considered by the *Jñānayogins* as total absorption into the Infinite Substance. We are warned that there is danger as long as any consciousness of separateness from that ultimate Reality exists. There is always cause for apprehension if there are two existences. If God and I are separate and distinct there could be so many moods flowing from one to the other. Furthermore, there is time, space and causation and as long as there are these three there is the possibility of transformation and change. So where is security, peace and perfection, in the presence of two?

It certainly is a wonderful state to remain concentrated and absorbed in the love of God, to enjoy the presence of the divine Being, but from the viewpoint of security you cannot say that one is absolutely "safe". Complete safety is attained when the worshipper and the worshipped, the human soul and the Divine Existence, become one and identical. We are not considering the question from the viewpoint of enjoyment; for if we ask for that we must stay in the dualistic state. But enjoyment is not always to be sought. A time will come when you are concerned more about security than mere enjoyment and there is no security, no rest, until one has transcended all consciousness of duality. It is true of course that by going through the state of enjoyment of God, one can eventually attain the state of Oneness. Man may start as a dualist adoring His Divinity, loving his God with his body, mind and soul, and enjoying the love of God showered upon him, but a time must come, in the course of the unfoldment of that soul, when he will attain that state of unity.

Now that unity, which is the goal of *Jñānayoga,* if it is unity at all, cannot be attained. Unity really cannot be attained. It must either exist all the time or it can never be found. If I am not one and the same with the divine Principle now, at this present moment, I cannot be so, say, two years from now. If I am not one and identical with that Principle at this present spot, travelling throughout the universe I shall never be able to reach a spot where I shall be able to become one with It. So, if we admit this proposition at all, that finally we have to attain our unity with the divine Principle, we must admit that we are one with it now. No separation ever took place. It is only our false conception regarding our self that has created this monstrous blunder that we think we are separated from the divine Substance. As a result of ignorance we are compelled to think that that divine Perfection is far, far away from us. When ignorance is removed we find that all the time, always, under all circumstances, we have been one and the same with It.

Herein comes the question of removing the obstacles. In other words, purification of the consciousness. Our consciousness is heavily burdened with impurities. As soon as those impurities clinging to the surface of the consciousness are eliminated, the inner lustre, the perfection, shines without hindrance. If we can successfully eliminate the impurities clinging to this so-called individual consciousness, this consciouness which I am calling 'mine', calling finite and imperfect, will attain the state of absolute Consciousness.

This truth must be very well assimilated. Look within and you will find that you are conscious of the existene of Something within, a power, a light, a force, (call it by any name), but of course we are reluctant to admit that that power within us is universal, is omnipotent. And the reason for that reluctancy is that the self has accumulated dust and dirt, as the result of which its inner, Absolute nature has been completely hidden. It is the same self, appearing as a finite imperfect entity. This consciousness of ours which we sometimes call our mind, our intelligence,—this is the divine Substance. You do not have to go anywhere to seek it. This is one hundred per cent divine. We have to eliminate the accumulated imperfections.

A beautiful illustration has been given—of the purification of gold. Gold intrinsically is pure and brilliant, but when it is mixed with other substances it may appear devoid of lustre; it may look like an ordinary stone. In order to make gold shine in its own purity we must know the process of purifiying it. This substance which we are handling every day—our inner consciousness—is like a pure, precious metal. What we have to do is to eliminate the impurities from the ore.

By analysing this 'ore' of our consciousness expert 'minerologists' have come to the conclusion that there are three things very impure, that cling to it. One is of a very gross nature. It is not compounded with the ore but it clings to it as a coating, just an external coating. To get rid of it you have to put the ore on the 'anvil' and hammer it, that cleanses it. There are other types of impurities that cannot be eliminated by the hammering method, because these impurities have almost formed a chemical compound. A strong 'chemical' has to be used to elimminate them. Then a very subtle form of impurity still persists. That can only be eliminated by putting it into the "fire". When it comes out of the "fire" it comes out as pure gold.

We are all going through these processes, willingly or unwillingly, knowingly or unknowingly. I do not believe that the path to perfection is strewn with petals of roses. It is beset with many difficulties. That is why, perhaps, we find in all forms of religious and philosophical thought, suffering has been glorified, extolled. But mere suffering as suffering is no glory! When suffering becomes a conscious process of purification then it is no more suffering. Only by going through that state of suffering one can atttain perfection, but mere suffering will not do. If that were so all the homeless, suffering, starving people would be the holiest. We cannot say either that those who have lived in luxury are nearer perfection. We have to go through that conscious process of purification. No soul can enter into the 'kingdom of heaven' without it. Gradually, going through that process of purification this consciousness gets rid of the different layers of imperfections, but even at the last stage of this process it has some defect clinging to it. Although it might appear to be absolutely pure and clear, if it retains the individual character, if it is still a unit by itself, it might be blessed but it is not safe. Again a whirlwind might overcome it and throw it again into a dust bin, because it is not yet the All. Unless and until it has become the All it is not safe.

That state of being the All has been called the state of *Nirvikalpa Samādhi,* a state where there is no duality of any kind. Even if your consciousness which is now full of grief and complaints becomes pure and abounds in happiness and power, that consciousness will still be the consciousness of an individual, in spite of the possession of those qualities. You will think : 'My consciousness is full of bliss, of peace.' It is still an individual consciousness, do not think that what has been attained will last for ever. Absolute security is attained by non-dualistic consciousness. If your ideal is one of enjoyment you will hate the thought of the non-dualistic consciousness. If your ideal is one of enjoyment you will hate the thought of the non-dualistic state. You will repeat with the *Bhakta* : 'I do not want to be sugar; I want to eat sugar.' All right, go ahead, eat sugar, but you might get a stomach-ache! You are not secure. Security is attained by being sugar.

That state is extolled in the following verses. You will find that Śaṅkarācārya is encouraging us not to stop until that final goal of *Nirvikalpa Samādhi* has been attained. Totally merge into that substance, into that infinite ocean of *Sat-Cit-Ānandam.* There is no compromise; that is the goal. There this container, our consciousness, will melt and will not exist any more, and there will not be any tendency to come back.

If that state were suddenly given to us most of us would resist it with all the force at our command. I am sure many of you have studied the life of Swami Vivekannada. Ramakrishna, by a mare touch, brought that condition of *Nirvikalpa Samādhi* to Swami Vivekananda when he was a young boy—and how he resisted! He has described what happened then in words something like this: 'There was a whirlpool that was moving the entire universe. I could see the heavens, the planets, being merged, My body was being disintegrated, and mother, family and friends had vanished.' And he cried out: 'What are you doing to me?'

Those who have gone into that *Nirvikalpa* state rarely come back. In history there is record of only a few who have done so. Shiva, for instance, and Shukadev (he could never grow old, he remained as a little boy because he touched that *Nirvikalpa* state). Of course, Ramakrishna could go at will into that state again and again and come back to normal consciouness. We have ample proof of that.

However, we must reconcile ourselves that the *Nirvikalpa Samādhi,* total absorption is the goal. Do not think that you do not believe in a heaven. You may not believe in a hell, for we can only think in terms of sense enjoyment. One has to convince oneself that there is no sense enjoyment which is lasting. Say : 'I only want to be what I am, I want to be absorbed in it.' There is suffering in heaven, perhaps, and quarrels and jealousies. In the realm of phenomena there is always suffering. To make up one's mind to attain that state of *Nirvikalpa Samādhi* is to reject any subject-object consciousness. That state has been described in terms of matter because we cannot talk in any other language. A poet says : 'If ten-thousand suns could shed their light at one moment it would appear weak before the glory of that Knowledge; if twenty million moons could shed their brilliance in one volume, that would not compare with the radiance of that Knowledge.'

(Question) : 'In that ocean of infinite bliss there would be no forms. Individual enjoyment would not exist there, how could we enjoy it?' (Swami) : 'The assurance has been given that nothing can be missed there. It is the sum total of all the bliss you can think of. Suppose you like to swim in a pool of water and you enjoy drinking from another, floating a boat in another—this gives you individual happiness. Now suppose one vast sheet of water includes all these pools which you enjoy in different ways, nothing is excluded from it. Nothing will be missed in that *Nirvikalpa Samādhi*. The individual enjoyment that we derive from the senses is just a little particle, but in that state is contained the sum-total of everything. So there is no reason to get discouraged.'

However, to continue, this consciousness of ours just

now, no matter how it appears, is the substance besides which ten-million suns and millions of moons look pale. We have to get rid of certain impurities that are clinging to it. So let us start with the hammering, rubbing, scrubbing and the fire-text processes with understanding and happiness, conscious that going through these stages we are purifying our 'gold.' It is not vain glorification of suffering. It is not self torture, which is a complex, but it is, perhaps, self-analysis. Understand the possibility of deriving benefit from all sorts of conditions you may find yourself in.

As gold purified by thorough heating in the fire gives up its impurities and attains its own lustre, so the mind, through meditation gives up its impurities of *Sattva, Rajas* and *Tamas,* and attains to the reality of *Brahman.*

—*Vivekacūḍāmaṇi,* 361.

This mind, now, is *Brahman,* but it has been covered up by three layers of impurities. The innermost is *Sāttvic,* the next *Rājasic* and the coutermost is *Tāmasic.* We get rid of *Tamas* by the hammering method, of *Rajas* by scrubbing, and of *Sattva* by applying the fire of discrimination and meditation.

'Desires are like knots.' Even the desire to see God is a knot which has to be cut. You remember when Sri Ramakrishna was going through the monistic practices with his Guru, Totapuri, he could eliminate all conceptions from his consciousness except the form of his beloved God, Kālī, and Totapuri picked up a piece of broken glass and pressed it between his eyebrows and said : 'Cut it with that.'

Again, 'When the seeds of *Karma* have been fried in the pan of *Nirvikalpa* you cannot sow them and get a harvest again,' so said Ramakrishna. Even the worship of God is *Karma,* the result of *Karma.*

And then when 'all work is at an end' one gets absorbed in that Substance which is one's own real nature. It cannot be described.

Now, hearing, reflection, assimilation and meditation are the processes of changing but they are little drops in the bucket compared with *Nirvikalpa Samādhi*. A child plays housekeeping, but what is that compared with real house-keeping? Reflection is *Manana*. It is superior to hearing, *Śravaṇa*. When you engage yourself in *Manana* it is a hundred times superior to Śravaṇa. Meditation, *Nididhyā-sana,* is a hundred thousand times superior to *Manana,* but *Nirvikalpa Samādhi* is 'simply infinite in its results'.

We may well remember here the trumpet call of Swami Vivekananda : 'Awake, arise, and stop not till the goal is reached.'

❑❑❑

13

THE GĪTĀ AND THE GAṄGĀ

R. Ramakrishnan

Every utterance of Swami Vivekanand is a jewel of a statement, an assertion of highly significant sense. It is an aphorism of condensed wisdom, a revelation of supreme truth. Not only in what he says, but in how he says it, it is of arresting import and of inspiring power. This is so because with Vivekananda words did not emanate from the tip of the tongue, they rose from the depths of his soul. With ordinary people words are very often shallow-rooted, but with Vivekananda they were really inmost thoughts expressed—subterranean ideas brought to the surface. His word were sparks issuing out of the flames of being. Though Vivekananda lived and moved among men and was very much human and refreshingly normal, he was really of a class apart; and his heroically-built body encased a super-soul, with ages of penance behind it; he was not one of the common multitude pushed into the arena of existence by the inescapable force of *prārabdha-karma* or destiny, to live a dull common-place life of daily littlenesses for less than two score years and then pass out unnoticed, unmourned, unmissed. He was, on the other hand, a gift to humanity from a compassionate Providence intent on a stupendous man-redeeming task. He was an associate to a God-man, one who came to earth, because he chose to come, in order to wipe out the tears of sorrowing men and open the path of enlightenment to harassed humanity. If Sri Ramakrishna was the Emperor of the Spiritual Realm Vivekananda was his Prime Minister and *Generalissimo.* Everything in and of Vivekananda was wholly Ramakrishna. Ramakrishna and Vivekananda were the two hemispheres of a Spiritual Globe. Vivekananda was the speaker word, and Ramakrishna the inner sense. It is not therefore in any way surprising that profoundity marks every one of Vivekananda's utterances, that there is the ring of undeniable truth in every one of his remarks, that whatever he says makes an irresistible appeal to the hearer or reader. For Sri Ramakrishna, his inspirer, was a Seer of Truth whose vision was not limited to this or that segment, but encompassed the totality of existence and striving and fulfilment. He saw all things wholly and completely, not in aspects and arts. Vivekananda's sayings are therefore not mere imaginings and conjectures and guesses about reality, but first-hand records and on-the-spot jottings of a discoverer and finder; faithful impressions of an eye-witness.

Another interesting point about Vivekananda is that no body knew India as he did. He was, for one thing, a condensed India in himself. He was the very Spirit of India incarnate. He was India's heartbeat, India' brainwave, India's soulfulness. He knew the Motherland inside and out, her past was an open book to him, her future lay in a clear vision before him. India was his chief passion. He had no problems other than India's to be solved. He had no ambitions other than India's, to be worked for and achieved. Her emancipation was his great mission. Her very dust was sacred to him, and he had been for years a pilgrim of the old style, a pedestrain pilgrim, an on-foot pilgrim, on her vast dust, traversing her from head to foot. He literally knew every inch of her. He had bathed in her holy waters, ascended her holy hills, inhaled the airs of her sacred *tīrthas,* mingled with all classes of her children, re-lived her days of the Vedas and Upaniṣads, conferred with her sages, drunk deep of her undying ideals, dedicated himself to the working out of the mission of that latest and most thorough-going efflorescence of Indian Culture, Sri Ramakrishna had become indistinguishable from what India was and is and will be. Therefore when Vivekananda says a thing about India, he knows what he says and means what he says; it is as if Mother India herself is speaking through him and telling us what she is and what she stands for. Here are a few such revealing self-assertions by India through Vivekananda's mouth:

"India's theme is religion .... Her life-blood is spirituality....... The national ideals of India are Renunciation and Service. Intensify her in these channel, and the rest will take care of itself... If there is any land on this earth that can lay claim to be the blessed *Puṇya Bhūmi,* it is India.... India's life is of the same nature as the soul, without beginning and without end, immoral and we are the children of such a country...... The banner of the spiritual cannot be raised too high in this country... India's gift to the world is the light spiritual...... The Gītā and the Gaṅgā constitute the Hinduism of the Hindus."

The last of these quotations (put in italics) occurs in a fairly long treatise of Swami Vivekananda entitled *Parivrājaka* penned in the course of his second journey to the West in 1900 and contributed to the pages of the Bengali journal *Udbodhan*. This has been rendered into English under the caption *Memoirs of European Travel* and forms a part of the *Complete Works of Swami Vivekananda*. Written in a light humorous vein the treatise is full of interesting observations on, and penetrating explanations of, men and things.

India is a land of rivers, but Swami Vivekananda singles out the Gaṅgā as typical of the Hindu. Indian religious literature is a vast ocean, but the Swami gives the pride of place to the *Gītā*. And he must have had his reasons for confining and concentrating Hinduism within these two glorious G's. What then is the speciality of the Gaṅgā, and what is the uniqueness of the *Gītā?*

Apart from the fact that the Gaṅgā is the great fertiliser of the Indian plains and that its perennial supply of silt and water are the basis of India's enconomic prosperity, the Gaṅgā is, to the Indian, a spiritual treasurehouse. It is not just one among the many rivers flowing in India; it is rather a current of culture, the life-blood of Indian faith, belief, wisdom and civilization. India is unthinkable without the Gaṅgā. India and the Gaṅgā are interchangeable. The Gaṅgā basin is physically the North Indian plain, but ideologically the Gaṅgā basin is coextensvie with India. The Gaṅgā is not the monopoly of the actual dwellers on its banks. The Hindu peasant in a village miles away from the Gaṅgā, as he takes his bath in the village rivulet or tank transports himself in spirit to the Gaṅgā waters and chants 'Gaṅgā, Gaṅgā' as he takes his pious plunge. And as attitude *(bhāva)* is the thing that makes a maṇ what he is, this faith-filled bather does get the merit of *Gaṅgā-snāna*. To the Hindu the Gaṅgā is not a mere river of earth, it originated in heaven. Lord Śiva is Gangādhara, and out of Śiva's locks flows out Gaṅgā's earth-purifying stream. It was Bhagiratha's marathon penance that made the divine Gaṅgā descent to earth possible. Starting as a rivulet from sacred Gomukhi in the Gangotri glacier the river triumphantly voyages over the expansive plains drawing to its bosom the waters of many tributaries, the Yamunā, hallowed by the association with Kṛṣṇa's Lila, being the chief of them. The shrines on the Gaṅgā banks are numerous, Banaras, the City of Śiva Mahādeva, and the Triveni confluence, being the most famous among them. Emires have come and gone; dynasties have risen and perished; ages have succeeded ages; but the eternal Gaṅgā has flowed on, ceaselessly purifying, ceaselessly enriching both soil and soul. A picutre of what the Gaṅgā signifies to the Hindu is given below in the words of Swami Vivekananda:

त्वत्तीरे वसतिं
तवामलजलस्नानम्।
तवप्रेक्षणं त्वन्नामस्मरणं
तवोदयकथासंलापनं पावनम्।

'O Gaṅgā! (I yearn for) residence on your banks, bathing in your pure waters, the sight of you, the remembrance of your name, the sanctifying talk about the story of your origin.'

Sri Ramakrishna was himself the Gaṅgā in many respects—in the perennial nature of his spiritual bounty as well as in his profusion and spontaneity, in his capacity to cleanse and save souls and in the ease with which he could be approached and availed of. Well has Romain Rolland described the Paramahamsa as 'This Ganges with its depths and its reflections, its liquid surface and its currents, its windings and meanders and the millions of beings it bore and nourished'.

The close link between Sri Ramakrishna and the Gaṅgā is well underlined by an incident in the life of the Holy Mother, Sri Sarada Devi. She once had a vision. And her visions were always of a deep spiritual import, and mystic significance. 'In a vision she saw Sri Ramakrishna getting down into the Gaṅgā and his whole body dissolving into the sacred waters of that river. Narendra (Vivekananda) was taking that water and sprinkling it on innumerable people with the cry, "Glory unto Ramakrishna!" The vision created a very vivid impression in her mind so much so that for long she felt hesitation in stepping into the water of the Gaṅgā with which the Master's body had become one. This vision of hers synchronised more or less with the inauguration of the great preaching activities of Swami Vivekananda.' And as for Vivekananda himself, well has Romain Rolland referred to him as "this son of the Gaṅgā"

If the Gaṅgā is thus Bhārat in liquid form, Kṛṣṇa is Bhārat's outstanding human symbol and representative. And the Gītā is Kṛṣṇa in word and phrase. He is what he preaches. Very aptly does a verse compare the Gītā to a goddess pouring the nectar of Advaita; another verse equates this nectar to milk of a superior quality, all the Upaniṣads being the cows, Kṛṣṇa being the milkman, Arjuna being the calf, those of mighty intellect being the enjoyers of the milk. In his telling way Sri Ramakrishna points out that when the word Gītā is repeated ceaselessly the word gets transformed into *Tā-gi* which is the same as *Tyaga* or renunciation; therefore the central teaching of the *Gītā* is that through renunciation the mind must be centred on God.

Here are a few of Swami Vivekananda's observations on the message of the *Gītā*:

Giver of delight to the gods in heaven!
Essence of Bliss, adored by the afflicted!
On me shower Thy compassionate love.
He who has made Thy bank his dwelling
Verily abides in Viṣṇu's realm.

—From Śaṅkara's *'Gaṅgāstotra'* Translated by Swami Nikhilananda.

It was the author of the *Gītā* who for the first time tried to harmonise the different paths. He took the best from what all the sects then existing had to offer and threaded them in the *Gītā*. The reconciliation of the different paths of *Dharma*, and work without desire or attachment—these are the two special characteristics of the *Gītā*.

If one reads this one verse

क्लैव्यं मा स्म गमः पार्थ नैतत्वय्युपपद्यते।
क्षुद्रं हृदयदोर्बल्यं त्यक्तोत्तिष्ट परंतप॥

(Yield not to unmanliness, O son of Pritha, this is unbecoming of thee. Scorcher of thy foes, shake off this despicable faint-heartedness and rise to fight)—he gets all the merits of reading the entire *Gītā;* for in this one *śloka* lies imbedded the whole message of the *Gītā*.

The greatness of little things—that is what the *Gītā* teaches, bless the old book!

The *Gītā* is the best commentary we have on the Vedānta philosophy.

The doctrine which stands out luminously in every page of the *Gītā* is intense activity, but in the midst of it, eternal calmness.

The *Gītā* teaches *Karma-Yoga*. We should work through *Yoga* (concentration).

Gītā no doubt has already become the Bible of Hinduism and it fully desrerves to be so.

The *Bhagavad Gītā* is the best authority on Vedānta.

These illuminating remarks of the great Swami give us an adequate idea of the prominent place which the *Gītā* holds in Hindu thought and faith.

Surely therefore is Hindu society or the Indian Community Gītā-nourished and Gaṅgāfed. And those of us who aspire to be truly Hindu or genuinely Indian will be near to the fulfilment of our aspiration to the extent to which we make ourselves Gaṅgā-soaked and Gītā-inspired.

14

THE SIX SYSTEMS OF HINDU PHILOSOPHY

Harold Barry Phillips

Philosophy is an 'insight' (*darśana)* into the nature and meaning of the universe; and just as the breadth of a view depends on the altitude of the viewer, so the depth of an 'insight' depends on the mental and spiritual development of the philosopher. Thus the validity of the traditional systems of philosophy will obviously vary. Traditionally, there are said to be six 'insights', and these may be grouped into three entirely distinct groups: (i) The Nyāya-Vaiśeṣika; (ii) the Sāṁkhya-Yoga; and (iii) the Pūrva and Uttara Mīmāṁsā.

(I) The Nyāya-Vaiśeṣika Philosophy

The Vaiśeṣika system is traditionally ascribed to Kaṇāda, and is named from the adjectival form of *'viśeṣa'*, meaning 'particularity' or 'individuality'. This is because it starts off with three eternal principles (actually there are more, but I simplify), atoms, souls, and ether *(ākāśa)*, of which the first two comprise an infinite number of individuals, each possessing its own particular characteristics *(viśeṣa)*. This philosophy starts off by taking a lump of something (say, chalk), crumbling it, and observing that it can be reduced to very fine particles, each of which is a minute *(aṇu)* fragment of the original whole. This word *'aṇu'* we translate as 'atom', although Kaṇāda's atoms have little in common with

Democritus's or Dalton's: they are really nothing more than minute particles of the original substance which had been crumbled. As one substance differs from another, so does each atom has its particularity; hence the name of this philosophy.

Now any observer knows that a unit volume of feathers is much lighter than a unit volume of lead, and this difference admits of an explanation by supposing that the latter contains more particles or atoms than the former. Hence, substances are composed of atoms joined into a structure by means of ether, which keeps them apart, so that different units of volume will have a different number of atoms. Basically, there are five categories of atoms, termed earth, water, light or fire, air, and ether. This classification is based on the following observation. From the vantage point of a high mountain, one sees the earth below as a sort of bowl, and in the distance is observed the circumambient ocean. An upward look reveals what appears to be a concave lid to the said bowl, before which move, by day and by night, various lights such as sun, moon, and stars. Experience reveals that the space in between the bowl and the lid is not empty, but is filled by winds. Hence, we have the earth floating on water, the crystalline bowl of the sky (conventionaly translated 'ether', but having nothing at all to do with the ether of modern science), and lights or fire moving and wind blowing in the interspace. Each of these five substances is supposed to be constituted by a predominance of a different type of atom, whence the fivefold classification referred to.

Earth smells, whereas normally water and air do not. Most liquids, which are taken to be forms of water, have a taste, and the Sanskrit word for 'taste', *rasa,* primarily means 'juice', a liquid. Light is obviously the source of colour, and air can only be distinguished by its touching the skin as the wind blows. Hence, allowing that all the elements are present in all substances, and that each is primarily distinguished by the quality *(guṇa)* mentioned, we can account for the full range of qualities displayed by substances as follows: Earth possesses smell, taste, colour, and tangibility; water possesses taste, colour, and tangibility; light or fire possesses colour and tangibility; air possesses tangibility; the first quality predominating in each case. As the universe is supposed to have come into existence by the word of God, and as ether is all-pervading, ether is made the substrate of sound. In this respect, it must be remembered that colour and sound as vibrations were unknown to the ancients; these qualities were regarded as subtle or extremely fine substances.

Besides these five elements, there were other four substances, namely, everything occurred in time and space; and besides inanimate nature, with which we have till now been dealing, there were also souls and minds, to account for life and consciousness. Souls were regarded as all-pervading, minds as atomic; and when any soul was in conjunction with a mind *(manas)*, it had its distinctive individuality and became conscious. This combination suffered rebirth again and again, this rebirth being determined by the result of one's deeds *(karma)*, deeds being the inevitable effect of desires. When, by an applied knowledge of the true nature of the universe, we are able to conquer desire, the soul becomes separated from the mind, is liberated from the cycle of rebirth, and exists wihtout any consciousness, and so without pain and sorrow.

With only unimportant differences in detail, the above system was adopted by the *Nyāya Darśana,* which concentrated on the question how we can know what we claim to know. The Nyāya is ascribed to Gautama (no connection with the Buddha), and the word means 'analytical investigation', since that is the essence of the system.

The Nyāya allows four sources of valid knowledge or *pramāṇas* :

(i) Intuition *(pratyakṣa),* which includes sense-perception and the apprehension of universals. This was explained by distinguishing two types of perception: when we look at something, we first see it as a simple whole without any subtle distinctions—indeterminate perception. A closer inspection reveals subtle distinctions (i.e. qualities, relations, etc.) which enable us to analyse and classify the conceptual elements in the thing—determinate perception.

(ii) We then pass from the perceived to the unperceived by means of inference *(anumāna).* The classical method of doing this is by means of the five-membered syllogism. In this, we commence by making a statement as the result of our perceptions, and say, 'The hill is on fire'. Then we justify our statement by adducing a reason: 'Because it smokes.' Then we express the basis of our reasoning, which is a generalization from a particular instance: 'Whatever is smoky has fire, like the kitchen.' Next we apply this generalization to the case in point: 'So is this hill.' Finally, we draw the conclusion, which corroborates our initial statement: 'Therefore the hill is on fire.'

(iii) Verbal testimony *(śabda)* is accepted either as based on the perceptions and inferences of others, or as based on scriptural revelation.

(iv) Comparison *(upamāna),* or argument from analogy, is included for the sake of completeness. Other systems, however, reduce this to a type of inference. The Vaiśeṣika follows this, but narrows verbal testimony down to memory *(smṛti)* thus denying revelation, and adds yogic perception (psi-phenomena!), which is accepted by some and rejected by other philosophies.

(II) The Sāṅkhya-yoga Philosophy

This philosophy proceeds from an entirely different basis. Instead of observing nature, it observes man's own self, and makes three initial assumptions: (a) the fact that there is knowledge entails the division of the entire universe into two categories: Subject or Knower, and Object or Known; (b) the principles of Man are the same as the principles of the Universe—termed Microcosm and Macrocosm respectively; (c) the true nature of man and the universe can be found by introspection into the process of awakening from sleep. As man awakens, the *seen* universe comes into existence, just as the real universe comes into existence from the Creator.

The Sāṅkhya is ascribed to Kapila and is named from its 'enumerating' (*saṅkhyā*=number) 25 principles, thus: There are two primordial principles, (25) *Puruṣa* (with which we shall deal presently) and (1) *Prakṛti*, representing subject and object respectively. *Prakṛti* is a kind of continuous stuff which is imperceptible, much like the modern concept of the luminiferous ether, I suppose. This has three constituent powers or *guṇas* (used differently from the atomistic sense of 'qualities') termed *sattva, rajas,* and *tamas*. When these are in a state of equilibrium, we have the cosmic equivalent of the state of deep sleep. When *Prakṛti* is illumined by *Puruṣa,* the equilibrium of the *guṇas* is disturbed, and a cosmic consciousness or (2) *mahat* comes into being; this is found also in the microcosm, where it is termed *buddhi* (intellect), and it represents the dawning consciousness as one begins to awaken. The next stage in awakening is the sudden realization that one is oneself, that is the realization of one's individuality. This is represented on both cosmic and individual planes by (3) *ahaṅkāra* (ego). The cosmos does not evolve further, but the individual develops (9) *manas* or mind, (10-14) the five sense-organs *(jñānendriyas),* and

(15-19) the five organs of action *(karmendriyas)* from the *sāttvic* side of *ahaṅkāra*, and from the *tāmasic* side, known as *bhūtādi*, (4-8) the five *tanmātras* or subtle elements. These evolve as follows: From the *bhūtādi* emerges the *tanmātra* of sound; from this plus more *bhūtādi* emerges the *tanmātra* of touch, with the attributes of sound and touch; and so on. Then from the combination of these *tanmātras* come (20-24) the five groups of gross atoms: ether, air, fire, water, and earth. These possess penetrability, pressure, light and heat, viscous attraction, and cohesive attraction respectively. The five sense-organs are obvious, and the mind is what correlates the data from the various senses to present the apprehension of an object. The mind also is needed to explain dreams, and why we can have the eyes open and yet not see, as in reverie. The organs of action are tongue, feet, hands, and organs of evacuation and reproduction. From the various combinations of the gross atoms appears the manifold variety of cosmic existence.

There is an infinite number of *Puruṣas*, and when these come into conjunction with a body, the *Puruṣa* becomes a *jīva* or individual soul. Actually the *jīva* is the *Puruṣa* associated with a subtle body consisting of *buddhi, ahaṅkāra, manas*, five sense-organs, five organs of action, five *tanmātras*, and rudiments of the five gross elements, from which it 'grows' a physical body in accordance with past desert *(karma)*. Liberation consists in freeing the *Puruṣa* from the subtle body, so that it remains a mere witness, solitary, indifferent, passive. The means of achieving this are not important, since the Sāṅkhya has been superseded by the Yoga system.

Now when an object excites the senses, the mind arranges the sense-impressions into a percept; the *ahaṅkāra* refers this to the self; and the *buddhi* forms therefrom a concept or modification, which, being illumined by the *Puruṣa* gives rise to thought. In dreams, the connection is severed between sense-organs and the *buddhi,* and the *buddhi* operates spontaneously, stimulated by its past impressions *(saṁskāras)* to cause dreams. In sleep, the connection between *buddhi* and *Puruṣa* is broken. Valid knowledge comprises perception (indeterminate, determinate, and yogic); inference, with the five-membered syllogism, and scriptural testimony.

The Yoga system is the work of Patañjali. *Yoga* usually means 'union', with God; but in this case, it is said to refer to the 'effort' which is required to achieve liberation by isolating the *Puruṣa* from *Prakṛti*. The Yoga follows the Sāṅkhya in all essential respects, except that *mahat* is termed *citta,* and its microcosmic counterpart embraces *buddhi, ahaṅkāra,* and *manas;* and that there is no subtle body, but the *Puruṣa* contracts or expands in association with various types of physical body, resulting in a contracted or an expanded consciousness. The main contribution which has been made by the Yoga is the eight-limbed or *aṣṭāṅga yoga,* usually called the 'King' or *'Rāja'* yoga technique.

The theory on which this rests is roughly that there are seven *cakras* or psychic centres placed up the spinal column or *suṣumṇā,* and there are two narrow channels ascending and descending on either side of this, termed *iḍā* (on the right) and *piṅgalā* (on the left). Of these *cakras,* the most important are the *mūlādhāra* at the base of the spine, the *anāhata* or lotus of the heart, the *ājñā* between the eyebrows, and the *sahasrāra* at the crown of the head. By controlling the *prāṇa* or life force in its passage up and down the *iḍā* and *piṅgalā,* pressure is exerted on the *kuṇḍalinī* or hidden energy, which lies at the base of the spine; and by raising this up the *suṣumṇā,* various states of superconsciousness or *samādhi* are attained.

But first, the aspirant must be prepared by an ethical discipline comprising *yama* (non-violence, truthfulness, honesty, continence,non-acceptance of gifts) and *niyama* (external and internal purification, contentment, austerity, and devotion to God); then having adopted a steady posture *(āsana)* the aspirant practises control of the vital force *(prāṇāyāma)* by means of rythmic breathing until he is able to direct it at will (which takes some doing); the next stage is to shut the mind against all outside impressions *(pratyāhāra),* fix the mind on a particular spot *(dhāraṇā),* and when this has been mastered, to induce an even current of thought on one particular object with all other thoughts being excluded *(dhyāna),* until this culminates in the ecstatic condition *(samādhi),* in which the aspirant posses over into another plane of consciousness. When one considers that these practices may lead to suspension of breathing and heart-beat, it will be realized that it is dangerous to attempt this discipline without the guidance of a properly qualified teacher *(guru).*

(III) Pūrva and Uttara-Mīmāṁsā

The Vedas or Hindu scriptures are not easy books, especially since the language in which they are written (Sanskrit) is no longer spoken. Hence arose the need to interpret them correctly. This gave rise to the Pūrva Mīmāṁsā (Earlier Investigation), associated with the name of Jaimini. His main preoccupation was not with questions of philosophy at all, but with details of ritual. But the whole concept of ritual performance rests on the assumption of *devas* or gods, to whom sacrifices are offered and an enduring soul to reap the results of the sacrifices performed. Hence, from the philosophical point of view, we find here a number of gods, a number of souls, and a world consisting of nine substances: five elements—earth, water, fire, air, and ether; time and space in which the world and all its works are situated. In association with a mind, the soul becomes subject to the round of birth and death; due to merit *(dharma)*, the soul separates from its associated mind, and resorts to the *Brahmaloka* or highest heaven, where it dwells until the end of days. But his is not so much a philosophy as a religion.

Philosophy is rather represented by the Uttara Mīmāṁsā (Later Investigation), later both in time and in the part of the Vedas investigated. Hence, it is generally termed *Vedānta*, which means the end *(anta)* of the Vedas, viz. the *Upaniṣads*, on which this type of philosophy is based—the *jñāna-kāṇḍa*, in opposition to the *karma-kāṇḍa* with which Jaimini had been chiefly concerned. This reached its culmination a little more than a thousand years ago; and since then it has expressed itself chiefly in three systems of thought. I shall reverse the chronological order of these three systems and represent them as an evolution.

Vedānta, then, begins (logically) with a dualism or *Dvaita* as represented by Madhva. In the beginning, there were *Īśvara* (identified with Viṣṇu), *Prakṛti*, and the *jīvas* or souls. This is called dualism, because the ultimate Reality is conceived broadly as two (dual): God and the world. Nearly all religious books deal with God and with God's creation of souls and the world, and so this dualism gives what is essentially the religious aspect of philosophy stated in its simplest terms. In the beginning was God; God created the world and men to live in the world; righteousness *(dharma)* leads to heaven, sinfulness *(adharma)* leads to hell. In all essentials, this *darśana* does not differ from Jaimini's: the real difference lies in this that Jaimini inculcates the observance of ritual performances or sacrifices in accordance with the instructions of the Vedas, whereas Madhva goes beyond this in urging us to attain a direct intuitive realization of God by means of meditation—*bhakti-yoga* or devotion.

Various modifications were introduced into this simple scheme in order to achieve more unity in the conception of the universe. These are best represented by Rāmānuja's qualified monism or *Viśiṣṭādvaita.* A sort of monism is avhieved by making the world *(jagat)* the outer and souls *(jīvas)* the inner body of God (*Īśvara,* as identified with Viṣṇu—or with Kṛṣṇa, according to Nimbārka and Vallabha). Then creation is reduced to God's supervision of the evolution of Prakṛti (which follows the lines of the *Sāṅkhya*) and His assigning souls to the resultant bodies in accordance with their desert. Liberation from the round of birth and death is attained by means of *prapatti* or resignation to the will of God. The valid sources of knowledge are the standard ones of perception (both indeterminate and determinate), inference (but now we have a three-membered syllogism, approximating to the Western form), and scriptural testimony.

But the most influential line of thought in Vedānta has been that worked out by Śaṅkara or Śaṅkarācārya. This is called Advaita (non-dual) Vedānta, to stress that the ultimate Reality does not admit of any qualifications,not even that It is One. This *darśana* accepts the evolution of the world from the *Prakṛti* (nature) of *Īśvara* along the traditional lines, but insists that the resultant world and universe of souls is not really real, but is *Māyā* (illusion); the really real is *Brahman* alone; and *Brahman* is absolutely without any attributes, is quite beyond the power of our intellects to comprehend. But the human intellect aspires to worship God, and cannot find any satisfaction in what seems to it a void. Hence it frames a symbol, a personal God, to represent the divine qualities which it vainly seeks to find in *Brahman.* The symbol is unimportant; only the symbolized is real. Hence, all religions are valid, as they represent so many different conceptions of the same ultimate Reality. But the worship which is associated with the various ethnic religions leads only to heaven, and when the reward for the worship that brought the individual there has been enjoyed, he returns to earth. Only the intuition or realization of Brahman *(Brahmānubhava)* can give liberation from the cycle of rebirth. This superconscious state is attained by a long discipline, of which the essence is meditation; and the whole discipline is called *jñāna-yoga*. The difference in the content of meditation between *rāja, bhakti,* and *jñāna yogas* is of course fundamental, but roughly speaking, the *rāja-yogin* meditates on parts or aspects of his own body; the *bhakta* meditates on the personal God of his choice *(iṣṭa);* and the *jñānin* meditates on the impersonal God, *Brahman*.

Advaita Vedānta can be summoned up, I think, by three aphorisms : (a) I am *Brahman;* (b) the world is *Māyā;* (c) liberation is obtained by knowledge *(jñāna)*, or by the destruction of ignorance *(avidyā)*. Let us expand these. (a) The soul of man is enclosed in three bodies: the physical body which it assumes at birth; the subtle body which accompanies the soul throughout its various incarnations; and the causal body which remains with the soul in *pralaya* (the state of virtual non-existence between any two world epochs or *kalpas)*. The causal body consists of the bliss *(ānanda)* of God. The subtle body includes this, and the consciusness *(cit)* of God, which uses as its instruments the *buddhi* with its modifications such as egoism *(ahaṅkāra)*, the *manas* coupled with the five sense-organs, and the five *prāṇas* or manifestations of vital force (such as breathing, circulation, digestion,evacuation, etc.) coupled with the five organs of action. And the physical body consists of the five gross elements, the existence *(sat)* of God, in which is located also the subtle with the causal body. Behind all these shines the *Ātman* shines out by its own light, and the Self realizes its true nature, and is freed from the round of birth and death, because (b) it now realizes that the world is not real, but is the product of *Māyā* (God's power of creating illusion). This is illustrated by the rope that one might mistake for a snake in the dark. When one realizes the true nature of the rope, there is no longer any snake; there is only the rope. So *Brahman* appears to us as the manifold universe, but when we realize *Brahman* (God) in *samādhi* or superconsciusness, the world vanishes and *Brahman* alone remains. As there is no longer any body, any world, there can be no more rebirth for that soul.

This can be made clearer, I think, by setting forth the extreme view of Gauḍapāda, Śaṅkara's spiritual grandfather. *Brahman* is the witness behind the three states of sleeping, dreaming, and waking,and so is the Fourth *(turīya)*. When *Brahman* sleeps, Its consciousness is termed *prājña* in the individual, *Īśvara* in the cosmos; when *Brahman* dreams, this consciousness, from which the world as *Māyā* is evolved,is termed *taijasa* in the individual, *Hiraṇyagarbha* in the universe; and when *Brahman* awakens, Its consciousness is *vaiśvānara* in the individual, *Virāṭ* in the universe. So the whole universe is merely the effect of imagination. There is, in fact, no creation at all; it is only imagined;and this gives the name *Ajātivāda* (No-Creation Theory). In contrast to this, Śaṅkara accepted the world as empirically real; he denied only its transcendental reality. This can be illustrated by dreams. To the dreamer, they seem real enough,but when the sleeper awakens, the dream is realized for what it is—the product of the mind. So the world is the product of *avidyā,* nescience.

❑❑❑

15

THE SUM AND SUBSTANCE OF ADVAITA VEDĀNTA

Swami Satprakashananda

As stated by Śrī Śaṅkarācārya, the greatest exponent of Advaita philosophy, the gist of the Vedāntic texts, numerous as they are, is this : '*Brahman* is real, the world is unreal; the *jīva* is verily *Brahman* and no other.' Since this statement is very often misunderstood, I shall make an attempt to bring out its significance in accordance with Śaṅkara. I shall dwell in its two parts successively.

1. The meaning of 'Brahman is real, the world is unreal'

In declaring the reality of *Brahman* and the unreality of the world, Advaita Vedānta repudiates the ultimate reality of the world experience, but not its empirical existence. When the *jīva* attains illumination and realizes *Brahman* the Absolute, the relative order disappears altogether. So, from his standpoint, the world is utterly false. But an unillumined person invariably perceives the phenomenal world and not *Brahman*. To him, the diversified universe is a fact of experience; it is not false in the sense that the son of a barren woman is false. Nobody ever perceives the son of a barren woman either in reality or in illusion. As long as a person dreams, the dream-world is real to him; dream-water allays his dream-thirst. He knows the dream-world to be unreal only when he wakes up. So says Śaṅkara : 'Empirical experiences are valid until the identity of the self with Brahman is realized, as are dream-experiences until awaking.' (*Brahma-Sūtra,* II. i.14, commentary)

To be explicit, the world, as characterized by Advaita Vedānta, is neither real nor unreal. It is not real, because it is sublated by the knowledge of non-dual *Brahman*. Yet it is not unreal, because it is a fact of experience for the unillumined. Thus the world-order can be viewed from the standpoint of the illumined and also from the standpoint of the unillumined. On the twofold world-view, Śaṅkara observes: 'This phenomenal world, caused by diversification and deceptive, is a fact for those who hold that things are different from *Brahman* and also for those who do not. The adherents of the supreme Truth however, while investigating, in accordance with the Śruti, the true nature of things, whether they really exist or not, arrive at the conclusion that *Brahman* alone is, the One without a second, beyond all relativity. So there is no contradiction between the two views. We do not maintain the existence of anything but *Brahman* in the state in which the supreme Truth is attained, as the *Śrutis* say 'One only without a second' and 'without interior or exterior'. Nor do we deny in the relative plane of name and form the validity for the ignorant of the empirical facts comprising action, its agent, its instrument, its result, and so forth. Therefore, the scriptural and the empirical outlooks rest on knowledge and ignorance. So there is no fear of contradiction between them. No school can deny that the existence and the non-existence of the phenomenal world depend on the relative and the absolute standpoint.' (*Bṛhadāraṇyaka Upaniṣad,* III, v. 1, commentary).

Sense-perception and the Śruti may appear to be mutually contradictory. But they are not. According to Śaṅkara, both are sources of valid knowledge in their respective spheres. The province of the *Śruti* is the transcendental Reality, which is beyond sense-perception. The suprasensuous cannot be reached by inference even. The reason is, that inferential knowledge depends on the knowledge of the invariable concomitance between the thing perceived and the thing inferred, and such a knowledge is lacking in the case in point. Nor can any other means of knowledge dependent on sense-perception acquaint us with the nature of the supra-sensuous. Therefore, the *Śruti* is the only source of knowledge with regard to the transcendental Reality.

Most philosophers and scientists recognize the inherent incapability of perception to probe into the fundamental Reality. Its province is the world of appearance. Sir James Jeans says in his book *Physics and Philosophy*: 'Our studies can never put us into contact with reality; we can never penetrate beyond the impressions that reality implants in our minds.' (*Physics and Philosophy,* New York, The McMillan Company, 1946, p. 15). It is with regard to the transcendental Reality that the *Śruti* declares: 'There is no diversity whatsoever in this *Brahman*.' (*Bṛhadāraṇyaka Upaniṣad,* IV. iv. 19) So it does not contradict sense-knowledge. When one person says, 'The sun moves', and another with his astronomical knowledge says, 'The sun does not move', the two statements do not contradict each other, but represent two different viewpoints regarding the sun. Similarly, the two statements, 'Man is mortal' and 'Man is immortal', mutually contradictory though they appear to be, are true from two different viewpoints, the physical and the spiritual. There is no conflict between them. But the value of either depends on the merit of its standpoint. This is so in all such cases. The following remarks of Madhusūdana Sarasvatī in his *Advaitasiddhi* (I. 18) are to the point: 'Only the empirical validity of perception and other allied means of knowledge is a proven fact; that is not controverted by the scriptures (*āgama*). What is controverted is its ultimateness, which is by no means a proven fact. Therefore, there is no conflict between perception and the scriptures (*āgama*).' (Nirnaya-sagar Press, Bombay, pp. 373-4)

The fundamental Reality is the substratum of the world-appearance. In fact, it is non-dual *Brahman* that appears as the manifold. The world, as it appears, is unreal; but in its essential nature as *Brahman* the world is absolutely real. So the *Chāndogya Upaniṣad,* (III. xiv. 1) says: 'Verily all this is *Brahman*.' As the supreme principle immanent in the universe, *Brahman* is its very basis and being. 'From Him all things originate, into Him do they dissolve, and by Him are they sustained.' (ibid.) The same non-relational, non-dual *Brahman* is in relation to the world as its originator, sustainer, and absorber. Transcendentally pure Being-Consciousness-Bliss, *Brahman* as immanent in the universe is its all-pervading, all-knowing, all-powerful, all-merciful Lord. So says Śaṅkara: 'Two kinds of *Brahman* are stated in the Upaniṣads: the one having as its adjuncts the diversities of the universe, the modifications of name and form; the other, its contrary, completely free from all adjuncts.' *(Brahma-Śūtra,* I. i. 11, commentary) The one is called *aparā* (the lower), the other *parā* (the higher). The one is *saguṇa* (with attributes), the other is *nirguṇa* (without attributes).

2. The identity of the jīva and Brahman explained

From the position of the *jīva*, the individual experience, the world of experience is real, and so is their supreme Ruler. The existence of the individual soul and the universe presupposes the existence of the supreme Lord, because neither of the two is self-existent or self-sufficient. These three are coexistent and inter-related, but are not on the same grade as manifestations of *Brahman*. None of the three has a beginning. As pointed out by Śaṅkara, their beginning is untenable. (*Vide* ibid., II. i. 36, commentary) The supreme Lord is the one Self of all. He holds the universe comprising the living and the non-living. So says Śaṅkara: 'To the contemplative, nothing other than the supreme Lord exists. He is manifest in the eightfold form of the unmoving and the moving, viz earth, water, fire, air, ether, the sun, the moon, and the individual soul.' (*Dakṣiṇāmūrti-stotra,* 9) In the inanimate He, who is intrinsically pure Being-Consciousness-Bliss, is manifest only as being; in the animate, He is manifest as consciousness as well. It is He who shines as the conscious Self in every individual.

One may pertinently ask : How does the undifferentiated One become differentiated, the Unlimited limited, the Changeless changeful? The question is possible only from the standpoint of the unillumined, who view the world-appearance as real. The point is, all differentiations, limitations, and changes belong to the realm of appearance. The transcendental Reality only *appears* to be different from what It is, but does not *become* so. The cause of this appearance, according to Advaita Vedānta, is *māyā* (lit. that which measures), a mysterious principle that apparently measures the Immeasurable, diversifies the Undiversified, mutates the Immutable. All transformations are in *māyā*, but are superimposed on *Brahman*. As is the effect, so is the cause. Just as the world-appearance is neither real nor unreal, so is *māyā*. It rests on *Brahman* without affecting Him in the least. *Brahman* associated with *māyā* is the supreme Lord of the universe, its originator, preserver, and absorber. He is also the all-gracious Saviour of the souls. He is the adorable One. *Māyā* serves Him as His power.

According to Advaita Vedānta, *māyā* is true so far as

the world-appearance is concerned. It does not inhere in *Brahman* as an ultimate principle. According to all monotheistic systems of Vedānta, *māyā*, the creative energy of God, inheres in Him. It is inseparably connected with His being. Nevertheless, Advaita Vedānta argues that in that case, any changes in *māyā* must mean changes in God Himself and the seed of imperfection of the world must be within Him; so this position is not tenable. The phenomenal world is real to the individual soul (the *jīva*), but cannot be reckoned as his creation. The existence of *māyā*, its origin, is a fact from his position. With individual *ajñāna* (ignorance) there must be cosmic *māyā* associated with the supreme Lord *(Īśvara)*. The one betokens the other as the fruit betokens the tree. This does not mean, of course, that cosmic *māyā* exists because of individual *ajñāna*. It is individual *ajñāna* that derives from cosmic *māyā*. Thus the *jīva* is identical in essence with *Īśvara*. But with their respective adjuncts, they are ever different from one another. By realizing the essential identity with *Īśvara,* the *jīva* becomes *Brahman,* what he really is. Verily, the knower of *Brahman* attains *Brahman*.

*Īśvara*hood is invariably linked with *jīva*hood. Both are manifestations of *Brahman* through *māyā* in its cosmic and individual aspects. *Īśvara* is ever related to the *jīva* as Ruler to the ruled. The one is the supreme object of worship, the other is the worshiper. The *jīva* can never be *Īśvara*. (Vide *Brahma-Sūtra,* IV. iv. 17, commentary) They are coexistent and without beginning. But neither is ultimate. As observed by Śaṅkara: 'And He *(Īśvara)* stands in the empirical realm in the relation of the Ruler to the cognizing souls called the *jīvas*, which are really one with His own Self (just as portions of ether inside jars are one with the universal ether), but are limited by the aggregates of the body and the senses made of names and forms brought forth by *ajñāna*. Therefore, the lordship of *Īśvara,* His omniscience, omnipotence, are relative to the finite beings due to limiting adjuncts derived from *ajñāna*; in reality, such expressions as the ruler, the ruled, omniscience, and so forth, do not apply to the Self from whose being all adjuncts are wiped out by right knowledge.' (*ibid.*, II. i. 14, commentary) Further he says: 'Moreover, when the consciousness of the identity (of the individual soul with the supreme Being) is aroused by such instruction of their identity as 'That thou art', then the finiteness of the individual soul and the creatorship of *Brahman* vanish at once, because all experience of difference proceeding from wrong knowledge is annihilated by perfect knowledge.' (*ibid.*, II. i. 22, commentary)

Beyond both *jīva*hood and *Īśvara*hood is undifferentiated pure Consciousness that *Brahman* is. The truth that the Śruti reveals by the terse formula, 'That thou art', is confirmed by reason and verified by the seer's experience.

❑❑❑

16

A NEW ANGLE ON THE PROBLEM OF UNREALITY IN ADVAITA

A.G. Krishna Warrier

The alleged acosmism in Advaita has long been a favourite target of critics, both well-informed and ill-informed. The latter, misled by the term *māyā* used profusely in the Advaita system, apprehend that life and its values can make little sense if, by definition, nothing is real except an acosmic Absolute from which, in the words of the *Taittirīya Upaniṣad* (IV. I), 'the mind together with the words recoils'. Some well-informed critics, on the other hand, solemnly and emphatically affirm that in the system of Śaṅkara 'unreal the world is, illusory it is not'. (Dr. S. Radhakrishnan: *Indian Philosophy,* Vol. II, p. 583) The host of writers who followed exponents like Gough have made it abundantly clear that *māyā* is not a theory or explanation of the world, but purely and simply a statement of the paradoxes of thought and action as also of the startling vicissitudes of the nature around. (*The Complete Works of Swami Vivekananda,* Vol. II, pp. 89ff., 10th edition) *Māyā* is the word for the way in which the universe is going on, or, as Swami Vivekananda pointed out with remarkable insight, the essence of *māyā* is relativity. (*'The Absolute and Manifestation', ibid.,* Vol. II, pp. 130 ff.) In the light of this explanation, 'life and its values' remain as secure as, in the circumstances, they may be. In this paper, a fresh attempt is made to examine and evaluate the objections raised against the doctrine of unreality, which occupies a prominent place in the Advaita system, and to focus attention on consideration that may do greater justice to Śaṅkara's own thoughts on the subject.

Arguments Against the Doctrine of Unreality

The views lucidly marshalled by Dr. Radhakrishnan in his *Indian Philosophy* (Vol. II, pp. 583ff. and p. 587) may be deemed as typical of the arguments against the Advaitic doctrine of unreality. The world is 'phenomenal but not an illusion, a creation of the mind'. It has been conceded that Śaṅkara often traces the plurality of appearances including *Īśvara* to *avidyā*.[1] In other words, according to Śaṅkara, plurality is the product of *adhyāsa* or superimposition, and, as established by him right at the beginning of the *Brahma-Sūtra-bhāṣya,* the unity of the ground or *Brahman* is not in any way affected by the superimposed plurality.[2] 'By that element of plurality which is the creation of *avidyā* characterized by name and form, which is evolved as well as non-evolved, which is not to be defined either as existing or nonexisting, *Brahman* becomes the basis of the entire changing world, while in its true real nature it remains unchanged beyond the phenomenal universe.' *(Brahma-Sūtra-bhāṣya,* II. i. 27) It is pointed out that this view, when exclusively emphasized, suggests that there is no plurality at all apart from the individual's *avidyā*. Dr. Radhakrishnan draws a gloomy picture of the consequences of the conclusion thus drawn. 'All change and motion,' he says, 'all growth and evolution, all science and speculation, are reduced to dreams, shadows, and nothing more.' *(Indian Philosophy,* Vol. II, p. 579) The Advaitic contention that *Brahman* is only the *vivartakāraṇa* of the world is held to confirm the fears expressed above. Śaṅkara holds that this world is only attributed to *Brahman* as the snake is to the rope. *(Brahman-*

Sūtra-bhāṣya, I. iv. 5; *Kaṭha-bhāṣya,* III. 12, IV. 2, etc.) Some of the illustrations used by Śaṅkara, when literally interpreted, suggest that all distinctions and differences are but a mirage produced by *avidyā* (or individual nescience). In continuation, it has been pointed out that later Advaitins like Vācaspati, Madhusūdanasarasvatī, and Citsukha have written in support of the view that *avidyā* is the cause, presumably, the material cause, of the world. So much so that a strong case for solipsism has been made out, and the *jīva's* consciousness has been declared to be the source of the world, which sinks into non-being with the cessation of subject-object consciousness.[3] Western criticism of Vedānta, such as that the *Brahman* religion only rose to a pantheism etc., has been provoked by a view such as this. *(Indian Philosophy,* Vol. II. p. 581)

The Vital Question

Dr. Radhakrishnan admits the force of this criticism, and points out that such a view makes a tragic joke of life renders meaningless many statements made by Śaṅkara himself about the world of experience. So, heroposes an interpretation of *avidyā* in Advaita with a view to disproving the illusory character of the world and establishing in its stead its phenomenal status. *Avidyā,* being as inert as the *Pradhāna* of the Sāṅkhya, cannot by itself be the cause of the world. Śaṅkara shares this view, as is evidenced by his trenchant criticism not only of the Sāṅkhya, but also of the *pratityasamutpāda* of the Buddhists which also starts from *avidyā.* It is equally patent from his elaborate rejection of *vijñānavāda (Brahma-Sūtra-bhāṣya,* II. ii. 28) that Śaṅkara upholds the externality of the world to the thinking subject. Existence of the world, according to Śaṅkara, does not depend upon the mental modes of any single percipient. It has a status distinctly different from that of the dreams. *(ibid.,* II.

ii. 18-21) *Avidyā* in Advaita is not a mere psychological force of ignorance, but has, as *mūlāvidyā*, an objective reality. It is one of the six factors held to have no origin in time.[4] Though negative in form, *avidyā* is a universal positive force, and is best identified with the will of God or *Īśvara*. Indeed, in Advaita, *avidyā, māyā*, and *prakṛti* are synonymous.

The non-subjective character of the world of experience is sought to be reinforced by an analysis of the analogous rope-snake phenomenon. It is urged that the rope appears as the snake, and when the illusion is shattered, the snake returns to the rope. (*Indian Philosophy,* Vol. II. p. 583) This statement, however, is metaphorical only, and it will be a grave error to rest the case for the non-illusory character of the world on this slender plea. For, actually the snake does not return to anything; the knowledge of the rope or substeatum just abolishes the snake, and shows it to have been non-existent even when it was experienced. The *bādhakapratyaya* or 'cancelling experience' shows, with reference to the snake, that it was *'Nāsid asti bhavi-ṣyati'*, neither was, is, nor will be. If this is so, and it is a point most emphatically maintained by Advaita, the further assertion, 'So does the world of experience become transfigured in the intuition of *Brahman'*, ceases to have much philosophical edge. 'The intuition of *Brahman'* obviously must mean *Brahmasākṣātkāra,* the integral experience of the absolute Reality. This implies *dṛśyoccheda,* the abolition of the objective manifold, which, in the language of the *Nyāyaratnāvali (Siddhāntabindu,* p. 12), is *'dṛśyādhikaraṇakṣaṇe dṛśyādhikaraṇakṣaṇa-pūrvatvā-nadhi-karaṇatvam'.* In other words, as soon as *Brahmasā-kṣātkāra* eventuates, there is an experience of a total stepping out of the stream of time. The time-conscousness with its divisions into past, present, and future, and the relations of before and after, completely vanishes. There is a liberation from the alien that besets us here. (Ennead, VI, xi. 10-11) Further, it signifies that *avidyānivṛtti,* from the point of view of the saint who experiences it, is not an effect produced by the operation of certain causes. It is realized as an eternal verity, and this should throw grave doubt on the status of the phenomenal world so-called.[5] The world, the realm of *avidyā,* ceases for the knower of *Brahman*. Of him who has experienced in the fullest measure his identity with *Brahman,* it may be truly said:

> And,like the baseless fabric of the vision,
> The cloud-capp'd towers, the gorgeous palaces,
> The solemn temples, the great globe itself,
> Yea, all which it inherit shall dissolve
> And, like this insubstantial pageant faded,
> Leave not a rack behind.
>
> (The Tempest, IV. i. 151-6)

The Advaitic doctrine, '*Jñānādeva tu kaivalyam*', of course, implies that the realization of *Ātman* as identical with the ground of the world or *Brahman* does not leave us with a transfigured world; indeed, nothing remainsor, if Advaita is right, can remain besides *Brahman* to shatter its non-duality or share in its unique status.

The state of nescience that enshrouds the *Ātman* is the sphere of plurality.[6] Due to *samyagdarśana,* the perception of plurality vanishes for good. The sphere of the many in which the self is, as it were, asleep *(Māṇḍūkya-kārikā,* I. 16) is abolished, when the Self wakes up to an awareness of its fullness and non-duality. Here is a universalization of the consciousness of identity, a perception of all things as *Brahman.*[7] This is the essence of the celebrated expression *prapañcapravilaya* or *prapañcopaśama*. In experiencing *Ātman* as the self of all, indeed as all, there is bound to be a total negation of the objective manifold in the very substrate where it formerly appeared to exist, *adhiṣṭhānaniṣṭhātyantābhāvapratiyogitā (Advaitasiddhi,* p. 382). Such is the effect of converting what was, in the state of *sādhanā,* only an intellectual view into an indubitable experience. In other words, such is the implication of the growth of the philosopher into the Advaitic saint and mystic. After the dawn of *Brahmajñāna,* according to Śaṅkara, the conviction 'I am the all' matures, no matter in what circumstances the sage finds himself. (*Bṛhadāraṇyakabhāṣya, IV. ii.* 20) In this integral experience, the two propositions *'Sarvaṁ khalvidaṁ Brahma'* and *'Ahaṁ Brahmāsmi'* are fully tested and validated. (ibid., IV. iv. 23) On the contrary, the perception of the slightest difference from the absolute Self, even to the extent of a 'hair's end' *(bālāgramātrāpi)* is nescience or *avidyā. (ibid.,* IV. iii. 20)

In the light of these facts urged by Śaṅkara, the affirmation that 'in the intuition of *Brahman* the world is not so much negated as transfigured' becomes hard to understand. The conception of *jīvanmukti,* the idea of *kramamukti,* the distinction of values, etc. may not be appealed to, to support the non-Advaitic contention that the integral experience 'merely transfigures the world and does not abolish it wholly'. The further assertion that 'unreal the world is, illusory it is not' and the supporting argument, 'In so far as Śaṅkara allows that, the Absolute may be realized through the practice of virtue', seem to confuse the issue. Without straining the final truth of *Brahmajñāna* as set forth above, it is possible to interpret the doctrine of unreality in Advaita and, at the same time, to find an honourable place in such a scheme for the recognized values of life.

It is true that, for Śaṅkara, the world is not a dream and that it has empirical reality. Nevertheless, the vital point to stress is not that it has such reality or that it is not illusory. The heart of the matter in Advaita is that the world is a variable, that its value and significance change with the culture and spiritual insight of the individual who evaluates it.[8] It may be allowed that in the final intuition of *Brahman* the world is transfigured. But how? Śaṅkara insists that, as shown above, the complete realization of *Brahman* does not leave us with two entities, viz *Brahman* and a transfigured world. Neither the knower nor the world, his empirical home, survives the all-consuming fire; only *Brahman* remains, the *bhūmā,* 'where one sees nothing else, hears nothing else, understands nothing else' (*Chāndogya-bhāṣya,* VII. xxiv. 1). The empirical world (*saṁvyavahāraviśayo lokaḥ*) experienced before the final realization is a sign of and due to *avidyā.* The conclusion seems inevitable that the question whether the world in Advaita is an illusion is not precise; it is at once misleading and naive. The vital question to ask, in my view, is: To whom is the world real, phenomenal, or illusory? No answer to this question can be legitimate without specifying the nature and achievements of the enquirer. To the perfected saint, as pointed out above, there is no world at all by the side of the Absolute.[9] To the Advaitic dialectician, even to the saint who returns to the awareness of the maniforld, the world may be accountable as an illusion. To the naive worldling, it is the sole reality.

Progressive Evaluation of the World

The last point may be slightly elaborated. The Advaitic evaluation of the world, of all entitites other than the non-dual Real, has been indicated by the use, with reference to them, of expressions like *avidyā, māyā,* etc. These latter refer to no single or stable principle of existence. It has been well pointed out that *avidyā* is a category *sui generis,* not real enough to set itself up as a rival to *Brahman,* yet not unreal like the hare's horn. *Avidyā* is an empirical fact, and its evaluation must differ with the competence of its evaluators. As the *Pañcadaśī* (VI. 130) says :

Tucchā'nirvāṇacintayā ca
vāstavī cetyasau tridhā;
Jñeyā māyā tribhirbodhaiḥ
śrautayauktikalaukikaiḥ.

'The man in the street deems the world of *avidyā* real, indeed, it alone as real; the intellectualist accounts it as neither real nor unreal; the man of spiritual insight discards it as naught or *tuccha*.'

These three broad divisions include, of course, infinite variations of attitudes to the world. The question of reality and unreality, thus, hinges on the position one occupies on the scale of spiritual development. This case may be likened to that of a hundred-rupee note. To the playful child, it is only a piece of paper as he is not aware of its worth and value; but to the adult who understands, it is not paper at all, but so much purchasing power. The Advaitin deems the world a problem that is solved only when the answer of God is wrung out of it. Once that answer is secured, the problem vanishes entirely. That Śaṅkara consistently speaks of the whole creation as a means to realize the sole reality of *Brahman* lends support to the solution of the problem of unreality suggested above.[10] In fact, according to Śaṅkara, the entire Upaniṣadic account of the creation of the world serves no other purpose.[11] It stands therefore, to reason that once the purpose is fulfilled, the objective manifold should vanish. To the extent this view is valid, Deussen seems to be right in asserting that to treat the world as real is to deny reality to God' *(The Philosophy of the Upaniṣads,* p. 160). Accordingly, as God-consciousness deepens, world-consciousness should sag and sink. As the inquirer constantly changes or progresses, an answering change in the world is bound to be experienced, till, having realized his identity with *Brahman,* he finds no world apart from *Brahman* to account for.

To describe the world's status, Śaṅkara employs the phrase *vyatirekeṇābhāva (Brahma-Sūtra-bhāṣya,* II. i. 14), i.e. non-existence as an independent entity. The implication of this phrase is that whatever truth and other values the world has, properly, pertain to *Brahman,* and that apart from *Brahman,* its ground, the world is naught. In and throughout the definitions of falsity offered by Madhusūdanasarasvati *(Advaitasiddhi,* pp. 139-40) shines the major Advaitic truth of the three levels or degrees of truth—the metaphysical, the empirical, and the illusory. The world as a whole has been widely held to possess the second type of *sattā* or existence. The relation of the empirical to the metaphysical is analogous to that of the illusory to the empirical. The world is a sort of mean proportional between the illusory rope-snake and the Absolute. The world, of course, is not eternally real, i.e. unsublatable; nor is it merely illusory. It has a pragmatic reality that continues to hold good in varying degrees, till the ground on which it is superimposed, viz *Brahman,* is fully realized. Till then, the activities of the world, both sacred and secular, remain valid.[12] The falsity of the world, in effect, is a task to be accomplished rather than a fact empirically given. The Advaitin stresses the fact that there is no stopping or rest for the fearless and ardent seeker after reality before he passes from the naive world-view of the worldling to the stable realization of the saint.[13] The world is a bridge he has to cross in the course of his pilgrimage to the Absolute;[14] as it is progressively crossed so it progressively vanishes, till, finally, *Brahman* alone remains.[15] Thus, we may conclude that the question of the world's being real or illusory is one of evaluation or axiology, and that its answer is altogether relative to the spiritual insight of the individual concerned. World-views such as those presented by *Dvaita, Viśiṣṭādvaita, Bhedābheda,* etc. may be treated as varying evaluations of the world in the course of an inquirer's progress to the summit of Brāhmic realization.[16]

Empirical Character of Jīva and Īśvara

It is well known that corresponding to the various degrees of reality associated with the objective manifold, there is a variety of views in Advaita regarding the nature and status of *jīva*. Depending on one's point of view, *jīva* may be, and indeed has been, identified with the body, lifeforce, mind, intellect, and spirit. (cf. Tai. U., II. 1-5 and Chā. U. VIII. 7 ff.) The concept of God in Advaita is equally fluid and relative. In the first place, it is vital to note that Advaita does not maintain that there are two *Brahmans,* one *nirguṇa* and the other *saguṇa,* the contention is that there are two angles of vision from which the non-dual Reality may be contemplated. *Nirguṇa Brahman* or the Advaitic Absolute refers to Reality as it is in itself, without distortion by the power of *māyā* or its product, the discursive mind of man. The contemplation of the same reality, logically, as the world-cause yields the concept of *Saguṇa Brahman*. Śaṅkara has important remarks to offer on this matter. In the introduction to his comment on *Brahma-Sūtra-bhāṣya* (I. i.12), he writes that in the Upaniṣads (vide Bṛ. U., IV. v. 15, II. iii. 6, and Ch. U. VII xxiv. 1), *Brahman* has been depicted in two different ways: (1) as qualified by the adjuncts of names and forms, and (2) as devoid of them all. In the sphere of emprical life or *avidyā, Brahman* becomes an object of religious and intellectual activities like worship and ratiocination, and, as such, is deemed *saguṇa* or *Īśvara*. The *Nirguṇa Brahman* is distinct from *Īśvara,* inasmuch as the former is beyond the sphere of all activities. Being the non-dual Reality, there is no question of relating it to time, space, and causality.[17]

It is of the essence of the problem under consideration to grasp that the concept of *Saguṇa Brahman* is essentially a human concept and is valid only in the human context, whereas that of *Nirguṇa Brahman* refers to Reality in itself. This truth is repeatedly brought out by Śaṅkara. Attributes such as the authorship of the world, omnipotence, etc. are ascribed to *Īśvara* to aid the mind of man in its efforts to comprehend Reality, and not to be taken as the final truth about that Reality. (*Taittirīya-bhāṣya,* II. 1) This position cannot be reversed by subordinating the teachings on *Nirguṇa Brahman* to those on *Īśvara,* because on realizing the former as the final truth of things, no further need, cognitive, conative, or emotive, remains to be satisfied. In other words, the knowledge of *Brahman* is the supreme end of life. (Tai. U., II. ix, 1; Bṛ. U., IV. ii. 4; Īśā. U., 7) That *Brahman* is free from all humanly conceived attributes is the ultimate truth, because these attributes are incidental to the human way of apprehending Reality.[18]

That the concept of *Īśvara* in Advaita is strictly a human concept with varying degrees of validity is well brought out in the celebrated verse of *Kalpataru* (I. i. 20):

Nirviśeṣaṁ Brahma
sākṣātkartumanīśvarāḥ;
Ye mandāḥ te'nukalpyante
saviśeṣanirūpaṇaiḥ.

'People of weak understanding who are not able to realize the Absolute, which is attributeless, are helped to think of It with the aid of forms with attributes.'

Hence in Śaṅkara's philosophy the postulate of *Īśvara* is empirical only; it is of the greatest practical consequence, no doubt, but none the less distinct from the plenary Reality. For Śaṅkara, personality, even of *Īśvara,* is not the ultimate truth; it is but a feature of the empirical world. To reach the absolute Truth, personality, so beloved of the dualistic mind, has to be transcended. The human mind may conceive *Īśvara* as the self-assertion of *Brahman,* the pure light, in the darkness of *māyā.*[19] To effect the transition from the concept of *Nirguṇa Brahman* to that of *Saguṇa Brahman* demanded by the problem of the world of *cit* and *acit,* matter and embodied consciousness, the Advaitins postulate the principle of becoming or *Māyā.* Does it not, in strict Advaita, involve self-contradiction. The answer is that in discussing *Nirguṇa Brahman* we are adopting a transcendental point of view, that of *parā vidyā,* for which no dualities exist; but in talking about the world and God we are shifting our position to the world of space-time, which demands a cause for its existence. From this latter point of view, the world of *māyā* is without beginning or *anādi;* by abstracting from it, a principle of change and becoming, the most characteristic feature of the world, may justly be postulated. In attempting to trace the genesis of the world, we are not positing an absolute beginning, a creation out of nothing or from pre-existing matter. We seek rather to account for the system of phenomena that constitutes the world of experience. It must be emphasized that in viewing the Advaitic Absolute from the empirical point of view, three principal factors are simultaneously posited, viz *māyā, jīva,* and *Īśvara.*[20] This fact seems to be the key to the problem of the doctrine of unreality in Advaita.

REFERENCES

1. *'Ekatvamevaikaṁ pāramārthikaṁ ... mithyājñānavijṛmbhitaṁ ca nānātvam.' (Brahma-Sūtrabhāṣya.* II. i. 14)
2. *'Tatraivaṁ sati yatra yadadhyāsaḥ tatkṛtena doṣeṇa vā 'ṇumātreṇāpi sa na sambadhyate.' (Adhyāsa-bhāṣya).*
3. *'Asyādvaitendrajālasya yadupādānakāraṇam ajñānaṁ tadupāśritya Brahmakāraṇamucyate.'*
4. *Jīveśvarau viśuddhacit tathā jīveśayorbhidā; Avidyātaccitoryogaḥ ṣaḍasmākamanādayaḥ.*
5. Cf. Within the single moment of time are enclosed all eternity, infinity. Hence Blake:
   To see the world in a grain of sand,

And heaven in a wild flower;
Hold infinity on the palm of your hand
And eternity in an hour.

6. Cf. *Bhagavad-Gītā,* V. 15: *Ajñānenāvṛtaṁ jñānaṁ tena muhyanti jantavaḥ;* (also ibid., II; Bṛ. U., IV. v. 15).
7. Cf. *Chāndogya-bhāṣya,* III. xiv. 1: *Evaṁ Brahmātmatayā triṣu kāleṣvaviśiṣṭaṁ, tadvyatirekeṇāgrahaṇāt.*
8. Cf. R.P. Singh : *The Vedānta of Śaṅkara,* p. 293: 'The concept of cause in Śaṅkara is axiological; it is the concept of essence.'
9. Cf. W.T. Stace: Time and eternity, p. 76: But looked at from within, the divine eternal moment is all-inclusive; nothing falls outside it to which it may bear comparison. The mystic therein is identical with all other mystics and God.'
10. *Brahmaṇo jagadākārapariṇāmatvādi yacchrūyate tadbrahmadarśanopāyatvenaiva viniyujyate. (Brahma-Sūtra-bhāṣya,* II. i. 14); see also *Aitareyabhāṣya,* II. i. 1 and *Taittirīyabhāṣya,* III.i.1)
11. *Sarvavyavahārahīnabrahmātma-bhāvapratipādnārthatveṣā pariṇāmaśrutiḥ; na ceyaṁ paramārthaviṣcyā sṛṣṭiśrutiḥ, avidyā-kalpitanāmarūpavyavahāragocaratvāt.*
12. *Prākcātmaikatvāvagateravyāhataḥ sarvaḥ satyānṛtavyavahāro laukiko vaidikascetyavocāma.' (Brahma-Sūtra-bhāṣya,* II. i. 14)
13. Cf. The parable of the wood-cutter in *The Gospel of Sri Ramakrishna,* Sri Ramakrishna Math, Mylapore, Madras, 1947, p. 35.
14. Cf. Akbar's inscription on the gate of Fatehpursikri : 'Said Jesus, may his name be blessed, "This world is a bridge, pass over it, but build no house upon it".'
15. Cf. *The Gospel of Sri Ramakrishna,* p. 345: 'It was suddenly revealed to me that everything is pure spirit. ... Man, animals ... all pure spirit.'
16. Cf. W.T. Stace: 'The world is unreal is a value judgement, and means that it is unblessed or worthless.'
17. *'Na deśakāladiviśeṣayogaḥ paramātmani kalpayituṁ śakyate.' (Brahma-Sūtra-bhāṣya,* IV. iii. 14)
18. *Samastaviśeṣarahitaṁ nirvikalpakameva Brahma pratipattavyaṁ na tadviparītam (ibid.,* III. ii. 11).
19. Cf. John. i. 5: And the light shineth in darkness.'

❑❑❑

17

ADVAITA-VEDĀNTA CONCEPTION OF THE SOUL

Roma Chaudhuri

'Who am I?' 'What is this world?'—these questions are, nay, have to be asked by all, by every rational being, and the very beginning of Philosophy lies in these, and these alone. But what are the replies, replies that will satisfy all of us, as well as satisfy all the sides of our nature,—thinking, feeling, willing, intellectual, emotional, practical? Are such replies at all possible?

Of course these are possible—at least every philosopher claims this when he formulates his own theories. But there are checks, there are tests. And what theory can come out unburnt out of this ever-burning fire of criticism?

It is in no spirit of exaggeration, or fantastic pride that we assert that the Vedānta Philosophy of India has indeed been able to reply to these fundamental queries in a manner at once incontrovertible and ingenious.

Let us turn to the very basis of the Vedānta Philosophy—the immortals amongst the mortals—the wonderful Upaniṣads, and see what they have to say with regard to this matter.

What thrilling reply we get here : *'Tattvamasi'*, 'That thou art', (Chānd, Up. 6.7.7). *'Aham Brahmāsmi'*, 'I am *Brahman*' (Bṛ. Up. 1.4.10). *'Sarvam Khalvidam Brahma'*, 'All this, verily, is *Brahman*' (Chand. Up. 3.14.1).

What exulting, exalting, exhilarating replies are at first sight, how unbelievable, how inconceivable, how unacceptable! For, how can 'I', this small and sinful and sorrowful 'I', ever desire to be, dare to be *Brahman* Himself? And how can the Universe, this mortal and material and mortified Universe also can ever do so?

But this is to the eternal glory of the Advaita-Vedānta System that it takes these supreme, sublime *Veda-Mantras* to be literally true.

And herein lies the beauty of the Advaita conception of the Soul: *'Ayamātmā Brahma'*, 'This Soul is *Brahman'* (Bṛ. Up/ 4.4.5).

Hence what *Brahman* is, *Ātman* too is—this is the one, and only one point in the benign Advaita-Vedānta conception of the Soul.

But is it, after all, so easy, and all that? What about your own direct experiences to the contrary? How can these be explained or ignored? For do we not directly feel that we are intimately connected with something physical, something material at every moment—with the physical world outside, with the physical mind-body inside? Thus, from all the sides of our nature, from the three fundamental sides, of thinking, feeling and willing, we are entirely dependent on all these. We need physical stimuli from the external physical world; we need physical stimulation of our organs and nerves and brain-centres of the internal physical body.

Thus, from the side of thinking, we are subject to ignorance, we have different degrees of knowledge, complete or incomplete, correct or incorrect and so on. From the side of feeling, too, we have pleasures, pains, anger, fear and the like. Finally, from the side of willing, no less, we have desires, strivings, successes, failures, and the like. But how can

Brahman, the Absolute ever have all these? How can *Brahman* be ever ignorant or have incomplete, incorrect Knowledge? How can He ever be subject to pain, fear, anger? How can He ever have unfulfilled desires, strivings for unattained ends, failures and frustrations? Is He not, according to all accounts, all-perfect, eternally pure, eternally full, eternally free, eternally satisfied—*Nitya-Śuddha, Nitya-Buddha, Nitya-Mukta, Nitya-Āpta*? Then how can such ordinary, empirical, worldly states be ever possible in His case?

Here we come to the crux of the whole matter: Is the Soul really what it appears to be? Apparently, the Soul is all these, but realily it isn't, never so. This fundamental distinction between what is only apparent and what is essentially real, constitutes the very basis of *Advaita-Vedānta.* This, in fact, is the fundamental *Advaita-Vedānta* distinction between the *Vyāvahārika* and the *Pāramārthika.*

The *Vyāvahārika* standpoint is the ordinary, empirical, worldly stand-point,—the standpoint of our ordinary daily experiences; the standpoint of the *Jīva,* as fundamentally distinct from the *Ātman.* Is such a *Jīva,* such an individual, really associated with and inseparable from a physical body and a physical mind?

First such a *Jīva* is a *Jñāna* or Knowledge or Consciousness as both its *Svarūpa* or essence and *Guṇa* or attribute. Such a knowledge or consciousness, as pointed out above, is only kind of ordinary empirical, worldly knowledge or consciousness, called *Buddhi,* dependent entirely on physical and physiological conditions. The science of Psychology deals with these, and these are called 'mental states or processes' *(Citta-Vṛttis)* and these, according to the Vedānta, never constitute real states of Consciousness. However, from the worldly point of view, these *Citta-Vṛttis* constitute our knowledge, and the *Jīva* is *Jñāna-Svarūpa,* as well as a *Jñātā* through these.

Secondly, the *Jīva* is a *Kartā*, too; for, from the ordinary standpoint, 'knowing' ends in 'doing'. Hence a *Jñātā* is necessarily a *Kartā* no less. And, like its *Jñātṛva,* its *Kartṛtva,* too, depends entirely on physical and physiological conditions. Thus, an external object arouses a desire in its mind; and that leads it to act in a particular way, necessitating corresponding physiological processes in the motor centres of the brain and the resulting in certain movements in the muscles and limbs.

Thirdly, the *Jīva* is a *'Bhoktā'* also. This needs no further elucidation, as according to the fundamental Law of *Karma, Kartṛtva* necessarily, involves *Bhoktṛtva,* otherwise the agent will get opportunities to escape from the just consequences of its own voluntary acts. Hence, an agent must necessarily experience the results or *phalas* of its own *Sakāma-Karmas;* and that is why, one who is a *Kartā* is also a *Bhoktā,* no less.

Fourthly, the *Jīva* is *aṇu* or infinitely small. Why? To make the *Bahutva* possible.

First of all the *Jīvas* are infinite in number. Thus, if there is to be an infinite number of souls, then each must be infinitely small, to make room for others. What other alternative is really there? Strange that even in India, opposite views have been held, e.g. by *Sāṁkhya, Yoga* and *Karma Mīmāṁsa* schools! According to these schools, souls are *vibhu* or all-pervasive; yet *bahu* or infinite in number. But, how is that ever possible?

These characteristics of the *Jīva* are, however, not its permanent, essential, absolute ones; but only temporary, accidental, conditional ones. And here, we once more come to the crux of the whole matter: What appears, is not necessarily real: The *Vyāvahārika* is not the *Pāramārthika*.

The *Vyavahārika* or the apparent, the empirical has not

a logical basis to stand upon. Apparently the Universe of Souls and matter is real, very real, eternally real. But how can its creation be ever explained to the fullest satisfaction of all? Details cannot be entered into there. But consider one fact only, viz., that if *Brahman* be ever-perfect eternally, then, what more can He ever need,—what is His motive in Creation? Nothing, and so Creation itself is nothing. Also, if *Brahman* be all pervasive, then *Jīva-Jagat* are there eternally as His parts, as His *Svagata-Bhedas,* or internal parts. So how can they be created a new? Further, if *Brahman* be *Nirvikāra* or unchangeable, then how can He have activity transformation at all? Hence how can there be any creation at all? Further, if *Jīva-Jagat* be *Svagata-Bhedas* of *Brahman*, then how can they be different from *Brahman*— for, can there ever be anything *'a-Brahman',* anything that is non-*Brahman* inside *Brahman?* That is absurd, for, inside the *Svarūpa* there cannot be at all something that is non-*Svarūpa,* as pointed out above.

All such numerous problems deluge us from all sides, but what is the way out—Yes, what? We pause for a reply, but in vain, for really no reply, no solution is possible.

So, let us better give up that vain effort, and admit straightway, if not joyfully, that there is no creation, no universe of souls and matter at all. Then?

Then consider anew : what are we, what is the world? If we have not been created at all, then what are we, after all? Are we non-entities *(asat),* are we false *(Mithyā)?*

We are neither—we are not *Jīvas,* that is perfectly true, still we are neither non entities, nor false—for, we are eternally what we are, we are *Ātman,* we are *Brahman,* the sole Reality. Why sole? Yes, sole, for duality is logically inconceivable. The ultimate Reality cannot be limited, or finite, it has to be all-pervasive, limitless. In that case, no second reality can exist outside It. And, inside It? As already pointed out above, inside a thing there cannot be anything which is not a thing. How can one ever go against one's own reality?

Hence, duality is impossible. Now, Oneness can be arrived at in two ways—negative and positive. Either, we say: The Universe of souls and matter is false and so there is only One *Brahman*. Or, we say: The Universe of souls and matter is *Brahman* and so there is only One *Brahman*. The Advaita-Vedāntists, adopt the negative method mostly, and that is why, *Advaita-Vedānta* has been unjustly stigmatised as *'Māyā Vāda', 'Mithyā Vāda'.* But really, it is neither—it is only *'Ātma Vāda',* it is only *'Brahma-Vāda',* it is only *'Brahma-Vāda'* in the most literal, most beautiful, most blissful sense of the terms.

'Ātma Vāda', 'Brahma Vāda'—these are the last words of the *Advaita Vedānta*—rather, not these, but this—this only, for *'Ātma Vāda'* and *'Brahma Vāda'* are one and the same, as *Ātman* is *Brahman,* as pointed out in the beginning and this is not a metaphorical flourishing. We repeat, it is not a poetic outpouring, not an emotional outbrust, but literally, actually, eternally true.

Thus, finally from the *Pāramārthika* standpoint, the Soul as *Brahman* is negatively *Nirviśeṣa, Nirguṇa, Niṣkriya, Nirvikāra, Nirañjana*—without distinctions, without attributes, without activities, without changes, without blemishes; positively, *Saccidānanda-svarūpa—Sat-Cit-Ānanda,* Pure-Absolute Existence, Pure-Absolute Consciousness, Pure-Absolute Bliss, in essence.

What an absolutely enthralling, enlivening, enchanting, conception! Who says that the Soul is non-eternal, momentary, mortal? Don't you know that it is eternal, full, perfect Existnece—with no beginning, no end; no birth, no death;

no changes, no transformations, no growth, no decay? Who says that the Soul is ignorant, subject to illusion and delusions? Don't you know that it is eternal, full, perfect Knowledge—Knowledge that has no Knower, no Known; that has no increase and no decrease, no degree and no fluctuations, that is wholly independent of a physical stimulus and a stimulated mind-body complex. Who says that the Soul is subject to endless sorrows and sufferings, failures and frustrations? Don't you know that it is eternal, full, perfect Bliss—Bliss that has no selfish desires, no physical satisfaction; that is entirely a kind of pure, perfect, fearless joy, happiness, fulfilment?

And such is the *Advaita-Vedānta* conception of the Soul. What can be more sublime, more inspiring, more gladdening?

And, such is the unique, wonderful, incomparable Humanism of *Advaita-Vedānta*—a Humanism that does not worship Man as Man; a Humanism that does not sing the glory of Man at the cost of that of God; a Humanism that has nothing to do with Materialism, Atheism, Sensualism; but a Humanism, that deifies Man, rather than destroying God; a Humanism that lifts up Man to God, rather than lowering down God to Man; a Humanism that worships Man as God, in the most literal, most real, most complete sense of the term.

What can be more sublime, we repeat, more inspiring, more gladdening?

And, at the end, let us, with reverence and joy, remember, anew the sweet and supreme message of the greatest Humanist of the Modern Age, Swami Vivekananda, who combined in an absolutely novel, peerless manner, Advaitism —generally associated with *Māyāvāda—Mithyāvāda,* over-indifference to the world at large, and over-Spiritualism, with Humanism, generally associated with Atheism and over-Realism:

'No books, no Scriptures, no Science can ever imagine the glory of the Self that appears as Man—the most glorious God that ever was, the only God that ever existed, exists or ever will exist.'

❑❑❑

18

THE CONCEPTION OF SOUL IN ŚAṄKARA'S *SŪTRA-BHĀṢYA*

P.K. Sundaram

The Nature of the Soul

The soul is of the nature of intelligence. As some others like the followers of the *Vaiśeṣika* or *Viāiṣṭādvaita* schools of thought think, intelligence is not a quality of the soul, either adventitious or inseparable and organic. The soul is nothing other than reality. The appearance of its limitedness is due to the limiting adjuncts. There are scriptural passages to this effect: 'himself not asleep' (*Bṛhadāraṇyaka,* IV. 3.11); 'That person is self-luminous' (*ibid.*, IV. 3.14). Sometimes it is argued that since in deep sleep consciousness is not patently perceived, soul cannot be said to be of the nature of intelligence. But the reason why a person who is asleep does not see anything is not that the intelligence is for the moment absent, but that objects are absent. This can be illustrated by the example of light. The light that pervades space with no object to illumine, cannot be said to be non-luminous. *Bṛhadāraṇyaka* declares: 'That he does not see (in deep sleep) is because although seeing then, it does not see; there is no cessation of the sight of the seer' (IV. 3.23).

The Size of the Soul

The doubt arises with regard to the size of the soul because of the fact that certain passages in the Scripture speak of the soul as passing out, going and returning, while some others speak of it expressly as atomic in size, and yet others as all-pervasive. From the passages like: 'When he passes out of this body, he passes out together with all these' (*Kauṣītaki* : III, 3); 'All who depart from this world go to the moon' (*Ibid* : 1, 2) ; and 'From that world he returns again to this world for action' (*Bṛhadāraṇyaka,* IV. 4.6), it is made out by some thinkers that the passing, going and returning would not be possible if the soul were unlimited in size. Limitation in size means only atomic size, since the medium size for the soul, as it is held by the Jainas, is not quite tenable. (This will be shown in the sequence). Śaṅkara's argument against atomicity of the soul is that the soul with the skin (viz. the sense of touch), sensations extend all over the body is not good. When one treads on a thorn, one does not feel the pain all over the body but only in a particular spot, where the skin is pierced by the thorn, Again, if it were contended that sensations can possibly extend over the entire body because intelligence is a quality of the soul, and this intelligence is not atomic and that like the light from the lamp, intelligence can spread out from the soul, it is replied that light is not a quality of the lamp, but is a substance in itself. Qualities are coincidental with their substances. Similarly, odour, for example, cannot exist apart from its substance. Moreover, the view that odour itself is only the dispersion of minute atoms, and, thus, is a substance, canot easily be set aside.

And, for those who hold that intelligence is the very nature of soul, if the intelligence of the soul pervades the whole body, it cannot be atomic. There is no reason why intelligence should not be taken as the very nature of the soul.

The question now is: Why then does the Scripture state the soul to be atomic in size? The soul, though infinite, is yet bound up with the qualities like desire and aversion, pleasure and pain which in fact belong to mind *(buddhi)* during the state of transmigratory existence. The *Śvetāśvatara* passage makes it clear: 'That living soul is to be known as part of the hundredth part of the point of a hair, divided a hundred times, and yet it is to be infinite' (V, 9). Here the conditioned existence of the soul when it is said to be atomic due to superimposition of the qualities of *buddhi* etc., on it, is first stated and then its true nature of infinity is revealed. So atomicity is only apparent, while infinity is real. Intelligence pervading the entire body is only the *buddhi* pervading the entire body. The *Kauṣītakī* passage; 'Having by knowledge taken possession of the whole body' (III, 6), must be taken to mean that the soul takes possession of the body through *buddhi* and does not mean that there is a difference between the soul and knowledge. Or else, the expression is only a metaphorical one as when one speaks of the 'body' of a stone where the 'body' itself is the stone and there is no stone apart from the body.

The references in Scripture to passing out, going and returning do not connote the soul in its essential nature, but only its adjuncts like the *buddhi*. The soul neither goes, nor comes.

The Jaina doctrine that the soul is of the same size as the body it happens to occupy, in any birth, is not considered to be satisfactory on the ground that this concept would mean the contraction and expansion of the soul which will render it unstable and impermanent. The analogy of the stream being permanent while the waters of the stream change will be suitable only to a nihilist viewpoint which is not desirable. Even the Jainas admit the permanency of the final size of the soul when it is released. It follows from this that the initial and intermediary sizes also like the final one must be permanent. This will entail the position that all three sizes are equally the permanent sizes of the soul. Then it is not known how the contraction and expansion of the soul takes place when it enters smaller or bigger bodies. So the size of the soul cannot be mutable and limited. It can only be infinite.

The Soul and Agency

The soul is not an agent in its essential nature. If it were an agent, then liberation will for ever be impossible, for, the soul can never get rid of its agency. Agency, which implies actions, is always painful just as fire is always hot. If it is said that just as fire, without fuel, does not burn, so the soul can abstain from action, it is replied that total abstinence from action, so long as there is association with the limiting adjuncts like *buddhi,* is practically impossible. It cannot be said that actions of such a nature that lead to release can be performed by the soul. For, whatever is secured by actions will not be permanent. Moreover, the Scripture declares that release is attained only by instruction on the true nature of the self, which is pure, free intelligence. This instruction will not be possible if agency were part of the true nature of the self. Self is described as 'Thinking, as it were', 'Moving, as it were' *(Bṛhadāraṇyaka,* IV. 3.7) and not really doing so. Again, 'The Self) in union with the body, senses and mind is called the enjoyer by wise people' *(Kaṭha:* I. 3.4). It is obvious then that the *Śruti* intends the self to be an agent only as associated with mind and sense organs and not in itself. The example of the carpenter is given here: So long as the carpenter is engaged in his bread-winning activity with his tools, he experiences pain, but once he has done the job and is free to go to join his family, he is joyous. Similarly the self, so long as it is involved in the wearisome cycle of actions feels pain. But once it is free from nescience it is all Joy. The falcon flying in the air is tired and comes to rest, then it is happy. So is the self. In the example of the carpenter, he is an agent only in so far as he uses his instruments in work, but not with regard to his body. Similarly, the self appears to be an agent only so long as there is nescience or *avidyā,* whose products are mind etc. In itself it is eternally free.

If the argument is, that certain passages in the Scripture do speak of the self as an agent of actions, it is replied that these passages do not propose to establish the self as an agent but presuppose that agency falsely imagined somehow, and prescribe actions accordingly. On the contrary, there are many passages in the Scripture that do deny agency to the self and speak of it as free.

Materialist Refuted

The materialist believes that consciousness is only the quality of the body. That this is wrong is obvious from the fact that after a person is dead, there is no consciousness, though the body is there. The materialist admits that the knower is different from the known. The body which is known, he should admit, is different from the knower. If consciousness were the quality of elements, it could cognize the body. It is contradictory that anything should act on itself. Fire does not burn itself. And though the body undergoes changes, consciousness continues to be the same and is capable of recognition as 'I saw this'. That the body is invariably associated with consciousness does not show that the latter is a quality of the former. Light and other auxiliaries are needed for any cognitive consciousness. From this it does not follow that cognitive consciousness is a quality of light etc. Moreover, the body is not a necessary auxiliary of consciousness for, in dream, consciousness is operative when the body is inactive. From all this, the soul is known to be different from the body.

The Soul is Dependent on the Lord

The soul, thus blinded by nescience, is dependent on God's grace for its release. It is true that God's control over human actions is not apparent in ordinary experience. Human actions have human motives for their immediate causes. All the same,God is the causal agent in all activity. As the *Śata-patha-brāhmaṇa* states: 'He who dwelling within the self pulls the self within' (XIV, 6.7.30). It is the Lord who leads the soul to higher status through good deeds, or to lower levels, through bad deeds.

This does not, however,mean that the Lord is sometimes cruel and unjust and sometimes kind and merciful quite arbitrarily, or that the soul reaps the consequences of the actions that it has not done. The Lord distributes the fruits of actions to people as they deserve. He acts as an occasional cause. The example of rain will illustrate what happens here. Rain constitutes the common cause of shrubs, bushes etc., which have different foliage and fruits and flowers. Similarly, the Lord only provides the favourable or the unfavourable circumstances for the souls according to their former efforts. The soul is that wich specifically acts, though it is the Lord who generally causes it to act. It is the soul that is addressed in all the injunctions and prohibitions of the Vedas, and not God. Moral responsibility is the soul's while the power of fixing the responsibility and evaluating it is God's own.

The Soul is a 'Part' of the Lord

The relation between the Lord and the soul is not that of master and servant, but that of the part and the whole. However, Śaṅkara adds that being part here is only figurative, for, Lord cannot have parts in the literal sense. This is in accordance with the Scriptural declarations. A certain *śākhā* of the *Atharva-Veda* has a *Brahma-sūkta* which says:

'*Brahman* the fishermen; *Brahman* the slaves; *Brahman* these gamblers.' This means that as everything is *Brahman,* there cannot literally be a partwhole relationship between the soul and Lord. The *Śvetāśvatara* says : 'Thou art woman; thou art man; Thou art youth; Thou art maiden; Thou as an old man totteres a long on the staff; Thou art born with thy face turned everywhere.' (IV. 3). Nondifferent intelligence belongs to the soul and the Lord alike, as heat belongs to the sparks as well as to the fire. Only in this sense, the soul is a part of the Lord.

It may be objected here that if the soul were a part of the Lord, the Lord will be subject to the pain of *saṁsāra.* This is not so because even the so-called pain that the soul is supposed to feel is not real but only apparent resulting from the mistaken superimposition of the mind, body and the senses on the self which is eternally free. This is obvious from the fact that a person feels pain not only when a part of his body is injured, but also when his dear and near ones get afflicted with some pain as though it has afflicted him. If in a gathering of ordinary men and saints somebody cries out suddenly 'The son is dead', the ordinary men get flurried but the saints remain unaffected. All this shows that perfect discriminating knowledge is useful even in ordinary life; how much more so should it be in the case of the omniscient Lord! Where then is the question of pain to the Lord? One can as well imagine that the sun trembles when its reflection in the cup of water is disturbed; or that light is straight or bent when objects limiting it are straight or bent. The *Muṇḍaka* text brings out the truth thus: 'One of them eats the sweet fruit; the other looks on wihtout eating' (III. 1.1.). The *Kaṭha* states: 'The one self within all things is never contaminated by the misery of the world, being himself without' (II. 5.11).

Reflections are many

The individual soul is only a reflection of the highest Self. There are as many souls as there are reflections. The experience of pleasure and pain by one soul does not mean the same experience in other souls. For, the adjuncts are different. The disturbance of one reflected image of the sun does not affect another reflected image. This position of many souls that are reflections of one Self must be sharply distinguished from the position according to which there are many Selves, and not one Self. In this latter case there will certainly result confusion of actions and results.

The *Bhāgavata* view of Soul not Satisfactory

The Bhāgavata doctrine holds that Saṅkarṣaṇa, the individual soul, originates from Vāsudeva, the highest self. But the soul that has origination will be impermanent and all the imperfections of the originated things will attach to it. Even release consisting in reaching the highest being will be rendered impossible. Nor is the doctrine of the Bhāgavatas that Pradyumna (mind) originates from the soul is satisfactory because it is nowhere observed that an instrument is produced from the workman. And mind is an instrument.

Soul at the Time of Departure

On departing from the body, the soul goes forth enveloped predominantly by water, though other elements also are present in water. These elements form a basis for the vital breath *(Prāṇa),* and organs. The soul goes to other spheres to enjoy the fruits of its actios. Even if it were born as minor deity it comes back to earth as soon as its good *karmas* are exhausted. As it is not possible to exhaust all the *karmas* in any one birth, the soul always is born with residual *karmas,* which are the cause of a new birth. While good actions lead the soul to the sphere of the Moon, bad ones lead it to world of Yama and the seven hells. After enjoyment in the sphere of the Moon, the soul descends quickly through the air, ether and the rest by means of rain drops. Thence, the soul enters into a state of conjunction with the bodies of plants, which are already animated by other souls. The temporary stay in the plants, for the soul returning from the sphere of the Moon, is thus not for enjoyment of pleasure or pain but is just a stage for passing on into new bodies. However, with regard to evil-doers, they are born as plants etc. and the plants etc., in their case are not merely a sojourn for them before entering into another new body. When the right time arrives, the plant is eaten as food by someone, the soul goes into the food, and through the father enters into the womb of the mother.

The Released Souls

The man of realization gets rid of all good and bad actions, and he does not go to any temporary abodes. He does not have the reason any more to reach any place. He, whose realization is a fact, whose wishes have been fulfilled, in whom the potentiality of all suffering is already destroyed, has nothing to look for but the dissolution of the body which is the result of the *prārabdha-karma*. If one wants to reach some village, he has to take a road leading to that village. But when one wants to be cured of a sickness, what he wants is medicine, and no movement is required. The realized soul does not go anywhere.

Certain souls, however, who have realized, yet might be appointed by the lord to fulfil certain duties for the sake of the world and their *prārabdha-karmas,* still unexhausted, may be utilized for their embodiment. *Apāntarātmas* is a case in point. These souls are, of course, free to move from one body to another at will and will be able to remember their identity and individuality whatever may be the bodies they occupy. *Sulabhā,* a realized soul, entered deliberately the body of Janaka to carry on a discussion with him.

The worshippers of *Saguṇa-Brahman,* who practise the *Upāsanas* and *vidyās,* go along the path of the gods, *devayāna* but do not however return to birth. The completely realized soul with *Brahman*-intuition has no need of a path. His *prāṇas* do not depart from the body (see *Bṛhadāraṇyaka:* III, 2.11), but then and there merge once for all. The bodily organs and elements of the realized soul of the worshipper of the *Saguṇa-Brahman* along with the organs comes to the heart. The heart is illumined, the passage of departure is lit up. The soul passes out through the *suṣumnānāḍī,* follows the rays of the sun whether it is night or day or whether it is *Dakṣiṇāyana* or *Uttarāyaṇa,* and guided by deities goes to *Brahma-loka*. From here, this soul gets its *Brahman*-intuition *brahman-sākṣātkāra* in due course. This is what is known as 'gradual liberation' *(Krama-mukti)*. However, it is not all worshippers of *Saguṇa-Brahman* that go to *Brahma-loka*. Those who worship *Brahman* in the form of any symbol do not go there but secure results according to the nature of symbols used in meditation. The soul getting release through the worship of *Saguṇa-Brahman* and residing in *Brahma-loka* can create bodies for itself by mere will. In fact, it has all the lordly powers except the power of creation. Both the realized souls and worshippers of *Saguṇa-Brahman* alike do not return to birth. A well-known verse attributed to Śaṅkara summarizes the nature of the soul, world and reality thus: *ślokārdhena pravakṣyāmi yaduktaṁ granthakoṭiṣu; brahma satyaṁ jagan-mithyā jīvo brahmaiva nā'paraḥ.*

❑❑❑

19

MADHUSŪDANASARASWATĪ

Anima Sen Gupta

Madhusūdanasaraswatī, the great Advaita scholar is the author of a booklet entitled *Advaitaratnarakṣaṇam* which has received attention of a very limited section of oriental scholars. In this important work, Madhusūdanasaraswatī made a special attempt to establish non-dualism of Śaṅkara after refuting the objections raised against Advaitavāda by the suppoters of the *bhedasat vada*. He refers to a number of *śruti* and *smṛti* texts showing how these are interpreted by the supporters of the *bhedasat vada*. Madhusūdan has also made an attempt to show the defects inherent in the interpretations of the opponent group thereby proving that all *śruti* texts should be interpreted from the Advaita point of view.

In an article published in "Darshan Internatioal" of Moradabad in its "Dr. S. Radhakrishnan Souvenir Volume", I made an attempt to present the views of Madhusūdanasaraswatī with particular reference to his views expressed in "*śrutīnā bhedaparatvabhangaḥ*" (*Advaita ratna rakṣaṇam*).

In this article I shall make an attempt to present his views with reference to his *sūtra* No. 4 i.e. *atha sarva buddhi-viṣayabhangaḥ*.

It is generally held against the Advaita Vedānta that the non-dual scriptural texts which are admitted by the Advaita-school as evidence for the declaration of the Highest Being as differenceless, cannot be accepted in that manner; because the sources of knowledge such as perception etc. which prove difference will then be opposed to these *śruti*-texts.

Madhusūdanasaraswatī in his *sūtra "atha sarva buddhibheda viṣaya bhangaḥ"* points out that this view of the realistic school is unsound. This is because perception can never reveal difference.

Incapacity of the Perceptual knowledge to Reveal Difference

Perception is generally divided into two forms—indeterminate *(nirvikalpaka)* and determinate *(savikalpaka)*. The Advaita Vedānta holds that *nirvikalpaka pratyakṣa* is incapable of revealing difference since it manifests only the differenceless pure being. Even *savikalpaka* perception which grasps a qualified object does not, in the Advaita opinion, reveal difference of one qualified object from another. When the jar is perceived, the determinative intellect or the *savikalpaka buddhi* only assumes the form of "this is jar", "this is cloth" etc. In other words in the determinate knowledge of the jar, the things present before the perceiver are, at the very first moment, the jar, jarness and the relation between the jar and the jarness etc. It is the *vaiśiṣṭya* in the form of the relation between the jar and the jarness which is grasped only in the full-fledged detrminate knowledge of the subsequent moment and there is no other thing present that can be admitted as difference.

It cannot be said that the difference is an ingredient of *vaiśiṣṭya* because we find that *bedha* and *vaiśiṣṭya* are always mentioned separately by different words. The realists may object by saying the *vaiśiṣṭya* should not be supposed as an extra-thing, different from difference, as in that case, the law of parsimony will be violated. *Vaiśiṣṭya* is to be regarded as a form of difference because it is the *vaiśiṣṭya* of the jar that differentiates the jar from all other things which are not jars. This is what is known also as *atadvyāvṛtti*. So the difference which is of the form of *ananyābhāva* is the same as *vaiśiṣṭya*. Hence, the knowledge of *vaiśiṣṭya* is the knowledge of difference. Udayanācārya has said: *atadvyāvṛtti vaiśiṣṭyamiti*. Here Madhusūdanasaraswatī raises a question : how does knowledge of *vaiśiṣṭya* in the form of *atadvyāvṛtti* arise in the case of the cognition of this jar, arising just after the passing away of the *nirvikalpaka* stage? He further assumes that the realistic school will perhaps try to answer his question by saying that just as prior to the knowledge of the qualified object in the *savikalpaka* stage, one has to have hypothetical knowledge of *viśeṣaṇa,* and also the recollection of the *saṁjñā,* in the same manner prior to the cognition of *vaiśiṣṭya* in the *savikalpaka* stage, recollection of *vaiśiṣṭya* has to be supposed. This possible answer of the realists, however, is not acceptable to Madhusūdanasaraswatī because *vaiśiṣṭya* in the Advaita view, must be something over and above the noun, adjective and their relation. Even in the *savikalpaka* stage (as we have seen) the knowledge of the first moment, is different from the knowledge of the second moment. In the first moment, we have the knowledge of stick, man and the relation, whereas in the second moment, we have the knowledge of a man with a stick *(Daṇḍī puruṣa)*. There is difference between cognitions of these two moments. There is something more in the second cognition (because *daṇḍa* is cognized as being related to *puruṣa* as an attribute) than in the first. This 'something more' is termed as *vaiśiṣṭya*. If we do not hold that there is something more in the second moment than there is in the first, then the knowledge of the first moment too will be the knowledge of a qualified object.

Since it is impossible to explain *savikalapaka* cognitions of the two moments without considering *vaiśiṣṭya* as something additional besides noun, adjectvie and relation and also as merging only in the second moment, the question of violating the law of parsimony does not arise at all.

In the opinion of Madhusūdanasaraswatī, *vaiśiṣṭya* cannot be regarded as a form of *atadvyāvṛtti* even from the point of view of the realistic *Nyāya* school. This is because unless there is the knowledge of non-blue, there cannot be knowledge of the difference from non-blue (i.e. *anīla-vyāvṛtti* or *anīlabheda)* in the case of the cognition of a blue lotus. If it is urged by the realists that here the memory of non-blue will serve the purpose, then too, the situation will not improve; because memory of non-blue is not possible unless there is prior knowledge of blue. How does the knowledge of blue arise in the first stage? Moreover, everything besides blue is included in non-blue and so it is not possible for any human being to have a full knowledge of the non-blue in one life.

We may ask what actually is meant by *anīla-vyāvṛtti?* Does it mean difference from blue? Or does it mean some positive thing that can be designated as *anīla?* If it is the former, then there will be the fallacy of mutual dependence. Blue is to be known as something different from non-blue and non-blue is to be known as something different from blue. Then how are we to know these two mutually dependent objects? If we accept the latter alternative (i.e. non-blue referring to something positive) then the knowledge of that positive thing is occurring without the knowledge of difference *(vyāvṛttijñāna)*. If this is so, then we can very well say that the knowledge cf blue too, arises without the knowledge of *vyāvṛtti*. Truly speaking, when we recognize the cow, our cognition takes the form of "cow" only and there is no knowledge of the negation of non-cow. *Gotva-vaiśiṣṭya* which is revealed in the awareness of the cow is positive and not negative. It is, therefore, not proper to explain cowness in terms of *agau-vyāvṛtti*. Again, if cowness is the same as *agau-vyāvṛtti,* then cowness as a universal will not be established and this will be prejudicial to the philosophical position of the realistic school.

The author of *Tattvacintāmaṇi* has said that it is only after one is aware of *daṇḍī puruṣa,* that he comes to cognize *adaṇḍa-vyāvṛtti* (negation of non-stick) in the *daṇḍī puruṣa.* Had the first moment of *savikalpaka* knowledge been the revealer of *vaiśiṣṭya* the word *anantara* would not have been used.

Comments

If we analyse critically the perceptual positions of the *Nyāya* and the Advaita schools in the light of what has been stated by Madhusūdanasaraswatī in this particular *sūtra,* we find that the two positions differ from each other in the following manner:

According to Advaita Vedānta, the first moment of the determinate knowledge reveals noun, adjective, relation etc. in unrelated units. It is only in the second moment that the knowledge of the thing (noun) as qualified by the attribute *(vaiśiṣṭyāvagāhi)* arises. So the knowledge of *vaiśiṣṭya* arises in the second moment of the determinate knowledge. According to the Nyāya school, the noun, adjective, relation etc. are cognized as unrelated units in the indeterminate knowledge which resembles to a great extent the first moment of the determinate knowledge of the Advaita Vedānta. The stage in which the substantive-adjective relation is established is known as the *savikalpaka* or the determinate stage by the Nyāya-school. Now this cognition of substantive-adjective relation is what is necessary for the knowledge of difference. Just as knowledge of two is at least necessary for having combination or relation between things (because *sva* cannot be relative to *sva*), in the same manner cogition of at least two things is necessary for having the knowledge of difference (*Sva* cannot be differentiated from *sva*). After the arousal of this cognition, the knowledge of difference arises easily, provided there is no *pratibandhaka* to prevent it. Now the positions of these two schools when analysed from the point of view of object *(sāmagrī),* stand as follows:

Advaita point of vews

1. *Jnāna-viśleṣaṇa:* First moment of determinate knowledge; knowledge of noun, adjective, relation etc. in unrelated conditions *(viśkalita jñāna).*

2. *vaiśiṣṭya-jñāna:* In this stage, there is an increase in knowledge.

1. *Sāmagrī viśleṣaṇa:* First moment of determinate knowledge: Noun, adjective, relation etc. as unrelated units.

2. Emergence of *vaiśiṣṭya* as relation between noun and adjective. In other words there is emergene of someting new as a result of *ghaṭa-ghṭatvasambandha.* So, there is an increase on the objective side *(sāmagrī-kṣetra).*

The Nyāya point of view

Jñāna-viśleṣaṇa:

1. *Nirvikalpaka* stage of knowledge where there is awareness of noun, adjective, relation etc. as unrelated units.

2. *Savikalpaka* stage of knowledge: knowledge of substantive adjective relation. (Increase in knowledge)

Sāmagrī-viśleṣaṇa:

1. *Nirvikalpaka* and *Savikalpaka* do not differ in their *sāmagrī* or object.

2. *Savikalpaka* unfolds all that is implicitly involved in the *nirvikalpaka* stage. So there is no increase in the object. The knowledge may be regarded as containing the seed of the knowledge of difference.

From the above analysis, it is clear that according to

both the schools the cognition of *vaiśiṣṭya* arises only after the awareness of the noun, adjective, relation etc. as unrelated units. Differences of opinion arise only in respect of the form of *vaiśiṣṭya.* The Advaita holds that when there is *vaiśiṣṭyajñāna,* something new and positive is added to the content or object of cognition. So, *vaiśiṣṭya* is not the same as *atadvyāvṛtti.* According to Nyāya, however, the object or content remains the same from the first moment to all the subsequent moments. In fact, when the undifferentiated whole is analysed and substantive-adjectiver relation is cognized, spade work for the knowledge of difference is done by the perceiver. *vaiśiṣṭya* in the opinion of the Nyāya-school, is the same as *atadvyāvṛtti.* So from the Nyāya point of view, there is no increase on the objective side of knowledge. Changes occur only in the knowledge-aspect.

The author of the *"Tattvacintāmaṇi"* has no doubt said that cognition of *adaṇḍa-bheda* arises after the cognition of *daṇḍī puruṣa;* but his statement truly implies that it is from the point of view of knowledge only that *atadvyāvṛtti* arises after *sambandha;* from the point of view of the object, however, there is no change. Again, the seed of *bheda grahaṇa* is shown as soon as the perceiver cognizes *daṇḍī puruṣa.* So there is no harm if one admits or does not admit *ānantarya* between *sambandha* and *atadvyāvṛtti.* According to Advaita, the noun, the adjective, the relation etc.nay, the whole of the object of knowledge is *vikalpa* (thought construction). When there is increase in knowledge, there is also an increase in the *viṣaya* of knowledge. According to Nyāya, however, the object of knowledge is real, it remains the same from the first moment of *sannikarṣa* till the end. Knowledge of the object may be vague or clear, *viśada* or *aviśada* but there can be no change in the real object of knowledge.

❑❑❑

20

THE PHILOSOPHY OF RĀMĀNUJA : SOME SALIENT FEATURES

R.K. Panda

Rāmānuja intended to present a philosophy founded on reason-based faith by synthesising *Brahman* of Vedānta philosophy with God worshipped in the field of religious devotion. For him, the *Brahman* of the Upaniṣads and the Sūtras, the Vāsudeva of Gītā, the Bhagawān of Pañcarātra and the arcā of the Ālvārs cannot be the same supreme self and insists on Bhakti-yoga as the direct means of knowing *Brahman*.

The ultimate reality, *Brahman* or God, according to Rāmānuja, is a realized truth. It consists in itself the variety of the world. Both the conscious soul and the unconscious matter are its essential and inseparable part. Consciousness and the matter both form the body of *Brahman*. All that is different from Paramātman, whether it is conscious or unconscious, forms the body of *Brahman*, and only that Paramātman forms the soul of that body. The soul, according to Rāmānuja, is not affected by the changes in the body. The soul is by nature pure and unchanging. The physical and worldly entities only cover the liminosity of the soul, they do not destroy its purity and unchanging nature. The physical and worldly entities are the creations of sin, but the pure soul cannot commit any sin. *Brahman* is both the material and instrumental cause of the universe which consists of the individual soul and the physical nature and the changes occur in the body of God. His soul is always devoid of all types of changes. Eternal and independent existence of individual soul is an essential part of Rāmānuja's Viśiṣṭādvaita philosophy. He has accepted the existence of all the three entities, God, idividual soul and physical nature, at the level of the same reality. As *Paramātman*, God is the soul of everything.

Rāmānuja admits a very close connections between *Bhakti*, *jñāna* and *karma*. He regards that knowledge is the cause of *Bhakti*. According to him, knowledge is the very foundation of *Bhakti* and it is *jñāna* that produces *Bhakti* and also nourishes and enriches it. In the process of attaining liberaion, an individual shoul, first of all, tries to acquire the true knowledge of the Ātman and then distinguish the soul from all its necessary accompaniments and also from all other inanimate objects of the world. *Karma*, according to Rāmānuja, is such a thing that it should not be abandoned at any stage of life. Rāmānuja emphasizes the performance of disinterested action.

According to Rāmānuja *Bhakti* is the supreme way of attaining God. But *Prapatti* is a secondary one. This is clear from his *Gītābhāṣya*. The general meaning of '*Prapad*', according to Rāmānuja, is "to take refuge in". This refuge may be either in God or in his human form, and is taken by following His commands. So it can also be applied to man's taking refuge in divine being as the principal object of worship. *Bhakti*, which presupposes *prapatti*, is the only means for the *aiśvaryārthin, kaivalyārthin* and *jñānin* to achieve their respective ends. The scheme of *prapatti* consists of six parts, viz. (1) *Anukulyasamkalpa* (2) *Pratikulyavarjana* (3) *mahaviśvāsa* (4) *kārpaṇya* (5) *Goptṛtvavarṇa* (6) *Ātmanikṣepa*.

Rāmānuja postulates the view that many shouls exist in

the world of God. These souls adopt various forms due to pure *sattva*. Similarly with the help of this pure *sattva*, the liberated souls give born to their thoughts and desires. Every soul, in the end, is sure to attain completenes but even then it will be dependent on the absolute *Brahman*. This absolute *Brahman*, due to its immanent nature, forms an organic unity with the different souls, but is not perverted due to it. Liberated souls are many in number. But their manifoldness is only numerical; they do not possess any qualitative difference. Qualitatively, all liberated soul are alike and also experience the bliss of *Brahman* in a like manner.

Rāmānuja believes in five stages of *mokṣa* which are as under:—

(i) Sālokya mokṣa
(ii) Sārṣṭi mokṣa
(iii) Sāmīpya mokṣa
(iv) Sārupya mokṣa
(v) Sāyujya mokṣa

As to the problem of the relation of Individual soul with *Brahman* Rāmānuja holds the view that God, the Puruṣottama desired to be in various forms and created the whole world constituting fire, water, etc. After that he created the various bodies, divine and human etc. which were made according to the merits and demirits of the individual souls. At the end, He entered the above souls according to his desire, and gave each of them a meaningful form, so that it could be expressed by a particular word. Thus the Individual soul is only a reflection of the whole reality. Every individual soul consists of the following: (1) The immanent *Brahman* i.e. that reality which shines in every living being. (2) the soul which is omniscient, and (3) the material ingredient through which the soul performs action. Thus every Individual soul depicts the tried in its individuality like *Brahman*.

According to Rāmānuja, *Śaraṇāgati* is the most sacred truth of all the scriptures. He gives highest significance to *Śaraṇāgati* in attaining *Mokṣa*. The progress of the aspirant to attain God, through *karmayoga, jñānayoga* and *Bhakti-yoga*, which are the successive stages of the same way culminating in the attainment of God, is for Rāmānuja, the fundamental teaching of the Gītā and *Śrībhāṣya*. At several places Rāmānuja says that devotion to God is the surest way of attaining liberation. The devotional service to God is the core of *Brahma-Vidyā* according to Rāmānuja. *Prapatti* and *Śaraṇāgati* are accessories to *Bhakti*.

In the stage of *Paramabhakti* the devotee visualises God, as one possesing infinite auspicious qualities, devoid of all faults, and by repeated meditation on God, the devotee gradually loses all sense of difference. The devotee becomes fully merged in the form of God. when an individual soul is liberated through devotion and divine grace, he loses his natural body and posses through *Vāyuloka*, *Varuṇa-loka*, *Ādityaloka*, *Indraloka*, *Prajāpatiloka*, *Brahmaloka* and finally reaches the eternal abode, Vaikuṇṭha. It is only in this state of emancipation that a liberated man becomes completely free from the influence of all his virtuous and vicious deeds and becomes similar to *Brahman*.

Rāmānuja does not believe in the concept of *Jīvanmukti* (liberated during life.). A knower of *Brahman* does not attain *mokṣa* so long as his body does not fall. He rejects Śaṅkara's doctrine.

❑❑❑

21
ŚRĪBHĀṢYA

Swami Vireswarananda

Section I

In the last two chapters, it has been shown that the Vedānta texts establish *Brahman*, the First Cause, which is free from all imperfections and endowed with an infinite number of good qualities and so different in nature from all other beings, as the proper object of meditation for attaining final release. In this connection, all objections based on the Smṛtis and reasoning against the Vedāntic view have been refuted and shown to be incorrect, and it was also shown that the so-called scriptural contradictions do not exist with respect to the Vedāntic view. The remaining two chapters prescribe the means and mode of attaining *Brahman*. This chapter particularly deals with meditation which is the means of attaining *Brahman*. But without a spirit of dispasssion for the world and a desire for *Brahman*, no one would be inclined to meditate on Him. In the first two sections of this chapter, the imperfections of the soul and the characteristics of *Brahman*, which is beyond all imperfections, are shown in contrast in order to create this dispassion for the world and the desire for *Brahman*.

Topic 1 : The soul, when passing out of the body at death, is enveloped with fine particles of the gross elements.

तदन्तरप्रतिपत्तौ रंहति संपरिष्वक्तः प्रश्ननिरूपणाभ्याम् ॥3।1।1॥

1. (The soul) goes (out of the body) enveloped (with

subtle parts of the gross elements) with a view to obtaining another of that (viz. a fresh body); (so it is known) from the question and answer (in the scripture).

The *sūtra* discusses whether in transmigration the soul takes with it subtle parts of the gross elements as the seed, as it were, for the future body or not. The opponent holds that it does not take them, for it is useless, becasue the elements are easily available everywhere. This *sūtra* refutes it. The words 'another of that' in the *sūtra* refer to the form or body mentioned in II. 4.17. The soul, when it goes out of one body and takes another, goes out with the subtle parts of the gross elements; that this is a fact is known from the question and answer that occurs in the scripture in the *pañcāgni vidyā*—the knowledge of the five fires. Do you know why in the fifth oblation water is called man? (Chā. U., V. 3.3). This is the question, and the answer is given in the subsequent texts which, after explaining how the five oblations in the forms of *śraddhā, soma*, rain, food, and seed are offered in the five fires (i.e. objects imagined to be fires for the sake of *upāsanā)*—the heavens, *parjanya,* earth, man and woman—end thus: 'For this reason is water in the fifth oblation called man', i.e. comes to be designated as man. From this, we understand that the soul goes out envelop-ed with water (same as *śraddhā*).

त्र्यात्मकत्वात्तु भूयस्त्वात्॥3।1।2॥

2. But on account of (water) consisting of three elements (all these elements are present and not merely water); (water alone is, however, mentioned) on account of its prepondera-nce.

An objection is raised that the text mentions only water and not the other elements as accompanying the soul. The *sūtra* says that, as the gross element of water contains the other two elements also according to the tripartite creation, all the three elements accompany the soul. As the watery portion in the body, however, preponderates, it alone is mentioned.

प्राणगतेश्च॥3।1।3॥

3. And because of the going of the organs *(prāṇas)* (with the soul, the elements also accompany the soul).

'When it departs, the vital force follows. When the vital force departs, all the organs follow' (Bṛ. U., IV. 4.2). Since the organs follow the soul, they must have a material base; hence also it is inferred that the elements follow the soul, thus forming a basis for the organs.

अग्न्यादिगतिश्रुतेरिति चेत्, न, भाक्तत्वात्॥3।1।4॥

4. If it be said (that the organs do not follow the soul), for the scriptures declare their entering into fire etc., (we say) not so, on account of its being so said in a secondary sense.

'When the vocal organ of a man who dies is merged in the fire' etc. (Bṛ. U., III. 2.13.)—this text shows that the organs are resolved in their presiding deities, and hence it cannot be said that they accompany the soul. This *sūtra* says that these statements are to be taken in a secondary sense and not literally, for the same text later says, 'The hairs of the body enter the herbs, the hairs of the head enter the trees', and this is obviously not true in the literal sense. Hence the text must be taken in a secondary sense.

प्रथमेऽश्रवणादिति चेत्, न, ता एव हि उपपत्तेः॥3।1।5॥

5. If it be objected on account of (water) not being mentioned in the first of the oblations, (we say) not so, because that (viz. water) only (is meant by the word *'śraddhā),* on account of the appropriateness (of such an interpretation).

An objection is raised that, as there is no mention of

water in the first oblation, it is not correct to say that the soul goes out enveloped in subtle parts of water. The text mentions only *śraddhā* and not water as oblation, and *śraddhā* is a mental attitude. 'On that altar the gods offer *śraddhā* as oblation' (Chā. U., V. 4.2). The *sūtra* refutes this and says that by *śraddhā* in the text water is meant, for in that case alone, there would be consistency between the question and the answer. The question asked is, 'Do you know why in the fifth oblation water is called man?' and the answer at the very beginning is that *śraddhā* is mentioned as the oblation in the fire of heavenly world. So *śraddhā* denotes water, otherwise there will be no syntactical unity of the whole passage. The word *'śraddhā'* is also used for water in the scriptures: *'Śraddhā* indeed is water' *(Taittīrīya Saṁhitā,* I. 6.8.1.)

अश्रुतत्वादिति चेत्, न, इष्टादिकारिणां प्रतीतेः।।3।1।6।।

6. If it be said that on account of (the soul) not being mentioned in the text (the soul does not depart enveloped in water etc.), (we say) not so, for the *jīvas* who perform sacrifices etc. (are understood).

An objection is raised that, in the *Chāndogya* text cited (V. 3.3), there is mention of water only, but there is no reference to the soul. So how can it be said that the soul departs enveloped in water, and is born again as man? The *sūtra* refutes this view, for there is reference to the mode of departure of the souls who perform sacrifices etc. later in the same chapter, it is said that those who have performed sacrifices attain the world of gods and become *Somarāja* (King Soma) and, on the exhaustion of their meritorious deeds, are reborn again as men. 'But they who, being in the village, practise sacrifices and works of public utility, and give alms, go to the smoke, from smoke to night, ... from *ākāśa* to the moon. This (i.e. this moon) is King Soma. This is the food of the gods. This the gods eat' (Chā. U., V. 10. 3-4). Earlier, we have the text, Out of that oblation King Soma arises' (Chā. U., V. 4.2). This King Soma is recognized in Chā. U., V. 10.4, which also mentions King Soma as quoted above. By the word 'water', therefore,the individual soul enveloped in water, and having the water for its body, is understood.

भाक्तं वाऽनात्मवित्वात्तथा हि दर्शयति॥3।1।7॥

7. But (the souls being the food of the gods in heaven is used) in a secondary sense, on account of their not knowing the Self; because (the Śruti) declares like that.

In the text cited in the previous *sūtra,* it is said that which goes by the path of smoke etc. becomes the food of the gods; and as the soul is not a material edible thing, how can those texts be taken as referring to the soul? This is King Soma. This is the food of the gods. This the gods eat' (Chā. U., V. 10.4.).

The word 'but' is used to remove this doubt. In the text quoted, the word 'food' is not used in the primary sense, but metaphorically, meaning objects of enjoyment; and the souls, in turn, enjoy in their company. That the souls become objects of enjoyment to the gods is known from texts like, 'He is like a beast to the gods' (Bṛ. U., I. 4.10).

Therefore the soul goes out of the body at death enveloped in the subtle parts of the elements.

❑❑❑

22

ŚATADŪṢAṆĪ OF VEDĀNTA DEŚIKA

B.H. Kapadia

Vedānta Deśika,[1] the author of *Śatadūṣaṇī,* was one of the promulgators of Viśiṣṭādvaita. He was born in A.D. 1268 at Himavana in Kanchipuram, in a Vaiṣṇava family known for learning and piety. Vātsya Varadācārya, a descendent in the line of Śri Rāmānuja, seeing the unparalleled genius of this child predicted that he will establish the doctrine of Viśiṣṭādvaita and will counteract the influence of the other doctrines.[2] The celebrated pupil of Vātsya Varadācārya, Atreya Rāmānuja was the maternal uncle of Deśika. He studied under his supervision and attained mastery at the tender age of twenty in all the branches of traditional sciences. In view of his dexterity and learning he was given the titles Vedāntācārya and *Sarvatantrasvatantra.* According to *Saṅkalpasūryodaya*[3] these titles were conferred on him at Śrirangam. His life[4] was extremely religious, simple and saintly. He spent his life in preaching the doctrines of Viśiṣṭādvaita, in writing philosophical treatises, and religious books. In the line of Śrī Rāmānuja he became famous as Venkatanātha. Even though he was of religious temperament yet his opponents used to harass him. He used to bear these hardships patiently.

He used to enter into disputes with scholars of other beliefs and win them over to his faith by his unparalleled art of disputation and sharp intelligence. His disputations are described in *Paramatabhaṅga* and *Śatadūṣaṇī*. On account of his mastery over the science of poetics and invincibility in argumentation he was given the title of *Kavitārkikasiṁha*. Like his erudition, his life also was inspiring. It was austere, like that of an ascetic. He lived on alms and despised wealth and fame.

Once in the alms which he obtained, a sympathetic follower of his, had mixed some gold coins. Desika threw them away the moment he found them out. This characteristic feature of his, i.e., Vairāgya, can be discerned in his *Vairagya-pañcaka:* a small poem of five verses, sent in answer to the invitation of Vidyāraṇya, the then minister of the king of Vijayanagara. His devotion to the Lord, and towards the doctrine of Sri Ramanuja were superb.

His principal treatieses in the field of philosophy are : *Tattvamuktākalāpa, Sarvārthasiddhi, Adhikaraṇasārāli, Nyāyapariśuddhi, Nyāyasiddhāñjana, Seśvaramīmāṁsā, Mīmaṁsāpādukā,* and *Śatadūṣaṇī*. In each of these, Deśika contributed something new. In *Tattvamuktākalāpa* he deals with *Jaḍa, Jīva, Īśvara, Buddhi* and *Adravya* according to Viśiṣṭādvaita. *Sarvārthasiddhi* is a *ṭīkā* in which Deśika has propounded the doctrines laid down in the above work. In *Adhikaraṇasārdvali* Deśika explains the topics of the *Adhikaraṇas* of *Śrībhāṣya* in verse. In *Nyāyapariśuddhi* he discusses the technical aspects of the *Pramāṇas* according to Viśiṣṭādvaita. The *Adhyātmavāda* dealt with briefly in *Nyāyapariśuddhi* is discussed in greater detail in *Nyāya-siddhāñjana. Seśvaramīmāṁsa* and *Mimāṁsāpādukā* are treatises about Mīmāṁsā. In the first work, Deśika elucidates the Mīmāṁsā Sūtras of Jaimini and he does this in such a way that they are not in opposition to the conclusions of Bādarāyaṇa. He posits that Pūrva and Uttara Mīmāṁsā are not divergent but they are one and *Akhaṇḍa*. In *Śatadūṣanī* he refutes in detail the Advaita doctrines.

His other works on philosophy are of the nature of commentaries. They are : *Tattvaṭīkā,* a *ṭīkā* on *Śrībhāṣya; Tātparyacandrikā,* a *ṭīkā* on the *Gītābhāṣya* of Rāmānuja; *Īśāvāsyopaniṣadbhāṣya; Rahasyarakṣā,* a *ṭīkā* on *Stotraratna* of Yāmunamuni and *Catuḥśloki* and *Gadyatraya* of Rāmānuja; and *Gītārthasaṁgraharakṣā,* a *ṭīkā* on the *Gītārthasaṁgraha* of Yāmunamuni. Over and above these, *Vedārthasaṁgraha-vyākhyā* on *Vedārthasaṁgraha* and *Nigamaparimala* on the works of the Ālvars are supposed to be from the pen of Deśika but they are not available.

Besides the above mentioned treatises, Deśika is the author of 32 works in Maṇipravāla[5] style. In these works, he propounds in a popular style the Vaśiṣṭādvaita doctrines. *Rahasyatrayasāra,* an unparalleled work of Deśika is written in the style. *Paramatabhaṅga* is also a work of this type in which besides Advaita 17 other beliefs are refuted. Kāvyas, Dramas, etc. are other works of Deśika. Among kāvyas *Yādavābhyudaya,* is about the life of Lord Śrī Kṛṣṇa; *Haṁsasaṁdeśa* is in imitation of Kālidāsa's *Meghadūta; Subhāṣ itanīti* deals with ethics; and *Pādukāsahasra* is about the feet of the Lord of Śrīrangam. *Saṅkalpasūryodaya* is an allegorical drama is ten acts. In this drama Deśika explains the efforts which a *Jīva* has to make to attain *Mokṣa.* He has written 29 devotional *sūktas* known as *stotras. Pañcarātrarakṣā, Nikṣekarakṣā* and *Saccaritrarakṣā* are religious works.

Vedānta Deśika's *Śatadūṣaṇī* is a critical work. It aims at refuting the Advaita doctrines. In the Pūrvapakṣa Deśika has put forth in detail arguments from works on Advaita coming from the pen of his predecessors. In this work Deśika tries to explain the differences between the two great Ācāryas, Śaṅkara and Rāmānuja. In *Advaitasiddhi* and in its gloss

Laghucandrikā and other works after Vedānta Deśika the objections raised forth in *Śatadūṣaṇī* are refuted. In our modern times in *Śatabhūṣaṇī*, a work written by Śrī Ananta-kṛṣṇa Śāstriar, in Sanskrit, *Śatadūṣaṇī* is controverted. To give and answer to *Śatabhūṣaṇī* Śrī Uttamura Viraragha-vacarya Swami has written an extensive and learned work *Paramārthabhūsaṇa.* Another such work is Varadācārya's *Tattvasudhā.* Dr. Dasgupta in his *History of Indian Philosophy* (vol. 3) makes a very brief review of Deśika's Vādas. Here 39 *vādas* are reviewed and they are not comprehensive.

Śatadūṣaṇī is of great importance to Viśiṣṭādvaitins. As is clear from the title of the work, it ought to attempt at a scientific discussion of a hundred topics of philosophy. From the opening verse of *Śatadūṣaṇī,*[6] and from *Tattvaṭīkā*[7] it can be inferred that the main object of this work is to refute the doctrines of Śaṅkara and his followers. The logic made use of here is of such works: One establishes one's point by refuting the view of the opponent and by evaluating one's own position. By refuting partial truths and wrong doctrines such works gain an importance. Compared to *jalpa* and *vitaṇḍā* this method is known as *vāda.* In *Khaṇḍana-khaṇḍakhādya* of Sri Harṣa *vitaṇḍā* is employed while in *Śatadūṣaṇī,* as in Citsukha's *Tattvapradīpikā, vāda* is employed. *Śatadūṣaṇī* being *khaṇḍanamaṇḍanātmaka* (refuting the opponent's viws and establisheing one's own) is a *vādagrantha.* It is compared to a sword, whereas *Sarvār-thasiddhi* is compared to a shield.[8]

The criticism levelled at Advaita in *Śatadūṣaṇī* is not the first attempt. Before Vedānta Deśika Śrī Yāmuna (in 916-1036) had converted the followers of Advaita to the doctrine of Viśiṣṭādvaita. Ātmasiddhi and Samvitsiddhi have criticised the important tenets of Advaita. After Yāmunācārya this work is carried on by Śrī Rāmānuja in the *Jijñāsā-*

dhikaraṇa of *Śrībhāṣya*. Before Yāmuna, in the first half of the ninth century *Māyāvāda* was severely criticised by Bhāskara. After Yāmuna Madhva was the foremost of the critics of Advaita.

Śrī Ramanuja and Madhva have taken an active part in the criticism of Advaita than any other doctrines because in their times this had a very great importance. Some light is thrown on this as can be gathered from the preliminary verses of *Vedāntasaṅgraha*. Even though in *Śrībhāṣya* a detailed and exhaustive criticism is levelled at Advaita, yet, after Rāmānuja the doctrines of Advaita still remained very influential. Śrī Harṣa, Ānandabodha and Citsukha are great thinkers of Advaita before Vedānta Deśika and after Rāmānuja. Therefore, Vedānta Deśika had to re-establish the glory of Viśiṣṭādvaita.

While criticising Advaita, Vedānta Deśika follows the thoughts of Śrī Ramanuja as established in the *Jijñāsādhikaraṇa* of *Śrībhāṣya*. At the end of many discussions Deśika quotes from *Śrībhāṣya*.[9] Even though the arguments of *Śrībhāṣya* are followed in *Śatadūṣaṇī*, yet the author has many points of originality to offer and while ridiculing the opponent he raises quite a few points[10] for discussion.

In *Śrībhāṣya*, the *Pūrvapakṣa* is very short, *Śatadūṣaṇī* amplifies it. (See *vāda* 36). The criticism is from various points and aspects. On account of his wide knowledge and on account of his astuteness in the art of dispute Vedānta Deśika has done a great job for Viśiṣṭādvaita. At the very outset of the work Deśika expresses his conviction that on account of the constant repetition of the arguments in *Śatadūṣaṇī*, the Advaitin could be easlily won over to his side. In any case, Deśika in *Śatadūṣaṇī* has re-established the glory of *Viśiṣṭadvaita* in a very fruitful way and on a logical basis.

At the beginning of every *Vāda*, while quoting the *Purva-pakṣa,* he cites from the *Khaṇḍanakhaṇḍakhādya* only and quotes from no other text pertaining to Advaita. He directly alludes to *Sūtrabhāṣya* of Śaṅkara, *Bhāmatī* of *Vācaspati* and *Iṣṭasiddhi* of Vimuktātman. In the Pūrvapakṣa of *Śata-dūṣaṇī* we can discern the impression of *Brahma-siddhi* of Maṇḍana, *Pañcapādikā* of Padmapāda, *Naiṣkarmya-siddhi* of Sureśvara, *Vārtika Vivaraṇa* of Prakāśātman, *Saṁkṣepa-śārīraka* of Sarvajnātman, *Tattvaśuddhi* of Jñānaghanapāda, *Nyāyamakaranda* of Ānandabodhācārya and *Tattvapradīpikā* of Citsukha. As can be gathered from the life of Deśika. *Śatadūṣaṇī* is the fruit of disputes with the opponents. While criticising Advaita, Deśika, *Śatadūṣaṇī* is the fruit of disputes with the opponents. While criticising Advaita, Deśika follows the style of *Khaṇḍanakhaṇḍakhādya.* In removing the doubts of common men he enumerates many alternatives. From the title of the work it should have 100 *vādas* but in the work there are only 66. Like *Tattvaṭīkā* and *Nyāyasiddhāñjani,* the works of Deśika, the remaining *vādas* must have been lost. According to one view 34 *vādas* were concerned with refuting the doctrines of Madhva and were not allowed to attain wide popularity. For this we have no proof and in the criticism of Advaita, Dvaita can have no room. According to one view there are only 66 *vādas* and *śata* is to be construed in the sense of many. But whenever Deśika uses *śata, sahasra* or *pañcāṣat* then he uses them in the true sense and hence we have to presume that 34 out of 100 *vādas* must have been lost. In these 66 *vādas* many points have been raised. They are : religious, ethical, philosophical, logical and spiritual. In every *vāda* there is talk about independent Advaita doctrine. In these *vādas* there is no definite order of arrange-ment of topics. As and when Vedānta Deśika had to argue with the opponents his arguments went to constitute the text of the *Śatadūṣaṇī*. Laghu and Mahāsiddhānta of *Śrī Bhāṣya* were kept in the centre and the disputes were carried on. In *Guruparampara* there is described the life of Vaiṣṇava Ācāryas. Here the life of Deśika also is depicted. According to it Deśika had to argue with the opponent for seven days. His pupil Perarulal Jeeyar took notes of it every day, gave over his jottings to Deśika on the eighth day who corrected them and gave out as *Śatadūṣaṇī*.[11] Second note about his life can be had from *Vaibhavaprakāśikā* (v. 47) and according to it Deśika himself, after the dispute was over, brought out the summary of the dispute as *Śata-dūṣaṇī*. Whatever that may be, it can be surmised from the nature of the work that it was composed from the disputes. The work has its own merit as a work of *Vāda*. Even though there is no order in the treatment and no methodology still *Śatadūṣaṇī* has its own value in the field of criticism of Advaitavāda. For the sake of convenienc, the 66 *vādas* can be grouped under the following eight heads: (1) *Pramāṇas,* (2) perception and its varieties, (3) characteristics of *Anubhūti*, (4) *Jīvātmā* and *Paramātmā,* (5) *Nirguṇabrahman,* (6) *Viśva,* (7) the principle of *Avidyā,* and (8) *Sādhana* and *mukti*.[12]

The *saptavidha anupapattis* or the seven-fold improbabilities or absurdities of the *nirviśeṣādvaita* of Śaṅkara as pointed out by Rāmānuja have been amply magnified here. Some of the refutations are not the refutations of the philosophy of Śaṅkara but of the cult of ritualism, of the sects of the Sanṅyasins of Advaitic persuasion. Moreover, the 66th *vāda* or the Sūtrasvārasya Bhangavāda pointing to the conflict between Śaṅkara's Advaita and the Brahma-Sūtras seems, in fact, to have been the concluding refutation.

The story that the *Śatadūṣaṇī* is the record of the Śāstrārtha of Vedānta Deśika with Kṛṣṇa Misra is nothing more than a myth as there is a gap of some 200 years between the times of Kṛṣṇa Misra and Deśika. What *Khaṇḍana-khaṇḍakhādya* of Śrī Harṣa is for the Advaita or the *Tarka Tāṇḍava* of Vyāsa Tirtha for Dvaita, the *Śatadūṣaṇī* of Deśika is for Viśiṣṭādvaita. The posterity takes Vedānta Deśika to be the only Viśiṣṭādvaitin Vedāntin, who, by his contribution, has given the Ramanuja Darsana, a high logical character, similar to that given by Śrī Harṣa, Citsukha, Madhusūdana-sarasvati and Appayya Dīkṣita to the Śāṅkara Vedānta. Vedānta Deśika is the only Viśiṣṭādvaitic dialectician who is on par with such great Madhva polemic writers as Jaya Tīrtha and Vyāsa Tirtha.

The work has a masterly commentary called the *Caṇḍa Māruta*. The author Doddācārya (16th century A.D.) is known as Mahācarya for writing this very commentary. The *Vedāntācārya-vijaya-campū* a prose-poetic composition on the life and wroks of Vedānta Deśika eulogizes the *Śata-dūṣaṇī* and its author in high terms. Many a Viśiṣṭādvaitic writer followed the *Śatadūṣaṇī* dialectic of Vedānta Deśika. The *Advaitavidyāvijaya* of Mahacarya is one such work. The *Brahmajnānanirāsa* of one Śrinivāsa mentions the *Śatadū-ṣaṇī* by name and discusses the points touched upon by Vedānta Deśika. Some other commentaries on *Śatadūṣaṇī* are : *Nṛsiṁha Rājiya* of Nṛsimha Deva and *Sahasrakiraṇī* of one Śrīnivāsācārya. These commentaries suggest the impor-tance of *Śatadūṣaṇī* in the polemics of Viśiṣṭādvaita.

REFERENCES

1. The life and a detailed discussion of his works can be gathered from a work written in Tamil on the works of Deśika. Besides, we get information from *Vaibhavaprakaśika* of Mahācārya and *Guruparamapara Prabhāva* of Parakala Swamin.
2. When his maternal uncle saw Deśika for the first time he gave the blessing :
प्रतिश्ठापितवेदान्तः प्रतिक्षिप्तबहिर्मतः।
भूयास्त्रैविद्यामान्यस्त्वं भूरिकल्याणभाजनम्।।

3. Cf. *Saṅkalpasūryodaya,* Act I, pp. 12 and 14 (Nigamaparimala Press) as well as the preliinary verse of *Adhikaraṇasārāvali.*
4. See *Vaibhavaprakāśika.*
5. In this style there is a mixture of Sanskrit and Tamil.
6. *Śatadūṣaṇī,* pt. I. p. 5
   वादाहवेषु निर्भेत्तुं वेदमार्ग विदूषकान्।
   प्रयुज्यतां शरश्रेणी निशिता शतदूषणी।।
7. *Tattvaṭīkā,* v. 5
   शातितः शतदूषण्यां शकरादिर्भुदाग्रहः।
   शारीरकशरीरं तु व्यक्तमत्र प्रदर्श्यते।।
8. Cf. *Saptiratnamālikā,* v. 48
   सर्वार्थसिद्धिः शतदूषणी च द्वे खेटशास्त्रे कथकायगानाम्।
9. इदं सर्व अभिप्रेत्य अभाष्यत वाद । अखिलमन्तर्निधाय ह (वाद 2) तदेतदाहुः (वाद 30) तदेतत्सर्वमुपक्षिप्तं भाष्ये (वाद 49).
10. See the discussion about Akhandārtha in Vāda 38.
11. See *Guruparmaparāprabhāva,* p. 136.
12. See *Śatabhūṣaṇī,* p.p. 11-12. Śrī Anantakṛṣṇa Śāstri has grouped the vādas under the following 10 heads : Sūtra Svārasyabhangavāda, Avidyā, falsity of the world, the meaning of the first sūtra of Vedānta, discussion about Brahmma and sādhanacatuṣṭaya, meaning of *tvam,* meaning of *tat, ṭīkā* of the Mahāvākya, Jīvanmukti and topics not correlated to Advaita.

❑❑❑

23

ŚRĪMAD-VIṢṆU-TATTVA-VINIRṆAYA OF ŚRĪ MADHVĀCĀRYA*

Kowlagi Seshacharya

In the evolution of Indian philosophic thought, Madhva appeared as an uncompromising critic of the Advaita of Śaṅkara in the thirteenth century. His system of thought is popularly known as Dvaita in view of the fact that it maintains difference between the finite and infinite even in the lst analysis, though the correct appellation of his system is *'Tattvavāda'*. Śaṅkara and Madhva are poles asunder in their systems of thought. If the essence of the former's philosophy is *'so'ham'*, the latter's is *'dāso'ham'*.

Besides his commentaries on the Upaniṣads, the *Gītā,* and the *Brahma-Sūtra,* Madhva wrote ten treatises on various philosophical subjects known as *prakaraṇas*. Including works on *Tantra* and *stotras,* Madhva wrote in all 37 works. To him Viṣṇu, who is flawless and abounds in all excellent attributes, is not only the God of religion, but the metaphysical absolute as well.

The book under review is the most important of his *prakaraṇa* works. This gives all the essential features of his system of thought in a brief yet stimulatingly forceful way and serves as a good introduction to those who would like to

* Edited and translated by S.S. Raghavachar, Foreword by Swami Adidevananda, Pub. by Sri Ramakrishna Ashrama, Mangalore-1, 1959, pages xxiii+98, Price Rs. 3.

read his major works. The work, as suggested by the title, establishes the thesis that Viṣṇu is the highest metaphysical principle on which the entire structure of thought is built up. Madhva opens his work with a salutation to Śrī Nārāyaṇa by enumerating His three attributes, each forming the theme of a chapter of the work.

The first attribute, viz., *sadāgamaikavijñeya* (Nārāyaṇa is to be known only through the instrumentality of the good and reliable *Āgamas),* represents the main plank. Considerable portion of the work is devoted to a full and comprehensive treatment of the scriptures as a competent means to reveal the nature of the Supreme. After detailing the right and reliable scriptures, Madhva argues that the Vedas have no human authorship; they are *apauruṣeya;* their validity is intrinsic. Non-postulation of these would render determination of *dharma* and *adharma* impossible, resultaing in chaos. Madhva contends that the scriptural texts proclaiming identity between the finite and the infinite need careful interpretation, in view of the other texts which emphatically affirm difference and the deliverances of perception and inference which unmistakably establish difference between the finite and the infinite. Moreover,the validity of the scriptures depends upon their compatibility with experience. Otherwise, they have no validity at all. Hence the texts proclaiming difference between the finite and the infinite are not only repetitive,but also confirm the truth revealed by the other *pramāṇas.* Hence, difference between the finite and the infinite is the fundamental import of the scriptures.

Madhva recognizes only three fundamental sources of knowledge, viz. perception, inference,and scriputres. The other sources of knowledge, such as presumption *(arthāpatti),* analogy *(upamā),* and conjecture *(sambhava),* are all varieties of inference. The supreme purport of all the scriptures, according to Madhva, is the transcendent greatness of Viṣṇu. Next follows a vigorous vindication of the concept of difference. Difference is the very form of object *(dharmisva-rūpa)*. When an object is perceived, its difference from others is also perceived. No logical quibble can dismiss difference as illusion. Difference is foundational.

The theory of error known as *'anirvacanīyakhyāti'*, propounded by the Advaitin, is subjected to trenchant criticism and ultimately scouted as logically untenable. Illusion is explained as misperception of the non-existent as existent and of the existent as non-existent. Next comes the consideration of some of the important passages of the scriptures, which are held by Madhva as proclaiming only difference and not identity between the finite and the infinite. Words such as *mahāmāyā, anṛta, asatya, avidyā,* etc., which apparently admit of Advaitic interpretation, are explained by Madhva as conveying some fundamental attributes of the Lord. Even the texts *'Ahaṁ Brahmāsmi'* and *'Soh'am'* do not convey identity between the self and the *Brahman*. They refer to the Lord as the inner ruler.

The interpretation of the famous text *'Tattvamasi'* may be cited as an instance of Madhva's magnificent interpretative insight. Without violence to the canons of grammar, Madhva takes the text as *'Atattvamasi'* (Thou art not that), so as to fall in line with his doctrine of difference and to do justice to the section of the Upaniṣad as a whole. *Ekajīvavāda* and *Anekajīvavāda* and the illusoriness of the world are all repudiated as illogical. The contention of the opponent that the world is the superimposition of the non-self on the self is challenged by Madhva, and it is successfully shown that the opponent's theory of illusion would, unmistakably and inescapably,land him (the opponent) in a distressing dualism, because the very theory of illusion has to admit two reals without which no illusion can arise. At the end of the chapter, Madhva concludes by saying that all the scriptures aim at revealing Nārāyaṇa, who is supreme and different from all else by His uniqueness, and that He is known only through the right scriptures.

The next chapter establishes the supremacy of Nārāyaṇa over both sentient and nonsentient entities *(samatītakṣarākṣara)*. The concluding chapter declares that Viṣṇu thus gets rid of this *saṁsāra* and enjoys bliss in proximity to Viṣṇu. Madhva maintains hierarchy among the emancipated selves,so that each enjoys bliss according to its own inherent capacity. Madhva ushers in an ontological principle known as *viśeṣa* to account for the possibility of conceptual and verbal distinction between the attributes of Viṣṇu and His substantive essence, which are not different.

The language of the *Viṣṇu-tattva-vinirṇaya,* though it looks simple, is difficult to grasp in its full significance sometimes, unless one has the aid of Jayatīrtha's commentary. In some places, Madhva uses well-known words as bearing quite a different meaning, for instance, *āgama* means the individual self. As an instance of Madhva's revolutionary etymology, the word *'prapañca'* is explained as that which consists of the great five kinds of difference (between God and matter, God and self, matter and self, matter and matter, and self and self). The style of the work no doubt suffers from extreme brevity, but even brevity becomes a beauty when one gets into its spirit. Madhva nowhere indulges in florid expressions, never deflects from the decorum of the debate by using vituperative vocabulary against the opponent. The way he silences his opponent by exposing his own logical inconsistencies is remarkable. Madhva hardly advances an argument or introduces an idea without effective and proper substantiation. His arguments are not merely persuasive, but bar the stamp of demonstrated assertion. These qualities mark him off as a philosophical debater par excellence.

It is significant to note that some of the ideas of Madhva have parallels in modern thought. The grand idea that God is to the world what the sun is to the rainbow finds cent percent echo in Carlyle. The doctrine that the individuality of the finite selves is not lost in God at any level of their existence, so ably advocated by Madhva, finds a pre-eminent place in the personalistic metaphysics of modern America (Vide Brightman, *The Problem of God)*.

Shri S.S. Raghvachar is well-known throughout the philosophical world by his scholarly contributions to various journals and editing of *Vedārtha-saṅgraha of Śrī Rāmānuja* with introduc-tion and translation, has added one more work to his credit. Shri Raghavachar's rendering of the original is not merely a translation, but mostly an exposition closely following the commentary of Śrī Jayatīrtha. His massive erudition in both Western and Indian philosophies, his intimate knowledge of the intricacies of Indian philosophical polemical language, his mastery over the English language have all combined in equal measure in the preparation of this work. Shri Raghava-char commands a stimulating style, which is in keeping with the dignity of the diction of the original. The critical presentation of Madhva's thought, which he has undertaken in his introduction, is refreshingly original. The entire text has been carefully edited and spilt into 464 convenient paragraphs. Each paragraph carries with it the English rendering. The joy and the relief that this text brings to those who have had the hardship in handling the *Dvaita Vedānta* texts printed purely to subserve orthodoxy can be better felt than expressed. Shri Raghvachar richly deserves our warmest appreciation for this distinctive service.

The Ramakrishna Ashram, Mangalore, commensurate with its catholicity of outlook, has placed all lovers of philosophy in general and the Mādhva public in particular under a deep debt of obligation by offering Śrī Madhva's *Viṣṇu-tattva-vinirṇaya* in a neat, handy, and attractive volume, at a time when printing of such books has become almost a luxury and a risky venture. The printing and the get-up are excellent. The paper used, the types selected, both English and Sanskrit, simply reflect the meticulous care and aesthetic sensibility which the publishers have bestowed on the publication. The manifestly low price can only be explained on the ground of love of labour. Though Dr. R.Nagaraja Sarma has given an exhaustive treatment of the ten *prakaraṇas* of Madhva in his *magnum opus—The Reign of Realism in Indian Philosophy*—yet this book does not savour of superfluity, in view of its serving entirely a different puropse. Hence this book will be another authoritative welcome volume on the philosophy of Madhva in English.

The reviewer wishes to conclude with the hope that the Mādhva pontiffs, who owe a spiritual duty to their Master Śrī Madhvācārya, would fully exploit the genuine interest aroused in non-Mādhva circles about Śrī Madhvācārya and his philosophy by bringing out cheap editions of all the works of Madhva, together with renderings in English, Kannada, and Hindi languages, and resuscitate Śrī Madhva from the unmerited oblivion to which he is subjected.

❑❑❑

24

BRAHMAN-JĪVA-JAGAT RELATION : A UNIQUE THEORY

Roma Chaudhuri

The question of relation is always a difficult one. For, if you come to think of it, what question, really, there is of any relation whatsoever between two or more objects external to one another? Is not each complete by itself, without any reference to, or relation with, any other? Apparently, yes. For, how can a chair, for example, need anything else, for its existence, than its own, its very own existence? Yet, strangely enough, all wise voices persistently decry this theory of self-existence, self-sufficiency, self completeness; e.g., Modern Physics, externally; Modern Psychology, internally. In fact, the Modern Age is an Age of Relativity, an Age when relation has become so very important as almost to devour even the Related Objects themselves.

And, what, in this respect, is the voice of wisdom of Indian Philosophy, of our venerable Indian Philosophy?

Leaving aside details, leaving aside logical quibblings, leaving aside philosophical profundities, it may, safely, be said, in a general manner, that according to our Indian View, the object itself is far more important, far more central Relation—even in the case of the empirical object, the ordinary object, not to speak of the transcendental one, the spiritual one, the supreme one.

However, whatever that may be, Indian Philosophers, specially Vedāntists, seem enamoured of one fundamental problem, in connection with the question of Relation, viz., the very difficult problem of the relation between the One and the Many; God and the World, the Absolute and the Universe. Apparently, this is an absolutely necessary, an entirely unavoidable, an eminently suitable question—for, if there be God, He has to be, willy nilly, brought into relation with the world. Why? Because, in the case of a chair and a table, who cares, scientists apart, if they are related or not? For, each seems to be quite self-dependent, quite capable of taking care of itself, quite satisfied with its own nature and status. But alas, here? Here the all-pervasive God is there, the All-powerful Lord is there, the All perfect Absolute is there. And, if there be anything else besides Him, it has to be accounted for, in such a way as not to jeopardise the all-pervasiveness of God, all-powerfulness of the Lord and all-perfectness of the Absolute. But how? that is the problem of problems—how?

For, if you come to think of it, how can all-pervasive being have any kind of relation whatsoever? Here, as we know, Indian Philosophers speak of *three* kinds of relation—*Sajātīya, Vijātīya, Svagata*; or, relation amongst similar objects, belonging to the very same class (e.g., amongst chairs); relation amongst dissimilar objects, belonging to different classes (e.g., amongst chairs and tables); relation amongst the internal parts of a whole (e.g., amongst fruits, flowers, branches, leaves, etc., of a tree).

Evidently, the all-pervasive Īśvara or Brahman cannot have anything outside Him, a second or, third, Īśvara or Brahman; similar to Him; or, a second or third demon or devil, dissimilar from Him. So there is, according to all views, no question at all of *Sajātīya* or *Vijātīya* Bheda in fis case. At best, the only kind of Bheda He can have is *Svagata Bheda,* or internal differences, as of parts, qualities, powers, and the like.

But, then that fundamental question; Can there be anything inside Brahman that is *different* from Brahman, or non-Brahman? For, there cannot, surely, be anything inside a thing which is not of the nature (*Svarūpa*) of that thing. Hence, if Jīva-Jagat be taken to be *Svagata-Bhedas* of Brahman, then Jīva-Jagat cannot be different in nature or essence or *svarūpa* from Brahman. That is, they, too, must be Brahman in nature, Brahman in essence, or Brahman-svarūpa.

Then, how can they be called *different* at all from Brahman?

The only way out is to say that they are different from Brahman in other respects, viz., in respect of *Guṇas*, etc. That is, they are identical with Brahman in *Svarūpa* or nature; yet different from Him in *Guṇas,* or attributes, powers, forms, functions, etc.

But all difficulties are not over; on the contrary, more difficulties flood in : Is *Svarūpa* more important, or *Guṇa*? If two things are identical in *Svarūpa*, yet different in *Guṇas*, do they, really, remain, ultimately, *different*?

The Advaita-vedāntists, say, No; the Tri-tattva-vādin Vedāntists say, Yes. Take that well- known Vedānta example of Devadatta. Devadatta's qualities, powers, forms, activities often change—now he has his limbs stretched out; now contracted; now he laughs; now cries; now he stands up, now lies down; and so on; but still, he himself does not change, he himself remains the very same, identical Devadatta all throughout. Then?

This is the crux of the whole thing—Which is more

important, more fundamental, more basic—*Svarūpa* or *Guṇa*?

No, let us try an ingenious solution, after Bhāskara, the not-al-all-well-known, yet a unique Vedānta philosopher of great merit.

Bhāskara's Āupādhika-bhedābheda-vāda :

To avoid the above difficulty of the inevitable conflict between *Svarūpa* and *Guṇa,* Bhāskara very cleverly adopts a new meaning of *Upādhi*—a term so very central, yet so very controversial, in Advaita-Vedānta Philosophy, all throughout.

Now, the Advaita-Vedānta meaning of *Upādhi* is that it is something that is entirely *Apāramārthika* or *Mithyā,* or false. That is, an *Upādhi* makes an apparent distinction between things, which are really identical; and so is not itself ultimately real. Take that well-known Advaita-Vedānta example of *Ghaṭākāśa* and *Maṭhākāśa*. The ether inside the Ghaṭa or pot, appears to be different from the ether outside in the *Maṭha* or field. But why? Because of the Upādhi of Ghaṭa—then, break off the pot; then the ether inside the pot and the ether outside will become absolutely identical with one another.

But Bhāskara's *Upādhi* is of an entirely different kind and on the basis of this unique *Upādhi-vāda,* he explains Brahman-Jiva-Jagat relation thus :

(i) During the Kāraṇāvasthā of Brahman, i.e., when Brahman is a pure, undifferentiated Unity, prior to creation or Sṛṣṭi, Jīva-Jagat, too, remain absolutely merged in Him, without any distinction from Him at all.

(ii) Then, during the Kāryāvasthā of Brahman, i.e., when Brahman creates, so to speak, Jiva-Jagat, out of Himself, *Jīva-Jagat* become different from Him. So, then, they are *Bhinnābhinna* from Him. This is the stage of *Sṛṣṭi-Sthiti*.

(iii) Then, during the stage of *Pralaya*, too, *Jīva-Jagat*, again, become identical with Brahman.

(iv) During *Mokṣa* also *Jīva* becomes identical with Brahman.

In this way, according to Bhāskara, the Abheda between Brahman and Jīva-Jagat is *Svābhāvika*, i.e., Satya and Nitya; while the *Bheda* between Brahman and Jīva-Jagat is *Aupādhika*, i.e., Āgantuka, due to Upādhis, and so *Anitya*, yet *Satya*.

Svābhāvika-abheda :

This is the original, eternal state of the Jīva-Jagat. As natural, Brahman being the cause, and the Jīva-Jagat His effect, Brahman himself transformed into the same. Hence, Jīva-Jagat must be *Brahma-svarūpa*, or Brahman in nature and essence. That is why, it can be said safely that Brahman and Jīva-Jagat are eternally identical. Prior to Creation, after Destruction, and during Salvation, Jīva-Jagat remain completely merged in Brahman; and are identical with Him. Also, during Creation, as just shown, Brahman, the Cause, and Jīva-Jagat, the effects, are identical in nature or essence or *Svarūpa* (though different in other respects, viz., Guṇa-Śaktis, etc.).

Hence, it is that the Abheda of Brahman and Jīva-Jagat is Svābhāvika, Nitya, Satya.

Aupādhika-bheda :

But the Bheda or difference between Brahman and Jīva-Jagat is neither original nor eternal; yet it is real. It is not original because prior to Creation, as shown above, Brahman and Jiva-Jagat are absolutely identical; after Destruction, also, Brahman and Jīva-Jagat become once again, absolutely identical; again during Salvation, too, the same is the case.

It is only during the state of Saṁsāra, i.e., the *Kāryāvasthā*, from the side of Brahman; and the *Baddhāvasthā* from the side of the Jīva, that Brahman and Jīva-Jagat become and remain different.

Why? Because of *Upādhis*. The *Upādhis* of Jiva are the same as those spoken of in Advaita-Vedānta, viz., the six *Upādhis—Sūkṣma-Deha, Sthūla-Deha. Indriyas, Prāṇa, Manas* and *Buddhi*. At the beginning of Creation, the Jīva comes to be associated with these *Upādhis*, due to its past *Sakāma-Karmas,* and is born again. Then because of these *Upādhis*, it becomes different from Brahman. Hence, it is held that the *Bheda* between Brahman and Jīva-Jagat is *Aupādhika*, i.e., due to *Anādi-Avidyā* and *Sakāma-Karmas*.

Thus, according to Bhāskara, what is *Svābhāvika* is original and eternal; what is *Aupādhika* is neither; yet both are equally real or *Satya*.

The Unique Conception of "Upādhi" :

Bhāskara's unique conception of *Upādhi* forms the basis of his strange Vedānta Philosophy. Thus, according to him :

(i) Brahman is *Nirviśeṣa-Nirguṇa-Niṣkriya* during *Kāraṇavasthā*, i.e., prior to Creation and after Destruction, and during Salvation; i.e., during *Pralaya-Mokṣa*. Then, He becomes *Saviśeṣa-Saguṇa-Sakriya* during *Kāryavāsthā*, or the state of Saṁsāra or Baddhāvasthā.

Here, Brahman's *Kāraṇa-rūpa* is *Svābhāvika*; His *Kārya -rūpa Aupadhika*.

For, before *Sṛṣṭi* or Creation, Brahman is an bastract Reality, with not even *Svagata-Bhedas*. So, during this stage, He has no difference, no qualities and no activities.

Then, during *Sṛṣṭi-Sthiti*, Creation-Preservation, Brahman becomes a Concrete Reality, with *Jīva-Jagat*, and the like, as His *Svagata-Bhedas*. So, then, He has internal differences, qualities and activities.

Then, finally, during *Pralaya*, Destruction, Brahman once again becomes an abstract Reality, not even with *Svagata-Bhedas*, like *Jīva-Jagat*. So then, He, once again, becomes *Nirviśeṣa-Nirguṇa-Niṣkriya*.

Thus, Brahman's *Nirviśeṣa-Nirguṇa-Niṣkriya-rūpa* is His *Svābhāvika-Ādi-rūpa*; while His *Saviśeṣa-Saguṇa-Sakriya-rūpa* is His *Āupadhika-Āgantuka-rūpa*.

Yet both are equally real.

(ii) In exactly the same manner, prior to *Sṛṣṭi*, or Creation, the Jīva is neither a *Jñātā*, nor a *Kartā*, nor a *Bhoktā*, nor *Aṇu*, nor *Bahu*. That is, it is not a knower, a doer or an enjoyer; not atomic or infinitely small, and many in number. For, then, it is absolutely identical with the purely abstract, *Nirviśeṣa-Nirguṇa-Niṣkriya Brahman*.

Then, during the states of *Sṛṣti-Sthiti*, it becomes all these.

Then, again, during *Pralaya-Mukti*, it caeses to be all these.

Thus, Jiva's *Jñatṛtva-Kartṛva-Bhoktṛtva-Aṇutva-Bahutva* are only *Aupādhika*, or *Āgantuka; Akaritṛtva*, and the rest, *Svābhāvika* or *Ādi*, original and eternal. Yet both are equally real.

(iii) In exactly the same way, as already shown, the *Abheda* between Brahman and Jīva-Jagat is *Svābhāvika*, Ādi; the *Bheda* between Brahman and Jīva-Jagat, *Aupādhika* or Āgantuka.

Yet both are equally real.

An Estimate : Bhāskara's Nirguṇatva-vada is Illogical :

The first attempt to bring down, tone down, soften down Śaṅkara's lofty, supreme, sublime Advaitism is found in Bhāskara. Of course, it is true that, by far the best and the foremost opposer of Śaṅkara was Rāmānuja of immortal fame, who as is well-known, most ably opposed Śaṅkara's Advaita-vāda, from the theoretical standpoint, by him own Viśiṣṭādvaita-vāda; and Śaṅkara's Śuddha-jñana-vāda, from the practical, by his own intense Bhakti-vāda. Yet, this courageous attempt of Bhāskara, generally supposed to be prior to Rāmānuja, as flourishing in the earlier part of the 9th century A.D., is a highly laudable one, from every point of view.

Now, we have three main views regarding the *Nirguṇatva-Saguṇatva* of Brahman, viz.,

(1) Brahman is always *Nirguna-Nirākāra-Nirviśeṣa*—a Pure Unity, and Bare Identity, and Abstract Whole.

(2) Brahman is always *Saguṇa-Savikāra-Saviśeṣa*, a Concrete Unity, and Identity-in-Difference, an Organic Whole.

(3) At first, or originally, or during His Causal State, Brahman is *Nirguṇa-Nirākāra-Nirviśesa*; but later on, secondly, or during His Effected State, He becomes *Saguṇa-Saviśeṣa*.

But here, we can accept, either the first, or the second alternative; never the third one.

That during the Causal State, the *Guṇas* and the *Śaktis* of Brahman remain in Him in an unmanifest form, is the common view of all Monotheistic Vedāntists. But this never implies that those Guṇas and Śaktis become absolutely merged in Brahman, and as such, absolutely identical with Him. In fact, even then, they remain distinct from Him as

His *Svagatabhedās*, just as, e.g., the burning-power of fire, though not manifested as actually burning some thing, yet remains distinct from fire, as its *Svagatabheda*.

Thus, either we have to say, here, that Guṇa being identical with *Svarūpa*, there is only *Svarūpa*; or, we have to say that, Guṇa being distinct from *Svarūpa*, is always distinct from *Svarūpa*. But, first, only *Svarūpa*, and, then Svarūpa and *Svarūpa-bhinna Guṇa*—is this kind of change possible and plausible on the part of Brahman?

Bhāskara' Upādhi-vāda is illogical :

According to Bhāskara, what is *Svābhāvika,* is eternal; what is *Aupādhika,* is transitory; yet both are equally nitya or real. But, this, inevitably, goes against the fundamental philsophical tenet of India, according to which what is momentary or transitory, is not a *Pāramārthika Satya*, not a real, transcendental eternal Relaity. For, what is *Satya* or Real, is, invariably *Sthira* and *Śāśvata*—steady and eternal; how can it ever be destroyed? As a matter of fact, Reality itself shines, for ever, in its own light, in its own glory, in its own beauty. Its existence and reality depend solely and wholly on itself; and on none else. Hence it is that reality is a space-less, time-less, condition-less, Absolute Existence; and not at all a merely relative one. So, what is momentary, what is transitory, can never be ultimately real.

According to his own, unique *Upādhi-vāda*, Bhāskara holds, as we have seen, that the non-difference of Brahman and *Jīva-Jagat* being *Svābhāvika,* is always present; while the difference between Brahman and *Jīva-Jagat*, being *Aupādhika*, is present only during the state of Saṅsāra. Still, such *Abheda* and *Bheda* are equally real. But how absured is this! "Bheda" that has no existence before creation and after destruction, is, surely, not so great and grand and glorious as to claim absolutely equal rights with Abheda, which, according to the above view, is eternal. As a matter of fact, how can that, which has no existence later on, ever aspire to have any ultimate value or validity at all?

Specially, according to all views, Mokṣa is the only end of life; and *Bandha* and *Mokṣa* are entirely different. Hence, the Bheda between Brahman and Jīva during Bandha, and Abheda between the two during *Mokṣa* being the *summum bonum* of life, the absolute and eternal identity between Brahman and Jīva must constitute the real *Svarūpa* or nature of Brahman; the conditional and temporary differences between them being only something that is adventitious and accidental.

Brahman is Unchangeable :

According to Bhāskara's unique *Upādhivada,* Brahman, Jīva, Jagat,—all become inevitably, subject to changes. Thus, *Nirguṇa-Nirviśeṣa-Svagata-Bheda-hīna Brahman* becomes *Saguṇa-Savikāra-Svagata-Bhedavan*. Aṇu or infinitely small Jīva becomes *Vibhu* or All-pervasive; the material world becomes non-material, or consciousness is essence. Still, in every case, the first and the second states are exactly similar in status and reality. For example, the *Aṇutva* or *Vibhutva* of Jīva are equally real—yet the one and the same Jīva comes to have two equally true *Svarūpa* or essences. In fact, the Jīva that was *Vibhu* prior to creation as identical with Brahman becomes *Aṇu* during creation and then, again, *Vibhu* during *Pralaya* and Mokṣa, Dissolution and Salvation. But, are not such change of Svarūpa or essence and destruction of prior Svarūpa or essence absolutely impossible?

Mokṣa is not Non-eternal :

According to Bhāskara's view, Mokṣa or Mukti becomes absolutely non-eternal : as it is taken to be "*Prāptavya*" or something to be attained. But, according to our Indian views, mainly, according to the Vedānta, Mokṣa is not something to be attained anew, or acquired afres or achieved anon, for the simple reason that Jīva is *nitya-mukta*. As a matter of fact, the Svarūpa, or nature or essence of something can never be changed, even in the midst of so many differences, seen all around.

The Inherent Conflict in Bhāskara-Vedānta :

This undeniable fact stands out in bold relief that Bhāskara though professedly a vehement critic of Śaṅkara, was, from the beginning to the end, inextricably under his spell. In fact, it will not be wrong to say that Śaṅkara's Nirviśeṣa-vāda, Nirguṇa-vāda, Śuddha-jñāna-vāda. etc. constitute the real doctrines of Bhāskara, however much he may try in vain to camouflage the same by the so called Doctrine of Upādhi. The fact is that Bhāskara could not accept, from his heart of hearts, the over-strong Advaita-vāda of Śaṅkara : yet he was incapable of formulating a new and a better theory of his own, counteracting the same. His unique "Upādhi-vāda" is a product of this conflict within his heart of hearts. He could not, under any circumstances whatsoever, accept the Doctrine of the Falsity of the World; and so he formulated, so to speak, half-heartedly, his own ingenious Upādhi-vāda. But still, he did not have the courage or inclination to accept a full-fledged "Bhedābheda-vāda". This, in fact, constitutes the main defect of Bhāskara's unparalleled system of vedānta.

However, just like the sun, spreading out its thousand golden rays in thousand directions, Bhāskara, too, spreads out his intensely luminous rays of knowledge all around, even through a single work of his, viz., Brahma-Sūtra-Bhāṣya.

❑❑❑

25

THE SCHOOL OF VALLABHA

G.H. Bhatt

There were several schools of the Vedāntic thought before Śaṅkarācārya (A.D. 788-820), and attempts have been made by scholars to collect materials that might throw light on these pre-Śaṅkara systems. It is, however, not possible to get a systematic account of their views, and consequently the history of the Vedānta really begins with the system of Śaṅkarācārya. The earliest known critic of Śaṅkarācārya is Bhāskara (ninth century who strongly attacks his doctrine of Māyā. Later on, a host of critics of Śaṅkara, such as Rāmānuja, Nimbārka, Madhva and Vallabha, appeared one after another. These thinkers, who happened to be followers of the Bhāgavata School, could not accept Śaṅkara's interpretation of the basic texts, namely, the Upaniṣads, the *Gītā,* and the *Brahma-Sūtra* and offered their own interpretations, thereby enriching the literature on the Vedānta. Moreover, the abstract, philosophical speculations of Śaṅkara could not naturally make much appeal to the masses who found suffcient spiritual food in the *bhakti* (devotion) Schools of Rāmānuja and others. In other words, *jñāna* (knowledge) lost its previous hold and made room for *bhakti* which had been progressively gaining in strength.

Śuddhādvaita and Puṣṭi-Mārga

Vallabhācārya (A.D. 1473-1531), a Tailaṅga of South India, was born in a family with leanings towards Vedic rituals and the worship of Gopālakṛṣṇa. He made more than one extensive tour in India and came in contact with leaders of other religious schools. He showed exceptional ability in philosophical disquisitons, won the title of an *Ācārya* (teacher) in the court of Vijayanagara, and found a good following in all communities. He spent most of his life in places like Kashi and Adel (about two miles from Allahabad), where he carried on his literary and religious activities. He tells us that, under the command of the Lord Kṛṣṇa, he devoted himself to the task of faithfully interpreting sacred texts, such as the Upaniṣads, the *Gitā,* and the *Brahma Sūtra,* which had been misrepresented by Śaṅkara.[2] Vallaba had tried to show that these basic works teach beyond doubt the doctrine of Advaita (non-dualism), pure and simple, without any reference to so called Māyā by Śaṅkara. The Advaita of the Upaniṣads is thus *Śuddha* (pure), unalloyed with Māyā, but the cause and the effect being pure and one, Vallabha's system is therefore known from the philosophical point of view as Śuddhādvaita (pure non-dualism).[3] As the system, again, strongly emphasizes *puṣṭi* (divine grace) as the most powerful and unfailing means of enjoying the highest bliss, it is also known from the religious point of view as *Puṣṭi-mārga* (the path of divine grace).

Four Basic Works

Vallabha accepted four basic works as authority : (1) the Vedas, (2) the *Bhagavad-Gitā*, (3) the *Brahma-Sūtra,* and (4) the *Bhāgavata*. The order of these works, we are told, is most logical, as the doubts in each preceding work are removed by the one that follows. The doubts in the Vedas are therefore to be removed in the light of the *Gitā* : those in the *Gīta* in the light of the *Brahma-Sūtra* and those in the *Brahma-Sūtra* in the light of the *Bhāgavata*, which has been aptly described as the ripe fruit of the wish-fulfilling tree, namely, the Vedas which have their root in the *Gāyatri verse* (ṚV. III 62,10) The Upaniṣads and *Brahma-Sūtra* may be classed together; while the *Gitā* and the *Bhāgavata* form another group. Just as the *Brahma-Sūtra*, is in a way, a commentary on the Upaniṣads, the *Bhāgavata* is to be considered a commentary on the *Gītā*. But though these texts are arranged in two different groups they are at the same time considered to be interconnected; and attempts have been made to show how the *Bhāgavata* really explains and develops all the points of the *Brahma-Sūtra*.[4] In fact every *Sūtra* of the latter finds an exact and detailed parallel in the *Bhāgavata*, and so there is a complete harmony between the teaching of these two sacred texts. These texts are thus the highest authority in philosophical matters, and all other texts and the various means of proof, such as inference, etc., are considered authoritative only insofar as they follow this highest authority. The *Bhāgavata*, which is a record of all the experiences of Vyāsa in meditation and which is therefore otherwise known as *Samādhi-bhāsā* (the language of meditation), enjoys the most important position in the Suddhādvaita system.

Literature of the School

Vallabha has written some works in the form of commentaries and some others as independent treatises for the elucidation of the teachings of the sacred texts. He tells us that he has written commentaries on the *Brahma-Sūtra*, the *Jaimini-Sūtra*, and the *Bhāgavata*, and has also composed some independent works.[5] Unfortunately, all his works are not available in a complete form. His commentary on the *Brahma-Sūtra*, called *Aṇubhāṣya*, is available only up to III 2.33, the remaining portion being supplied by his second son, Viṭṭhalanātha.[6] Vallabha seems to have first written a more extensive commentary on the *Brahma-Sūtra*, which may be described as *Bṛhadbhāṣya* (long commentary),[7] and then made a summary of this in the form of what is known as *Aṇubhāṣya* (short commentary). The only available commentary on the *Jaimini-Sūtra* is on I.I.I. and II. I, and it begins with forty-two verses, which summarise the discussion of the *Bhāṣya* on the first *sūtra.*[8] The Commentary on the *Bhāgavata* called *Subodhinī,* as now available, is on the first three *skandhas* (books), a part of the fourth *skandha* (viz. six chapters and a portion of 13 verses only of the seventh chapter), the tenth *skandha*, and a part of the eleventh *skandha* (viz. four chapters and only one verse of the fifth chapter). There is also another important work called *Tattvārthadīpa,* popularly known as *Nibandha,* with Vallabha's own gloss called *Prakāśa,* which is divided into three parts known as *Śastrārtha, Sarvanirṇaya,* and *Bhāgavatārtha.* The *Prakāśa* is complete so far as the first two parts are concerned; but of the third part it is available only up to the thirty-third verse of the fourth section. Viṭṭhalanātha tried to fill up the gap by supplying the gloss on the sections following, but unfortunately even his commentary is available only up to the 135th verse of the fifth section. *Sāstrātha* discusses the content of the *Gitā*; *Sarvanirṇaya* discusses different philophical topics; and *Bhāgavatārtha* explains the subject matter of the *Bhāgavata* in a very general way. Vallabha, following Bopadeva,[9] holds the view that he who makes a critical study of the *Bhāgavata* and realizes the fact that one and the same topic is discussed in all the seven different parts of the *Bhāgavata* enjoys liberation; These seven parts are Śāstras (scriptures), viz. *Bhāgavata*), *prakaraṇa* (topic), *adhyāya* (chapter), *vākya* (sentence), *pada* (word), and *akṣara* (syllable).[10] *Bhāgavatārtha* gives the meaning of the remaining three. Vallabha does not seem to have written independent commentaries on the Upaniṣads and the *Gitā*. He has, however, written small works such as the sixteen treatises, *Patrāvalambana, etc.;* which are very helpful in understanding his system. The literary activities of his school have been carried on with great vigour up to the present day by his descendants and followers, who have produced a very rich literature, not only in Sanskrit but also in some of the vernacular languages of India, such as Hindi, Vraja, and Gujarati, and have exercised a great influence over millions of people in northern and western India.

Philosophy : Parabrahman

Vallabha has evolved his philosophy solely on the authority of the verbal testimony (*apta*) and has thereby shown that dry logic has no independent place in the discussion of philosophical problems—an attitude which is responsible for his strong criticism of Śaṅkara. His philosophical views are as it follows.

The highest entity is Brahman, which is Sat (existence), Cit (knowledge), Ānanda (bliss) and Rasa (sentiment). He is Pūrṇa (perfect) Puruṣottama (the best of beings); and is therefore personal in nature. He possesses many divine qualities, of which *jñāna* (experience) and *kriyā* (activity) are the most prominent. He also possesses contradictory qualities. He is devoid of worldly or material qualities, and the negation of qualities in Brahman, mentioned in the Upaniṣads, refers to the absence of material qualities in Him. He possesses sort of body totally made up of *ānanda*. His *ānanda* is infinite. He is omnipresent and eternal. He is both *kartṛ* (agent) and *bhoktṛ* (enjoyer). For *līlā* (sport). He has created the universe out of himself, and is thus both the efficient and the material cause of the universe which is natutally sustained by Him and absorbed in Him at the end. Although the world is full of people, both happy and unhappy, and comes to an end at particular periods, Brahman is not open to the charges of practising cruelty and creating inequality, simply because He has created the world out of Himself in *līlā*. Again, He does not undergo any change even when He transforms Himself into this world—a doctrine known as avikṛtapariṇāma (unchanged transformation). The *kriyā-sakti* (power of action) of Brahman is described in the *pūrva* (first or ritualistic portion) of Vedas, while His *jñāna-śakti* (power of knowledge) is described in the *uttarakāṇḍa* (latter portion, i. e. the Upaniṣads). Brahman is, again, described in His grandeur in the *Gitā* and the *Bhāgavata*.

Akṣara

Next to and lower than *Parabrahman* is Akṣara (immutable) or Aksara Brahman. He possesses *sat, cit,* and *limited ānanda* (as against *infinite ānanda* of Parabrahman). He is the *dhāman* (abode of Parabrahman. He appears in various forms according to the different aspects of the latter. He may appear as *Vaikuṇthaloka* when Parabrahman, the Lord, appears as residing in Vaikuṇṭha. He may appear as the *charaṇa* (foot) of the Lord when the latter appears in the form of *antaryāmin* (the inner controller) and also in the form of an *avatāra* (incarnation). He also appears as the foot in the *adhidaivika* (celestial forms of the Lord. The Akṣara is further described as the *puccha* (tail) or the *ānanda-maya* (blissful) Lord, and is the *ādhyātmika* (corporeal) form of the latter. When the Lord wants to give *mokṣa* (liberation) through *jñāna*, He manifests four forms, viz. *akṣara, kāla* (time), *karma* (action), and *svabhāva* (nature). *Akṣara* then appears in the forms of Prakṛti (Primal matter) and Puruṣa (soul); and this Prakṛti develops through diffferent stages into the universe, and is therefore called the cause of all causes. The negative descriptions of Brahman in the Upaniṣads refer to this *Akṣara Brahman* which become the subject of meditation of *jñānins* alone.

Kāla, karma, and *svabhāva* are *akṣara,* different forms

of the Lord inseparable from Him, and serve some purpose in the creation of the world. There are, again, twenty-eight *sattvas* (cosmic intelligence), *ahaṅkāra* (egoism), five *tanmātras* subtle elements, five *mahābhūtas* (gross elements), five *karmendriyas* (organs of action), five *jñānendriyas* (organs of knowledge), and *manas* (mind). But though *akṣara, kāla, karma,* and *svabhāva* exit even before the creation of the universe, they are not included in this list of the *tattvas* as they are general causes *inseparable* from the Lord. The twentyeight categories are called *tattvas* as they represent in the world the causal capacity of the Lord.[11] The Lord, as the cause of the whole universe, expresses His causal capacity in the form of these twenty-eight categories which, in spite of the same nomenclature, have to be clearly distin-guished from the categories of the Sāṁkhya system.[12] For instance, the three *guṇas* (qualities), which constitute the Prakṛti of the Sāṁkhya, are distinct from Prakṛti in this system; the *indriyas* (organs) are developed from the *rājas ahaṅkāra,* and their *devatās* (presiding deities) from the *sāttvika ahaṅkāra;* and *indriyas* and *manas* are atomic and eternal.

Soul

The Lord was alone, without a second, in the beginning of a cycle. He desired to be many for the sake of pleasure and as He desired thousands of souls came instantaneously out of Akṣara Brahman like sparks from fire. In special cases the souls may emanate from the Lord Himself. The soul is thus an *aṁśa* (part) of Brahman and is eternal. With a view to enjoying sport, the Lord suppressed the element of *ānanda* (bliss) in the soul, and the soul consequently became subject to bondage and wrong knowledge. The soul is never created, nor does it ever die. It is only the body which is created and destroyed. As long as the soul is associated with the body, are metaphorically predicated of it. The soul is atomic—it is neither omnipresent, nor does it vary in size according to the body it inhabits. It experinces everything in the body through its quality of *caitanya* (intelligence) which pervades the whole body. It knows, does and experiences various things in the world; but these qualities of the soul are, in fact, derived from the Lord. The soul is thus quite real, and not a product of nescience. The Lord, in order to bring about variety, which is essential for the sake of pleasure, makes the souls varied in nature. Consequently, the souls can be grouped into three classes, viz. (1) those that are busy with worldly matters, (2) those that follow the Vedic path according to the letter of the Vedas, and (3) those that worship the Lord out of pure love engendered only through divine grace. These three types are generally described as *pravāha, maryādā,* and *puṣṭi* respectively.

The Universe

The universe is the effect of Brahman and is real and nondifferent from Him. It represents the *ādhibhautika* (material) form of Brahman. The element of *sat* is manifest in it, while the other elements of *cit* and *ānanda* are latent. The Lord has created the universe out of His own self for the sake of sport (*līlā*) without suffering any change whatsoever, and is related to it as the spider is to its web. The origination, existence and destruction of the world of experience is completely different in nature from the world of dreams and is therefore not unreal like the experiences in a dream. The universe (*jagat*) is clearly distinguished from the unreal word (*saṁsāra*) caused by the *avidyā* (nescience) of soul. For the sake of diversity, the lord makes the souls subject in His power of *avidyā* which is the root cause of the ideas of 'mine' and 'thine'. *Saṁsāra* which is solely made up of *ahantā* (I-ness or egoism) and *mamatā* (My ness or the idea of possession), has to be destroyed by means of knowledge, devotion etc.

Puṣṭi Contrasted with Jñāna and Karma

Three paths have been generally recognized as leading to *mokṣa,* viz. *Karmamārga, Jñāna-mārga*, and *Bhakti-mārga*. The several schools of the Vedānta differ from one another in laying differential emphasis on the elements of *Karma, Jñāna,* and *Bhakti,* According to the Śuddhādvaita system, the Lord manifests Himself in the five forms of *Kriyā* (Vedic sacrifice), viz, *agnihotra, darśa-paurṇamāsa, paśuyāga, cāturmāsya*, and *somayāga*, in the *pūrva-kāṇḍa*, and in the form of *jñāna* in the *uttara-kāṇḍa.* He who performs the Vedic rites and obtains the knowledge of Brahman as prescribed in the Upaniṣads, enjoys *mokṣa* in the form of divine joy. To such a man the Lord, described in the Vedic literature as possessing the six forms (the five of sacrifice and the one of *jñāna*) manifests Himself. He goes by the path of the gods (*devayāna*) and gradually attains *mokṣa;* but if he happens to enjoy the special grace of the Lord, he gets *mokṣa* immediately after death. He who does not attain the knowledge of Brahman but performs the Vedic rites without any motive, pleases all the gods concerned in the sacrifices and enjoys *ātmānanda,* (the bliss of the soul). The term *svarga,* used in this connection in the sense of *ātmānanda,* etymologically means that which is perfectly earned', or the happiness of the soul which is unmixed, eternal, and inferior only to the supreme divine joy which is the privilege of those who enjoy the favour of the Lord. But he who performs different sacrifices, simply with a view to fulfilling different desires, goes to the popular *svargaloka* (heaven), where he enjoys different kinds of happiness till his merit is exhausted and then returns to the world of mortals to move again in the cycle of birth and death.

It should be further noted that he who attains the knowledge of Brahman and realizes that everything in the world is Brahman, is a real knower of Brahman. But he is absorbed in Akṣara Brahman, and not in Parabrahman or Pūrṇa Puruṣottaṃa, because, as already stated, he meditates upon Akṣara Brahman and considers it to be the final stage of reality that has no higher. But if this knowledge of Brahman is associated with devotion, the knowing devotee is absorbed in Pūrṇa Puruṣottama. This stage is, indeed, higher than the stage of absorption in Akṣara Brahman. There is, again another stage which may be described as the highest. When the Lord desires to favour a particular soul and be it remembered that in showing His favour He is not guided by any other consideration than His own will He brings out the soul from Himself, gives him a divine body like His own and plays with him for all time. In this play, which is called *nitya-līlā*, the Lord, remaining subordinate to the devotee, gives him the pleasure of His company which is generally known as *bhajanānanda* (the bliss of devotion) or *svarūpānanda* (the bliss of the lord Himself) which is referred to in the *Taittiriya Upanisad,* the *Bhāgavata,* and other Purāṇas.

It is most interesting to note that this divine bliss is purely a gift of the Lord and cannot be obtained by any human effort. In is this very idea of the gift of divine grace that is called *Puṣṭi* in the Śuddhādvaita system.[13] The best illustration of divine grace (*puṣṭi*) is found in the case of the *gopīs* of Vṛndāvana, who are rightly described as the spiritual teachers who have opened the path of *puṣṭi* to the world at large. Those who enjoy this divine grace automatically begin to love the Lord and lock upon Him not only as their Lord, but as everything. The doctrine of regarding the Lord as everything called *sarvātmabhāva* (all-in-oneness), which should be distinguished from the *sarvātmabhāva* (one-in-allness) of the *jñānins*. In the *sarvātmabhāva* of the *jñānins*, men of realization see Brahman in all things, while in the other case the devotees see everything in the Lord. The *gopīs* possessed this attitude in a remarkable manner, and Lord Kṛṣṇa had therefore to remain quite obedient to them. The experience of *svarūpānanda* which is decidedly superior to that of *Brahmānanda,* is according to Vallabha, the highest conception of *mokṣa*, the *summam bonum.* The Lord is full of *rasa* (sentiment), and out of the eight *rasas* (love, heroism, fury, humour, wonder, pathos, and horror), *śṛṅgāra* (love) is the most prominent. As *śṛṅgāra* has two aspects, viz, *saṁyaga* (union) and *viprayoga* (separation), there are two stages in this *rasa* which the devotees enjoy. In the company of the Lord the devotees enjoy the happiness of union, while in His absence they suffer the misery of separation and think of Him all the time, so much so that they cannot see or experience anything but Lord Kṛṣṇa. According to some, the stage of separation is therefore superior to that of union.

Puṣṭi and Maryādā

Vallabha has clearly distinguished the Puṣṭi-mārga, from the Maryādā-mārga. In the latter, an individual has to follow the dictates of the Vedas, and practise the different types of *bhakti*, such as *śravaṇa* (hearing), etc. until he begins to love the Lord, who, taking his efforts into consideration, grants him *sāyujya mukti* (mergence in His body). In the Puṣṭimārga, however, through the operation of divine grace only, one starts with loving the Lord and then practises *śravaṇa,* etc. out of that love, and not with a view to generating it. The Maryādā-mārga is open only to the males of the first three classes, viz., Brāhmaṇas, Kṣatriyas, and Vaiśyas, while the Puṣṭi-mārga is open to all without reservation. This knows no distinction of sex, caste, creed, or nationality; it is universal religion : and this aspect is clearly borne out by literary and historical evidence. In short, whatever is done by the devotee of the Maryādā-mārga is done on the strength of the voice injuctions and in conformity with them, while the devotee of the Puṣṭi-mārga does everything out of his natural love and for the sake of the Lord.

Vallabha saw that his own times were most unfavourable to *karma, jñāna,* and Vedic or *śāstrīya bhakti,* and that people in general, and women and śūdras in particular, had no chance of ameliorating their status from the spiritual viewpoint. The duties of the different *varṇas* (classes) and *āśramas* (orders of life) could not be satisfactorily discharged; and the Vedas, though most effective in the past, had ceased to be so, not because they were useless, but because the people could not put the Vedic teaching into practice and perform sacrifices. The Ācārya has tried to show that over and above the paths of *karma, jñāna*, and Vedic *bhakti,* there is one more path, that of divine grace which, if once enjoyed, makes our life divine. The doctrine of grace is clearly referred to in the Upaniṣads, the *Gītā,* and the *Bhāgavata;* and although Rāmānuja and others admit it to be an all-saving factor, it must be said to the credit of Vallabha that the way in which he has dealt with this question is unique. The followers of the other Vaiṣṇava schools also believe in the power of divine grace, but their mode of worship is māryādika, as they look upon the Lord as the great awe-inspiring God, endowed with infinite qualities and possessing great powers. Their worship is not prompted by love, which is possible only through the grace of the Lord. The followers of the Puṣṭimārga however, worship the Lord, not because. He is the Paramātman or the highest Entity, but because they ardently love him. The worship of these devotees is therefore *snehātmaka* (consisting of love) and the Lord who is thus loved and worshipped is called Gopijanavallabha (the beloved of the *gopīs*), a term which is very significant in the system. The *gopī*) are the pioneers in this line, and others who follow them enjoy the same divine bliss. The mode of worship that has been followed in this system upto the present day is based on the spirit of the *gopīs*. One who follows the Puṣṭi-mārga aspires to be a *gopī* and worships the Lord with that attitude. In fact, all souls represent the feminine Principle and have the Lord as their spiritual husband.

Spiritual Discipline

As regards the daily life of a devotee of this type, the Ācārya tells us that he should first of all dedicate his own self and all his belongings, all the members of his family, to Lord Kṛṣṇa, who appeared in the world for the uplift of people of all classes, and particularly those who are not in a position to attain *makṣa* by their own efforts. There is a *saṁskāra* (sacrament) called *Brahma-saṁbandha* which has to be performed by the Jīva (soul) to re-establish the lost contact with the Lord to remove thereby the weaknesses of his nature, and to qualify himself fully for worship. The devotee, after performing this sacrament, worships the Lord, making an unreserved use of his own body and property, and thereby destroys *saṁsāra*, which is of the from of 'I' and 'mine' (i.e. ego-centric). This sacrament can be performed by all persons irrespective of caste and creed. The unreal *saṁsāra* is thus removed by the dedication of the body and wealth to the cause of the Lord, and not by the renunciation of the world. We are told by the Ācārya that in the *Kaliyuga* formal *sannyāsa* (monasticism) without the spirit of renunciation is detrimental to spiritual progress, and that it is justifiable only when one is unable to bear the pangs of separation from the Lord. The Ācārya himself took *sannyāsa* in his last days, when he felt that he could not live in the Lord and that family life was an impediment to the highest bliss, which he wished to enjoy in the company of the Lord. The worship of the Lord requires the services of all members of the family, and they are promised the highest bliss that always results from worship or *sevā* (service). This mode of service makes the whole family free from worldly ties even when leading a householder's life, and their whole life becomes divine. If the head of the family finds that some of the members of his family are not supporting him in this, he is advised to leave them and pass his time in *sevā* quite alone. The highest form of *sevā* is mental; in this stage the devotee thinks of the Lord alone.

The duties of four *varṇas* and *āśramas* cannot be satisfactorily performed in moedrn times; and if they are carried out mechanically, they fail to give any reward. When there is a conflict between the *Bhagavad-dharma* (the service of the Lord) and the *varṇāśrama-dharma,* a devotee of the Puṣṭi-mārga must choose the former : he may perform the duties of *varṇāśrama* when he finds leisure from his *sevā*, but under no circumstances at the cost of the service of the Lord. This is the real *ātma-dharma,* duty relating to the soul, while the duties of the *varṇas* and *āśramas* are simply duties relating to the Ātman and the body, the former is decidedly the superior.

It is thus obvious that a follower of the Puṣṭi-mārga devotes his own self and all his belongings to the Lord, passes his whole time in His service. He completely loses his independent existence in the world and cannot therefore possess any property. Whatever he requires for personal use he first dedicates to the Lord and then makes use of it with His permission. Since everything is dedicated to the Lord, the devotee cannot in any way exercise the right of ownership over anything. It is also impossible for a follower of the Puṣṭi-mārga to be immoral for this path is based on renunciation, not enjoyment. Although its doors are open to all—men and women, people of the upper three castes and Sūdras, and even those who are morally fallen (*patita*) and seem to have lost all chances of spiritual uplift, it does not encourage immorality. It should not be looked upon as a licence for doing immoral actions without responsibility; it simply promises safety to all who would follow its doctrines. The essence of the Puṣṭi-mārga is to establish connection between the soul and the Lord, and this is possible in many ways. One may be constantly angry with the Lord and still get *sāyujya*. It is immaterial whether it is anger or jealousy or devotion or passion that serves as the connecting link; what is required is connection, it should, however, be noted that those who are connected with the Lord through love (*sneha*) enjoy the privilege of participating in the *nitya-lilā* of the Lord and of enjoying *bhajanānanda,* while others simply get *sāyujya.* If for any reason this kind of *sevā* is not possible, one should not be disappointed. The Ācārya tells us that such a man should throw himself at the feet of the Lord and remain at His mercy. This method is called *prapatti* or self-surrender.

The Deity for Worship

The form of the Lord that is generally worshipped in this system is known as Śrī Govardhananāthajī, popularly called Śrī Nāthajī, who is the embodiment of the twelve *skandhas* of the *Bhāgavata,* and whose shrine is situated at Nathadwar in Mewar. In other words, Śrī Nāthajī, represents the very form of the Lord which is taught by the *Bhāgavata.* The twelve *skandhas* of the work are identified with the twelve parts of Śrī Nāthaji's form, the tenth *skandha* which describes the *rāslīlā* being identified with the heart. The image of Śrī Nāthajī was, according to the traditions of the School, reveated to the Ācārya on the hill of Girirāja and was later on brought to Nathadwar.[14] It represents the highest form of the Lord known as Pūrṇa Puruṣottama. All other images represent the *vibhūtis* (powers) and the *vyūhas* (manifestions), and not the highest form. The worship of the Lord is called *sevā,* while that of the *vibhūtis* is called *pūjā.* The Śuddhādvaita system, again, accepts the four *vyūhas,* vis. Vāsudeva, Saṅkarṣaṇa, Pradyumna, and Aniruddha, with their respective functions of giving *mokṣa,* removing the burden of the world, creating, and establishing *dharma.* These *vyūhas* are inferior to Pūrṇa Puruṣottama, to whom belongs the privilege of lifting up even those who are entirely helpless. In the different activities of Kṛṣṇa one can easily determine from the nature of His actions, whether the particular form assumed is the highest one or a *vyūha* or a *vibhūti.* The Ācārya has laid down the criterion for distinguishing one from another. Applying the criterion, he very emphatically recommends the *sevā* of Śrī Nāthajī and this constitutes his originality. He is not indebted to any of his predecessors in his teaching of the Puṣṭi-mārga, and the belief that Vallabhācārya simply carried on the traditions of one Viṣnu Svāmin is therefore untenable.[15]

A note of Warning

The Ācārya, when he placed before the world the conception of *puṣṭi* as illustrated in the *rāsalīlā,* anticipated certain difficulties owing to misunderstanding and its evil consequences, and he therefore freequently sounded a note of warning. He tells us that the episode of the *gopīs* and the Lord is both real and allegorical. If it is taken to the real, it must be clearly borne in mind that there is no tinge of sensualism in the *rāsalīlā,* even though its description in the *Bhāgavata* appears to be more or less worldly. Moreover, he who listens with devotion to this account of the gopis and the Lord becomes free from all the pangs of the heart and enjoys bliss. Some of the verses written by Vallabha in this connection deserve careful study. If one is disposed to interpret the *rāsa-līlā* as allegorical. One can say with him that the *gopīs* represent the Śrutis, and when they are said to enjoy the company of the Lord it simply means that the Śrutis teach only one thing and that is the Lord. The Ācārya has considered this most important question from all points of view and has asked his followers not to imitate the Lord, but to serve Him and hear the account of His doings, nay, when he was on the point of leaving this world, standing on the Gaṅgā near the Hanūmān Ghāt in Kāśī, he gave a massage to his sons and followers in words that should be written in letters of gold. He said, 'My dear followers, you should always serve the Lord to the best of your ability; you should not look upon Lord Kṛṣṇa as an ordinary worldly master; once you become His, He will always take care of you. But if, somehow or other, you forget the Lord and think of worldly matters, you will fall.'[16] The message of the Ācārya as embodied in his teachings is indeed sublime and inspiring, and will serve as an infallible guide to all lovers of truth in the realization of the ultimate end of human existence.

Contributions to Vedāntic thought

It is obvious from what has been said above that Vallabha has made a special contribution to the Vedāntic thought. The conception of Parabrahman as full of *rasa,* although found in the Upaniṣads, first received systematic attention from the Ācārya. Again the idea of Akṣara Brahman, founded as it is on the basic works received full treatment for the first time at the hands of the Ācārya. The doctrine of grace, the ideal of self dedication, and the sublimation of human life are some of the peculiar features of the teaching of the Ācārya. And what is still more remarkable is the attitude of the Ācārya towards the Vedas and the allied literature. He has accepted the Vedas as the highest authority and followed them most faithfully, with the result that logic can never get the better of faith. It is because of this attitude that Vallabhācārya differs from Śaṅkarācārya.

REFERENCES

1. Mm. Kuppuswami Sastri, 'Ācārya Sundara Pāṇḍya', *Journal of Oriental Research,* Madras, 1.5; 'Baudhāyana and Dramiḍācārya', *Proceedings of the Third All-India Oriental Conference,* p. 465. Prof. M. Hiriyanna, 'Bhartṛprapañca,' *Indian Aniquary,* June 1924, p. 77. *Proceedings of the Third-All-India Oriental Conference,* p. 787, Mm. Dr. P.V. Kane 'Vedānta commentators before Śaṅkarācārya', *Proceedings of the Fifth All-India Oriental Conference,* pp. 937-953. Mm. Dr. Vidhusekhara Bhattacharya, The *Agama-śāstra of Gauḍapāda,* Introduction, pp. 103-113.
2. *Aṇubhāṣya* on the *Brahma-Sūtra,* II, 2.26; *Subodhinī,* I.I.I.
3. The term is explained in two ways : (i) Pure non-dualism and (ii) Non-dualism of the two—cause and effect which are pure.
4. *Brahma-Sūtra* with *Śrīmad-Bhāgavata-bhāṣya,* Calcutta Oriental Series, No. 15.
5. *Tattvārthadīpa, Śāstrārtha,* 5.
6. G.H. Bhatt, 'Double Authorship of Aṇubhāṣya' *Proceedings of the Fourth All-India Oriental Conference,* pp. 799-806.
7. A portion of the commentary on the *Brahma Sūtra,* III. and III. 2.1-12, published in an old magazine, now defunct, *Puṣṭi-Bhakti-Sudhā* (Vol. V. Vo. 19 to Vol. VI. No. 6), was claimed to be a fragment of Vallabhācārya *Bṛhadbhāṣya;* but the claim is unjustifiable as the printed text is a fake, written by some modern scholar.
8. The available portion is published in the magazine *Puṣṭi-Bhakti-Sudhā.* Vol. V, 2; Vol. VIII, Nos. 2-4.
9. Bopadeva, *Harilīlā,* XII, 17.
10. *Tattvārthadīpa, Bhāgavatārtha,* 2; *Subodhinī* 1, I.I.I.
11. *Tattvārthadīpa, Sarvanirṇaya,* 85.
12. *Tattvārthadīpa,* 94.
13. For a fuller conception of *Puṣṭi,* cf. G.H. Bhatt, The Puṣṭi-mārga of Vallabhācārya, *Indian Historical Quarterly,* IX, pp. 300-336.
14. Vallabhācārya inherited from his father, Lakṣmaṇa Bhatta the image of Madanamohanaji accompanied by Rādhā on one side and

Lakṣmī on the other. This represents the form of Kṛṣṇa which is associated with the *rāsa-lilā*. In the course of time when Viṭṭhalanātha divided his property amongst his seven sons, he gave each of them an image for Sevā. These are still worshipped in different places by his discendants. All the seven *rūpa* (images) are included in the perfect and original form of Śrī Nāthjī. The later writers of the School have tried to show that these different forms represent particular *līlās* of Kṛṣṇa. Although Rādhā is worshipped in the company of Kṛṣṇa in this School, she does not enjoy as much prominence here as she does in the Vaiṣṇavism of Śrī Caitanya.

15. G.H. Bhatt, "Viṣṇusvāmī and Vallabhācārya", *Proceedings of the Seventh All-India Oriental Conference*, pp. 449-465, *Proceedings of the Eighth All-India Oriental Conference*, pp. 322-323.
16. G.H. Bhatt, "Last Message of Vallabhācārya", *Annals of the Bhandarkar Oriental Research Institute*, XXIII, pp. 67-70.

26

THE CONCEPT OF THE ABSOLUTE IN VEDĀNTA

Swami Tapasyananda

Two types of minds, both talented and belonging to the same race, but situated in different lands with varying climatic and natural conditions, started on the long and endless mission of understanding the nature of things and the significance of life. The Greeks, living in their small fertile peninsula surrounded by silvery seas and beautified by low mountains and small rivers, found the image of perfection in that which is limited and defined by fixed boundaries and which could, therefore, come under the purview of human thought, speech and effort. Thus to the Greek the circle was the perfect figure, the limited City State the field for realizing the good life, and Nature visible to the senses the absorbing object of study. There was on the other hand the ancient Indian whose lot was cast in the sweeping limitless plains of a huge subcontinent with its mighty rivers and lofty mountain ranges. His mind spurned the finite as imperfect and worthless, and sought perfection in that which is limitless, all-inclusive, infinite and transceding thought and speech.

While among nations and among systems of philosophy it is possible to note an extreme stress on the one or the other of these tendencies, it is true to say that they are both inherent in the very structure of human thought. With our eyes, ears and thought we grasp discrete and well-defined forms, but the forms are changing from one condition to another centering round something more fundamental, vast and stable, namely, the material cause out of which they are formed. Thus there are various things like pots, toys, bricks, etc. made of clay. The pots, toys etc., are the changing forms of their comparatively stable cause, the clay. Clay itself is the effect of still more subtle and relatively sutble substances that have combined to produce it. In this way when the gross changing forms are traced to their subtler causal conditions, we finally arrive at an absolute changeless substratum which is the ultimate source of all changeful phenomena. Without reference to this changeless substratum, the very phenomenon of change cannot be grasped by thought.

To view the same problem in another way, when we see a thing we experience it as a series of attributes—sounds, shapes, colours, etc. Each one of these attributes is different in itself from the others, but they are all held together, as it were, in a common object of reference, which may be called substance. We do not see the substance, we only see the attributes, but yet we are bound to accept the idea of a substance behind these attributes, as their unity in a common object of reference is otherwise inexplicable. Thus that which is obvious, definite, palpable carries with it the implication of its own self-transcendence into a changeless substratum or universal causal substance which is not involved in, or exhausted by them. Here we are up against the concept of the Absolute, a concept so abhorrent to the practical headed man of common sense, but which he has none the less got to accept if he is to be a consistent thinker.

It is the same compelling inner necessity, may not be so much of thought as of life, that has led to the origin and persistence of the idea of God among mankind. The God of the relgious man and the Absolute of the philosopher form one and the same entity in two different perspectives. This is not, however, often realized both by the religious man and the philosophic thinker, consequently leading to the degeneration of religion into dogmatic cults and philosophies into mere speculative abstractions. It is the uniqueness of the Indian system of Vedānta that it has evolved a system of thought in which both these concepts are harmonized so as to form a non-dogmatic yet vital faith that is fully justified by reason and satisfactory to emotions.

We shall now discuss how this is achieved. The idea of God that is natural to an unphilosophical religious mind is that of a all powerful will that is external to, and exclusive of the universe. He is conceived as an extra-cosmic being either producing the universe out of nothing by a fiat of His will, or as manipulating an already existing material stuff out of which He forms everything. Such a conception may be sufficient to meet the emotional and ethical needs of man, but it fails to satisfy the philosophical quest after an unchanging substratum that sustains all change without being involved in it—a universal substance which includes everything in itself. It is only when the concept of the Absolute informs and interprets the God of religion that the latter becomes really meaningful to human intelligence. But there seems to be an inner contradiction between these two concepts. God is a person and power beneficiently disposed to man, but necessarily limited, being separate from the universe. The Absolute on the other hand is unlimited and all-inclusive, but it has no reference to human destiny, and therefore reduces itself into a mere intellectual assumption so far as man is concerned. To harmonize these two and give man a God, who is also the absolute, is the task before the great Vedāntic thinkers.

The Upaniṣads which contain the records of the highest

spiritual experiences of the *ṛṣis,* the illumined sages of India, declare boldly the Absolute of philosophy and God of religion to be one and the same entity—the Impersonal-Personal Deity, *Brahman*. He is indeterminate *(Nirguṇa)* and acosmic *(Niṣ-prapañca)* in His impersonal aspect, and *Saguṇa,* (with determinative attributes) and *Saprapañca* (with cosmic manifestation) in His personal aspect. They achieve this synthesis through the acceptance of two stand-points, the *Pāramārthika* and the *Vyāvahārika*. The *Pāramārthika* represents the way *Brahman* experiences Himself; and the *Vyāvahārika* the way living beings see Him. The former is ultimate, eternal, and transcendental, while the latter is empirical, temporal and relative. Being the self-intuition of the Absolute, thoughts and words, whose sphere is the relative and limited, cannot give an actual description of the *Pāramārthika* but only an indirect and symbolic word-picture of it. Thus the Upaniṣads speak of *Brahman* as *Satyam* (Truth), *Jñānam* (Consciousness) and *Anantam* (Infinity). Truth means the ultimate causal substance, the changeless substratum which forms the implication of all changeful phenomena and which endows the phenomena with what ever reality value they possess. Such a substratum, even if granted, may be akin to the inertness of objective reality. To ward off this it is stated to be the *Jñānam* (Consciousness) and *Anantam* (Infinity). Truth means the ultimate causal substance, the changeless substratum which forms the implication of all changeful phenomena and which endows the phenomena with whatever reality value they possess. Such a substratum, even if granted, may be akin to the inertness of objective reality. To ward off this it is stated to be the *Jñānam* (Consciousness). But it is not to be mistaken for the little light of consciousness within us, as it is next described as *Anantam,* Infinite. It is thus excluded from everything finite and described by implication as that

Infinite—the Pure Consciousness—of which our little individual consciousness is a faint perverted expression through the medium *(Upādhi)* of the intellect, mind and senses. Nor is it is to be understood as an entity before us, an object before the philosophizing mind to be observed, understood and described. Being the substratum-consciousness, it is the core of the knowing self, and as such the real power of awareness itself. It is therefore impossible for it to be known as an object, just as it is impossible for the eye, the seer of all things, to be itself an object of sight. An absolute known is no longer the Absolute, but a limited entity related to a knowing subject. The Absolute is in truth *Nirviśeṣa,* without determinations, and *Nirupādhika,* without limiting adjuncts i.e. without the characteristic marks of all objects of thought and descriptions.

The Absolute discussed above should not be mistaken for *Śūnya,* a nihil, or an empty thing. The opposite concept of *Pūrṇa,* the full, is nearer the truth in so far as it is the substratum of all objective phenomena and the matrix of the self-conscious individual. The concept of *Ānanda,* Bliss-unending, is also applied to it in order to negate the common man's notion that pure being is pure nothing, and to show that it implies the summit of all values and not the denudation of them all.

The Absolute conceived as partless and indeterminate, as unchanging and non-objective, must necessarily be relationless. Yet it is spoken of as the Ultimate Substratum and the Eternal Witness, giving the idea that it is causally related to the phenomenal universe. But it has really no causal relation with it, since the changing phenomenal universe is only an appearance, so far as the Absolute is concerned. When a substance, say, a rope, appears as a snake to an onlooker, there is no real relation between the rope and the illusory snake, in spite of the rope being the substratum of the snake. Similarly *Brahman*, from the point of Its own self-intuition (the *Pāramārthika*) is relationless and transcendental, in spite of Its being understood as the cause of all by the individual consciousness that considers itself separate from It.

This doctrine of apparent manifestation is the crux of the philosophy of the Absolute, as the double status of reality represented by *Pāramārthika* and the *Vyāvahārika,* the ultimate and the empirical views, can be linked and justified only in the light of that doctrine. The illusory phenomenon of the snake-rope can illustrate the position. For the rope, the snake is non-existent. That represents the *Pāramārthika* view of the Absolute. But to the snake-conscious onlooker, the snake is a fact, and, though all the time he is seeing only the rope in reality, the rope as such is non-existent for him, it being displaced by the snake appearance as far as he is concerned. The snake consciousness represents the *Vyāvahārika* experience, apprehended as factual so long as the basic ignorance of the Reality lasts, but actually non-existent even during the time of experience, though this is realized only on the dawn of knowledge. Thus the absolute and acosmic being, the *Nirguṇa Brahman* of the *Pāramārthika* view, is apprehended in the *Vyāvahārika* state as the All-inclusive Whole,—the *Saguṇa Brahman* or the Absolute in association with its latent *Māyā Śakti* or creative power. This condition is unreal to the Absolute, but real to the *Jīva* or finite intelligence. The *Saguṇa Brahman* represents the highest conception of the God of religion. He is the creator and sustainer of the universe as also the object of worship and devotion. The philosophy of the Absolute is not therefore a negation of God as many imagine but an interpretation of Him. It is an effort to reconcile reason with religion.

Śrī Rāmānuja, a great Vedāntic thinker made an effort in later times to effect the reconciliation without the doctrine of *Nirguṇa Brahman,* its thorough-going spiritual monism and the ultimate denial of distinction between *Jīva* and God. These implications are completely hostile to this devotional spirit. He is a thorough-going realist to whom all experience is real, and plurality and change ultimate facts. He accepts the ultimacy of the three entities—matter *(Achit),* soul *(Chit)* and *Īśvara* (God), the last being the Divine Lord and Master of the others and possessed of infinite auspicious qualities. Though equally real and ultimate matter and souls are absolutely dependent on God He is not their creator, but yet their relationship with Him is so intimate and fundamental that had it not been for God, the other two could not have existed separately. They cannot last even for a moment in isolation from Him. They are thus entirely sustained and controlled by Him and their sole purpose is to be utilized by Him. This relationship is illustrated by the example of an organism and its body. The central dominating principle of life and will in an organism represents *Īśvara,* and the different limbs and organs of it, existing solely for it and subserving its purposes and perishable in isolation from it, represent the world of matter and souls. The all, included as an inseparable organic Whole, with God indwelling, sustaining and controlling it in its entirety and in parts, is the Pan-organistic Deity, whom Rāmānuja represents as *Brahman*, the Absolute of the Upaniṣads.

While this conception of the Absolute is found very congenial to many a devotional mind, it has one grave defect. If it provides for the all-inclusiveness of the Absolute, it fails obviously to secure its partlessness and immutability. It would seem that both these demands of reason are satisfied only in the Advaitic system of Śaṅkara through its doctrines of two stand-points and its two fold conception of *Brahman* as *Niṣprapañca* (the indeterminate, acosmic supra-personal Being) and as *Saprapañca* (the Cosmic Person with attributes and power of manifesting the universe of names and forms). There is, however, no reason why Rāmānuja's Pan-organistic doctrine should not be accepted as the most satisfactory interpretation of the *Saprapañca* aspect, without questioning, as Rāmānuja actually does, its acosmic and indeterminate aspect from the ultimate point of view. That at least seems to be the ideal of a true and satisfying philosophy of religion.

❑❑❑

27

VEDĀNTA AND THE DEMOCRATIC SPIRIT

Swami Swahananda

Indian culture down the ages has been influenced so much by Vedāntic ideas that it has become synonymous with Vedānta. Vedānta has some unique ideas. Democracy too, specially during the last two and a half centuries, has developed some peculiar ideas and approach to life. Democracy has two aspects, political and philosophical. Rousseau spoke about the General Will of the people. Thomas Paine spoke about the Rights of Man. Abraham Lincoln popularised the idea of the Government of the people, for the people and by the people. They all spoke the tongue of politics. Based on these ideas democracy developed its economic and political theories. Politically democracy gives to every person the right of being an equally important entity in the social context. Philosophically, it is more or less dependent, originally at least it was, on the religious thinking, on the spiritual nature of man.

Vedānta in all these aspects has got a definite message to give and we do feel that *Vedānta* can be the philosophical basis of political democracy. Here democratic idea is a creed, but the most important thing is to create a temper, a mental climate, a mood in the average man of society to react to a particular situation with an attitude. That is what democracy as a way of life does. It is not at all foreign to the nature of

Indians. In the olden days, the Vedic Aryans were a community of elders having equal share in conducting the work of the society. Later there were the *saṅghas* and the *sabhās*. The *Mahābhārata* as well as *Pāṇini's Aṣṭādhyāyī* bear witness to it. These have also been referred to by the Greek travellers in their travelogues. We read of them in the Buddhist literature too. The Lichhavis, in which tribe Lord Buddha was born, as also other tribes were small Republics.

Equality of man, in the sense of equality of voice of every man in society, in running the Government is possible only in very small communities, as in Swiss Cantons. Democracy has, therefore, in modern times taken a turn to a sort of representative democracy, a limited democracy. A vast body of people select a group of people in legislatures, and probably, also the top executives in some countries. Every man is equal, politically speaking, in giving this opinion. It is true that there is difference between man and man. The contribution of an ordinary individual eking out a precarious existence may not be the same as the contribution of a highly gifted individual—a scientist, a social engineer, a man having special skill, for instance. Still, before the eyes of democracy, every man is equal and has one vote. So a rort of equality is practised.

Now, this particular type of political system, if it is to succeed in practice, in any particular given context, the society must be permeated with a democratic spirit. Otherwise, the path for totalitarian or autocratic Governments will be paved, as we have seen in various countries. So, unless the majority of the people are imbubed with this particular idea, particular view of life, it is not possible for democracy to thrive in its real sense. To cultivate this temper is the duty of the thinkers of society and the propagators of ideals.

We find in most of the developing countries the hunger for the good things of life so great and the fall from the ideal so steep, that it has led to the formation of some type of totalitarian Governments. In India alone, among the newly freed countries, democracy is still struggling. It is necessary that we strengthen this spirit, because the alternative in modern context is totalitarianism; and totalitarianism believes, as one great thinker said, in the atomisation of man. What totalitarianism wants is the total control by the state of all the affairs of individuals, even his thinking,. Free thinking and expression are obstructions in its path. Hence they insist on the atomisation of man.

Sorokin, the great sociologist, in *'The Reconstruction of Humanity'* makes a very significant remark that the modern scientific and technological development in Europe and America, has ushered in the big corporations. Huge societies or corporations or business houses control the life of millions of their employees and their dependents. These big corporations, he says, are the harbingers of totalitarian Government. Now his argument is that if there are big corporations, then, the smaller ones gradually get merged in them. Thereby you get better efficiency no doubt, and for the sake of better efficiency, you go on merging the small units in the bigger units. As a result a time may come when 10 or 15 corporations may control the economy of the entire country. Now, if there is a conflict of interests between these groups, there is civil war. Or these big corporations also will be compelled to merge themselves or be fully controlled by a totalitarian form of Government. So Sorokin says, it is very peculiar that America, the most advanced democratic country of the world, is at the same time, fostering the forces which will ultimately nullify its idea of democracy. Any way, all thinkers agree that the assurance of continuance of democracy is in the temper of the people. If the vast majority of people are temperamentally democratic in their outlook and behaviour, democracy cannot be wiped out.

Political democracy is guided by people because everybody has got a vote. Government is a summation of individuals. When the majority of people want a particular type of Government, they can have it. So it is necessary, and it is accepted in democratic thinking, that a good amount of discussion should be there. Democracy has been defined by some thinkers as Government by discussion. People start with initial doubts, they discuss the problems and come to a conclusion. So this openness of the mind is a characteristic of democracy.

Now, this type of mental climate, attitude or approach towards problems is more or less normal in Indian thinking. But it can be fostered more and more by popularising the Vedāntic teaching. For on five or six counts *Vedānta* is definitely superior to any of the political theories in its capacity to impart this democratic spirit: of sharing, of discussion, of free thinking, of taking into consideration the view of the other man. India has been guided by this idea, throughout its history. India gave great freedom in thinking, though not so much of freedom in doing. As Swami Vivekananda says : India did not give freedom to society. As a result, Indian society did not develop much and could not have a variety of experiments in the social context. But it gave freedom to thought. As a result India excelled in wonderful efflorescences of thought-patterns evolved here. India gave freedom of discussion and that is why, to our astonishment we could see atheists preaching their philosophy right at the gates of temples. This shows how much freedom was allowed to thought, though there was no freedom for anybody to choose any way of life; it laid down the social habits and costoms and manners and all had to conform to it. But in their thinking, they could have any type of thought they liked and they had perfect freedom to preach that idea as well. This freedom of discussion and patience to hear the other man's points of view is a pre-requisite for all democratic development. The Indian thinkers never stifled independent thinking. Whenever a Vedāntic teacher tried to expound his theory he began by quoting the views of other people and then tried to answer the objections and establish his own view. There was always an attitude of readiness to understand the other man's viewpoint and an attempt to accommodate his views as far as possible. That is why the Vedāntic theory, as developed by Ācārya Śaṅkara, could draw upon some of the concepts of *Sāṅkhya, Yoga* and other philosphies.

Liberalism and evolution of synthesis was the effect of Vedānta. If Vedānta tried to harmonize the different religions, it was because of its Indian temper. Many people find it difficult to define Hinduism; it is a conglomeration of faiths like Vaiṣṇavism, Śaivism, Śāktism, and the like which were really speaking, different religions in the same manner as Islam and Christianity are different. But they were all harmonized because of the synthesizing power of Vedānta, a power which came from its democratic spirit of recognizing the truth, no matter where it lay.

Vedānta said that the Ultimate Reality, in the final analysis, is formless, but then, by some mysterious means It can take any form It likes because It is all-powerful. So It can take the form of Śiva, of Kṛṣṇa, of Devī, in short whatever form a devotee wants to see. So there should be no question of quarrels among the votaries of the different religions. The particlar form you are worshipping is the same as the other form being worshipped by the other man and both are the same Ultimate Principle, 'the chosen deity'. Every one can have his own *'Iṣṭa'*, but at the same time, each should know that all the different *Iṣṭas* are really the manifestations of the one God who can be either formless or with form. With that one theory, Vedānta harmonized the different religions and changed them into different sects within Hinduism. The same principle could apply to the other religions also.

Vedāntic ideas were gradually being absorbed by the other religions. The evidence is seen in the coming up of the Sufis, an Islamic sect. It absorbed so much of Vedāntic idea of oneness of beings that it was becoming one with Hinduism in its fundamental aspects. That is why in the Indian context you do not find any struggle in the mind of a Hindu to go to a Muslim fakir, if he is a realized soul, or a Muslim does not find it uncomfortable to go to a Hindu saint for inspiration. Akbar's *Dīn-Ilāhī* was a sort of piecing together the best things in different religions and an attempt to create a new religion. In later days, the Brahmos and others also tried to find out the best things from different religions and produce a new synthesis, free from all defects. But a vital religion cannot be created in this way. It requires a saint of enormous magnitude and great realizations to create it. Vedānta worked out a synthesis by a better method than the eclectics. It pointed out that all the accepted *Iṣṭas* are really reducible to the One. And it gave Hinduism the sense to recognize the truth in an opponent's views and its capacity to harmonize various views.

It will be a matter of not a little astonishment if it is said that this same idea of toleration was at the root of the much decried system of *'Varṇas'*, which in later days came to be called as the caste system. It is this principle of harmonization that played not a small part in developing it. It might seem strange; all the same, it is true. For look into the history of mankind, the moral standard of early days of man's life was such that when a particular City State conquered another, though equally cultured and having equally sensible type of religion, customs, manners etc., still after the conquest, all the male folk of the vanquished City State were either butchered or made slaves. Such was the moral standard then in Greece. We need not apply our moral standard of the 20th century to the people of bygone days, almost 3,000 years ago. The same thing was practised even later in other parts of the world, where the original tribes were practically exterminated. As against this, look at the great humaneness of the Aryans. They came here, probably, from outside India and conquered its original inhabitants. Yet they did not exterminate the conquered people, did not even make them their slaves, but gave them only an inferior position and at the same time accepted them in their society.

Even in the twentieth century, if a country conquers another naturally the conquering people will consider themselves superior and the conquered not worth any respect. This is the norm even now. If, therefore, thousands of years ago the Aryans treated the conquered race better, does it not speak for the nobility of the Aryans? Then originated the concept of the Brahmins, Kṣatriyas, Vaiśyas and Śudras—different groups doing different functions of the society. All of them are equally important. It is not that the Śudras really issued from the legs of the Creator, as conceived in the image of the *Virāṭa Puruṣa*. The statement was just symbolic. Without legs man cannot move. So the *Virāṭa Puruṣa,* the Indian society, could not function without legs, without the people who would be producing wealth. Therefore they should be given a recognition: that was the concept. I would repeat, the stress, at that time, was on the positive aspect of the concept, on recognition.

The inferior position was rationalized by the conquered people's lack of power or initiative or incentive but that did not prevent their absorption in the larger body politic. This absorption was effected by a theory called re-interpretation. They said: You need not be completely absorbed in our society beyond recognition. Form a society of your own and take part in the bigger society. Retain your manners, customs, deities, food and everything else. At the same time, find out finer and higher meanings for them. If it is your habit to worship a tree, do it by all means. If it is your habit to worship the stone, do it by all means. But just think that you are worshipping not the tree nor the stone but the God who is behind the tree, the god behind the stone: i.e. re-interpret your object of worship.

In this way gradually the Aryanisation took place, giving a higher and higher interpretation to ordinary things of worship, ordinary manners and customs.

In this way also, gradually, higher and higher standards of morals were brought into the society and the absorption took place. That was the origin of caste: separate groups of people retaining all their characteristics and yet remaining part and parcel of a single society.

In a way it looks peculiar, but will not if I give an analogy. In India we have people speaking, say, 13 or 14 major languages. Everybody is allowed to have his own. Still we form a body, the greater Indian society. We do not find any disharmony in that, no peculiarity in that. Similarly, in those days, these Aryans said to the others: Have your own manners and customs, your own food habits, own deities, own method of worship, but still you are part and parcel of our society. If today, the existence of linguistic groups as part of a bigger society is possible, the caste groups of the ancient days need not possibly be denounced, more so because the standards of the caste in the lower positions were being raised and they were being increasinlgy absorbed in the larger body politic.

Vedānta played a very important part in this absorption of people of different groups. It declares, that there is the One Spirit in everybody; that there is God in every human being, God whose manifestations can be various. There can be various forms and names. That is why creation means varieties of names and forms, although intrinsically there is oneness. In all these thousands of varieties you find out a common point also. This is the unity of existence, which means, everybody is basically divine.

The Vedantic idea of tolerance was extended to all tastes and expressions of dress, of food and the like. Variety is the spice of life. Even now, in our own being we have got this temperament of consideration for the other man's view. For Vedānta has prepared our mind for it. You can move in any dress you like in the Indian streets. But, even a few years ago, you could not move in many foreign countries without being jeered at, if you went in a dress unfamiliar to them. Even now, that is by and large the case. That means they lack the catholicity in regard to other people's tastes. That means they are not able to put into practice the spirit of freedom that democracy assures to every man even when this freedom does not disturb the general social order.

Variety is necessary in life. Unless there is variation in temperature there will be no storms, no rains, no grains, and therefore no life. So there must be variety; it is, in fact, in nature itself. But does that mean that there will be complete dissociation between one variety and another? No. Then also, there will be complete chaos. So, search for unity is also necessary.

As we allow for varieties, we must try to find out unity

also. And this unity was provided for by Vedānta through its theory of unity of consciousness, of the One Spirit indwelling in all. With this idea, Vedānta fostered the basis for this great ideal of unity in variety. In democracy you require this ideal. Unity must be there, so that all the people of the different groups, in a country, can feel some common bonds. Somewhere one must feel a common aspiration, common ideals and the like. But at the same time a variety in culture, in expression, in food habits and clothes etc. has to be allowed.

In the political context also varieties of manners and customs and varieties of group loyalties can be allowed provided there is the national consciousness. But if you allow only variety without unity, without cohesion at the social, temperamental and ethical levels, there will be fragmentation of society and total atomisation of man: Every man will be directly related to the State and unity will be sought only at the political level,which is the goal of some of the politicians.

In the Indian society people are accused of being too much attached to the families. They are not easily transferable from one place to another. This is not good from the point of view of economic development. But there is another side to it. It shows cohesion within the family and unity within the environment. In some countries, thousands of people have been overnight sent to outlying areas, completely cut off from their families. There the politicians have in a sense brought about absolute mobility. They can take one group of people at a moment's notice to another part of the country for quick economic development and quick material achievement. It is quite good so far as economic eficiency is concerned. But the goal of a Government is not merely economic efficiency, and turning people into automatons but also finding out ways of development of the heart. People shorn off of all sentiments and emotional bonds will be turned into automatons, or demons or reduced to atoms in the process of atomisation. A thinker has nicely put it as the 'insectification of man'. Like insects men are conducted to whatever part of the world without consideration to any of their human sentiments.

It was against this insectification that Vedānta fostered liberalism in the Indian thinking itself. And this liberalism is the basis of all democratic concepts. What was the important idea which Vedānta or spiritual conception of the universe gave? Vedānta said that there is a moral order of the universe, that the entire universe is guided by a divine scheme, which is called *'Ṛta', 'satya'* or *dharma.* Its liberalism consisted in its recognition of different values of life. So in Hinduism we have a four-fold ideal of life, four legitimate goals of man : *Dharma, Artha, Kama, Mokṣa.* It is said that search for the pleasures of life—pleasures, physical, aesthetic, artistic and intellectual—is a legitimate goal. Now to enjoy these pleasures, we require wealth. So search for wealth is also a legitimate goal. But both must be controlled by the conception of *dharma,* by a moral law so that in trying to acquire money for the sake of pleasures we do not flout the rights of other individuals. Man must, whenever he tries to get these pleasures and wealth, give an equal consideration to the other man. He must not adopt immoral means. An individual should not behave in a way that disturbs the social fabric. If the social fabric is disturbed he himself, as a part of the society, will be disturbed today or tomorrow. When the vast majority of people in a society does not observe moral laws that society collapses.

The question is asked : Is religion necessary? The necessity of religion can be explained from various standpoints, one of them is its social necessity, which hardly anybody can doubt, because religions, down the ages, have fostered the development of higher virtues. Speaking truth is one such virtue. It is very difficult to speak truth now-a-days, they say, and that we cannot manage without telling lies. They may or may not be true in the context of a particular situation, but it cannot be a social ideal. If all the members in a particular society subsist on lies, then that society cannot go on for long. As they say, even dacoits have a norm: they have got a standard of mutual regard. People say, truth is not possible in business. But even then there is a standard of truth. Otherwise things cannot go on. So also with other higher virtues. In a family if every one is selfish, and each pulls in his or her own way, how long will that family keep together? Similar is the case with society. Of course, the impact is not felt immediately as in a family. If the vast majority of people in a society became selfish a limit will be reached, which, if crossed, will bring about a total collapse of that society, as it happened in the case of the Roman Empire.

It was a complete collapse of the character of the Roman people that was the cause of the decline and fall of the Roman Empire, though it had the vigour to rule for a thousand years. So it is necessary that some values are recognised and constantly kept up before our eyes. And these are generally provided by religion.

The Vedic thinkers believed that there is a spiritual scheme of the universe and most of us also normally, if not definitely, believe that there must be some purpose. There are two major theories in the field. In the materialistic theory, there is no purpose in life : you are only a link in the larger chain and your function is to pass on the racial characteristics to later generations. Your duty is finished there and if you want to live at all, live in your progeny. That is the materialistic conception. The idealist conception throughout the world—and this is stressed in the Vedānta—is that there is a divine spiritual scheme of the universe, and a spiritual purpose in life. It is not meaningless, not 'a way to an abyss'. Whatever may be our approach, this idea gives us much consolation, great strength and energy to fight the battle of life. Life is not all smoothness. So if you come to know that there is a goal, a purpose in life, you will hesitate to resort to questionable means to acquire the things of the world and thereby disturb the whole social fabric. If I know my whole life is finished within 25 years, naturally I would be anxious to get all I can in a short time and I would not discriminate between the means. The result would be disastrous for the society.

When Aristotale was asked this question: What is the use of philosophy—philosopy in the sense of thinking? Aristotale said: It enables you to do things, without being commanded, what other people do by being commanded. Some people think of doing things without being commanded because they are convinced that it is intrinsically good to do good; naturally these people become good. Other people become good by the fear of the law. Now, society gives some latitude; it allows you to tell some lies. But if this latitude is turned into licence and if thieves become numerous, the police force will have to be made larger; if law-breakers are more, the military will have to be increased. Society directs through law and enforces its authority in a particular way, and the individuals follow this norm willingly or unwillingly. But unwilling action is no ethical action. When you are goaded and compelled by a situation to follow a particular path, there is no morality involved in it, although you may do it out of fear. So it is said in ethics that if you coscientiously think of the pros and cons, you have got a free will to do either a right or a wrong thing and if you do the right thing, then you are a good man. When, however, compelled by the situation, you do a good thing, you are neither good nor bad. So willingly we should follow the higher ideal.

As already said, Vedānta provides us with a philosophy of life and a scheme of the universe. If you believe in this, you naturally try to behave in such a way that in your progress in life, in getting good things of life, you do not become a source of tyranny. Of course, Vedānta does not say that all people can be simultaneously and equally happy in material possessions. It is an impossibility. An affluence somewhere means poverty and penury somewhere else. Swami Vivekananda was once asked: Is it possible to do good to the world? Swamiji said: 'In an absolute sense, no; in a relative sense, yes.' To explain this he told a story:

There was a poor man who wanted some money, and, somehow, he had heard that if he could get hold of a ghost, he might command him to bring money or anything else he liked; so he was very anxious to get hold of a ghost. He went about searching for a man who would give him a ghost, and at last he found a sage, with great powers, and besought his help.

The sage said, 'Don't disturb yourself, go home'. The next day the man went again to the sage and began to weep and pray. At last the sage was disgusted, and said: 'Take this charm, repeat this magic word, and a ghost will come, and whatever you say to him he will do. But beware; they are terrible beings, and must be kept continually busy. If you fail to give him work he will take your life.' The man replied, 'That is easy; I can give him work for all his life.'

Then he went to a forest, and after long repetition of the magic word, a huge ghost appeared before him, and said, 'I am a ghost. I have been conquered by your magic;

but you must keep me constantly employed. The moment you fail to give me work, I will kill you.' The man said, 'Build me a palace,' and the ghost said, 'It is done; the palace is built.' 'Bring me money,' said the man. 'Here is your money,' said the ghost. 'Cut this forest down, and build a city in its place.' 'That is done,'said the ghost. 'Anything more?' Now the man began to be frightened and thought he could give him nothing more to do; he did everything in a trice. The ghost said, 'Give me something to do or I will eat you up'. The poor man could find no further occupation for him, and was frightened. So he ran and ran and at last reached the sage and said, 'Oh, sir, protect my life!' The sage asked him what the matter was, and the man replied: 'I have nothing to give the ghost to do. Everything I tell him, he does in a moment, and he threatens to eat me up if I do not give him work.' Just then the ghost arrived, saying, 'I will eat you up,' and he would have swallowed the man. The man began to shake, and begged the sage to save his life. The sage said: 'I will find you a way out. Look at that dog with a curly tail. Draw your sword quickly and cut the tail off and give it to the ghost to straighten out.' The man cut off the dog's tail and gave it to the ghost, saying : 'Straighten that out for me.' The ghost took it and slowly and carefully straightened it out, but as soon as he let it go, it instantly curled up again. Once more he laboriously straightened it out, only to find it again curled up as soon as he attempted to let go of it. So he went on for days and days, until he was exhausted and said: 'I was never in such trouble before in my life. I am an old veteran ghost, but never before was I in such trouble. I will make a compromise with you,' he said to the man, 'you let me off and I will let you keep all I have given you and will promise not to harm you.' The man was much pleased, and accepted the offer gladly.

Swamiji said, 'This world is like a dog's curly tail, and

people have been striving to straighten it out, for hundreds of years; but when they let it go, it has curled up again.' As long as you hold it, it is kept straightened. Much improvement is there, social and other progress and much happiness too. As soon as you leave it, it goes down. Thus a particular part of the world will be prosperous, but another part will be less prosperous. But then much of this inequality can be removed by proper distribution. Vedānta can foster a mood of distribution of wealth. A favourable climate of opinion, a mental disposition to share wealth with others is a necessary condition for that. In Vedāntic thinking, the idea of sharing is predominant. Vedānta did not believe in any privilege. Swami Vivekananda speaking about 'Vedānta and Privilege' says, 'Vedānta does not believe in any privilege—whether it is privilege of birth, or wealth or any other'. Complete equality is the ideal, but veriety is allowed because it is in the nature of things. The ideal is to strive for equality in the full knowledge that disparity is in the very nature of things—a knowledge which must not, however, deter efforts to mitigate as far as possible the sufferings of people. Vedānta tried to foster this idea in the people by the idea of *Dāna*. If you read the Gītā which is an important Vedāntic classic, you find three important ideas—*yajñā, dāna* and *tapas*. Every now and then Śrī Kṛṣṇa speaks about these. Achārya Śaṅkara defines *dāna* as 'sharing'. We are already convinced that there must be fair distribution of the good things of life, that we must have a socialistic type of society. At least, the means of production must be socialised so that the equal distribution also can be more efficiently organized.

An example of how the idea of sharing had taken hold of Indian people may be cited here. When the Zamindari Abolition Act was being passed in the State of West Bengal, a great foreign dignitary who was in Calcutta was astonished that there was no rioting, no bloodshed. Land reforms meant hundreds of people were being deprived of privileges which they were enjoying for a long time. Their main means of life were being taken away by legislative acts. Yet there was no bloodshed. He asked the then Chief Minister of West Bengal about it. The reply was that it was the idea of the Indians to consider accumulation of wealth as a kind of cheating. If you procure too much wealth, it is as if you have deprived the other man. That idea is so much in the Indian consciousness that even the rich feels that their wealth is not legitimately theirs.

There is a verse in the *Bhāgavata* which says you should have just enough property to maintain yourself. If you have more than that, it is equivalent to stealing others property. As a result of constant repetition, this idea is deeply imprinted in the minds of the Indian people. And that is why, as Tagore said, Indian philosophy taught the kings of India to relinquish their kingdoms at the approach of old age.

Swamiji says, the Europeans take pride in feeling that they are the descendants of the robber barons, whereas Indians try to trace their ancestry to the Ṛṣis. That shows the temper of our people. Wherever there was sacrifice, we have given respect. An Indian does not spurn enjoyment; so he requires wealth. But at the same time he knows a man who renounces his wealth is a greater man than himself. That is why in Indian thinking, the Brahmin was given the highest prestige. He did not have enough to eat; his was a life of sacrifice for the benefit of the society; at the same time he was the brain of the society. He gave the laws. If he had wealth, a vested interest would have been created in him, as a result he would have tried to frame laws in a way that safeguarded his interests. It would then have been no good law. So the first condition for earning the right to be the law-giver was that you did not have any property. You renounced all your rights and courted poverty. If you opted for poverty, it is true that you would not get the good things of life like other men, but the society said : 'We would give you the compensation.' This compensation was in the form of prestige.

Honour is a great incentive to work. Why should men work if there is no personal property, it is often asked. That is the argument given against the communist principle. But then, prestige is an equally potent force. Up to a certain extent, you want property, security, wealth, but a state comes when wealth does not satisfy. Then man begins to give away wealth, because he wants honour. Otherwise, how can you account for the benevolence of some of the capitalists? Their whole life is spent in amassing wealth. All the joys of life they have practically denied themselves only to acquire money. Yet, at the fag end of their life, or at the height of their money-power, they give in charity, found schools or colleges. Why? For name and fame. Name is a great motive force in guiding man.

Vedānta created consciousness that there is a higher goal and that a stage must come in everybody's life when he must transcend the hungers for these pleasures, and be dedicated to higher and higher causes. This mood has been created by constant preaching, over thousands of years. Man knows by instinct that it is good to be of a sacrificing type, but it is also necessary that he must be able to feed himself first. I am sure, no type of totalitarian society that stresses material prosperity to the exclusion of human values can gain ground in India if only the basic needs of man are provided.

Vedānta has thus created in us what can be rightly termed a democratic temperament, of sharing, of discussion, of seeing the other man's viewpoint, of finding a unity in all these varieties of manifestations. And all this is important to make a political experiment with democracy a success. So, if we clearly know the demands democracy makes on the society for its success, and how Vedānta has been of service in creating that particular mood, we will find that Vedānta has already done a great service. It can do still better service if we popularise these ideas, preach them to the masses of India, and let the masses know these basic ideas of Indian philosophy, religion and life.

❑❑❑

28

THE DYNAMIC POWER OF VEDĀNTA

Swami Gnaneswarananda

The most powerful dynamo of strength and power, the infinite and inexhaustible source of eternal perfection, beauty and truth is man. The sun, the moon, the planets, the oceans and mountains, fire, ether, electricity—all these are but by-products of this great Power which is man. A Vedāntist, for that reason, worships man above any other power, any god, demi-god or spirit. He recognizes in man the immense possibility of the highest type of power and perfection. All his endeavour is concentrated on the awakenment and manifestation of the real man within. It is not the apparent man, the outer surface, which he considers to be the reality. He goes beyond these appearances and tries to find out that essence which sustains phenomena, and realizing that underlying Principle he finds the Divinity of man.

Above all other expressions of nature man has greater possibility of manifesting that Divinity. Vedānta certainly recognizes the presence of the Divine everywhere. It does not say that the cosmic spark is present only in man, that it is not in beasts, birds, trees and stones. Vedānta declares that from the highest down to the lowest the same one Reality is present everywhere, equally, without any distinction. The reason a Vedāntist worships man above all other manifestations is that in him Divinity finds greater expression than in other entities. Vedānta asserts that after going through millions of births and deaths, deriving experience from all kinds of existences, high and low, a soul at last incarnates as man, and in human life alone it can attain the highest perfection and illumination.

But, as in the case of all kinds of power, Divinity may remain in a static or a dynamic form. When power struggles, manifesting strength and vigour at every step of its progress, we call it dynamic; when it remains in a static form we hardly recognize its presence, as it does not express itself, as it is sleeping. When, in the case of this immensely powerful dynamo of man, that infinite storehouse of power remains in a static condition and does not manifest, we call it the degraded, degenerated or sleeping condition of man. By a skilful method static power can be transformed into dynamic power and the dormant Divinity in man can be aroused and manifested. That makes the difference between a saint and a sinner. According to the philosophy of Vedānta the same perfection is present in the murderer and in the sage, only in a sinner, so-called, the power is obstructed and does not manifest itself. If a lamp is covered with something opaque and dark we will not see any expression of light. But for that reason are we to infer that the light is not there? The light with all its power and effulgence is there but some external influence is thwarting its expression. In order to see the light we do not have to do anything with the lamp. All that we have to do is to remove that dark, opaque shade. The power of Divinity is certainly present in all, the weak, the depraved and the degraded people of the world. But in order to manifest it they must remove the dark coverings. The endeavour of Vedānta is to aid man remove the obstructions that hide the effulgence of the glorious *Ātman,* the soul, within. Again, Vedānta does not propose to give you something which you did not already possess. It helps to remove the obstructions to the manifestation of that perfection which is hidden within you. It is always within you but it is hidden. The method is caled Yoga, and there are several forms to suit the taste, temperament and aptitude of different individuals.

To be able to apply the power of this dynamo of the Spirit constructively we have to have a highly developed sense of discimination. If a huge dynamo of mechanical power is entrusted to one who has not sense of right or wrong or the slightest power of discrimination, he can turn that power to a destructive end; whereas, if a person of discrimination controls and manipulates it he can accomplish something of greatest good. Witlr the power of the Spirit also, different ends can be achieved. The power can be applied even in a destructive way. Spiritual power is applied by many for the attainment of worldly ends. And what is the result? Like all destructive forces it not only destroys in the outside world but it eventually devours the mover of the force. So the most important thing is to know how to apply this gigtic dynamo of power.

In order to illustrate this truth a beautiful story is told in the Upaniṣads. The king of the Devas, Indra, and the king of the demons, Virochana, wanted to find out the eternal and infinite source of power, by possessing which they would be able to accomplish anything they desired. With that end in view they approached Prajapati, the Creator. Making no distinction between them Prajapati taught both the very same truth: 'Thou art the infinite source of all power and strength. Know thyself, and the entire power will be at thy command.' Both the students retired and contemplated upon this truth, given to them by Prajapati. The demon king, Virochana, saw nothing beyond his physical self. He recognized only his body and mind, and meditating on physical matter he attained what we call material power. He developed gigantic strength in his body, enormous resources, unconquerable military force and in short, everything that contributes to the power of enjoying the world. He was greatly satisfied by attaining all this and he taught this materialistic philosophy to his people. His kinsmen and descendants are the demons, who see nothing beyond the physical body and material power.

The other student, Indra, contemplated deeply, and sat for meditation over and over again. At first the idea came to his mind that perhaps Prajapati meant the body and mind as the source of all power, but he was not satisfied. He argued within himself: 'This body will perish. It was born; it had a beginning, and for that reason it must have an end. Its life may be prolonged but one day it certainly will end. So the infinite and inexhaustible source of power cannot lie in anything physical.' He argued the same way about the mind. It was changeable, did not exist in deep sleep, and so on and so forth. He went back to the teacher and asked him, Master, did you mean that my body and mind were the source of all perfection? The teacher smiled and said: 'Thou art the source of all perfection. Know thyself and immense power will be thine.' Indra went back again to his meditation. He went deeper and deeper until he unfolded the inner spirit. Realizing That, he found that it was never born and it would never die. The *Ātman* was infinitely glorious, eternally existing, the source of all power and perfection. He found *Brahman* everywhere, in everything from the highest down to the lowest.He perceived himself in everything, and realizing his larger Self in every atom he remained immersed in infinite bliss. That is why he is called a *Deva*. This story is a beautiful illustration of how one can misuse power and wrongly interpret any teaching.

Vedānta sounds a note of warning to man not to become attached to things that are perishable. 'Do not rust appearances,' it says. 'Remove the veil of Māyā and behind appearances discover the Reality.' Vedānta does not teach you to hate this world; it only asks you to find out the Reality of it. Do not get attached to a thing unless and until you know what it is. If appearance attracts you, stop and analyse it and see what is influencing you. Is it only the surface which is fascinating you? Or do you know what it really is? If you analyse every phenomenon that is presented before you, you will find that, instead of being wrongly influened, you will go deeper and deeper into the reality until every manifestation will reveal to you the light of truth, the depth of wisdom, and the vastness of absolute peace. Therefore the culture of discrimination, analysis, and contemplation have been emphasized over and over again by the philosophy of Vedānta.

The trouble is that although this great power is present everywhere, although we are higher than gods, although we can do anything we like, there is a great force pressing us down. Being gods we move about in this world like so many insects. Why? What is that negative power that has converted us, gods, into so many little earthworms? Vedānta has arrived at the definite conclusion that it is, fundamentally, ignorance, manifesting itself in the form of fear. Fear is the first-born of ignorance, through the influence of which we, gods have been dethroned from our kingdom of heaven. Analyse how this one demon, fear, has invaded every department of life, cramping all endeavours, spoiling and devastating the beauty and the magnificence of the wonderful edifice of human life. Study the history of religion, for instance. You will find that almost all the religious systems of the world have originated from fear. Fear has been magnified, eulogised and deified by the church and priesthood of every religion. Whenever I come across the common expression, 'a God-fearing man,' I resent it. As if one who fears God is a very wonderful man!

Vedānta is the only philosophy that declares at the top of its voice that if there is even a small particle of fear existing anywhere within your system you are in the realm of darkness, and so long as ignorance remains light cannot reveal itself. Light and darkness cannot exist at the same place at the same time. Know that you are the only Reality that exists and all fear will vanish. We are overpowered by fear. We are afraid of suffering, we are afraid of death, afraid of losing money, social position, prestige or a little ease or comfort, and that is why destructive forces get the better of us. Try to analyse the mentality of a little child who has the habit of lying. Why does he start to lie? You will find that someone has put the poison of fear into his system, and it is expressing itself in the form of that disease of lying. Analyse every bit of weakness, depravity or sin from which humanity is suffering, and without a single exception you will find that fear is at the back of every evil.

If Vedānta recognizes anything as sin it declares fear to be the deadliest of all. It says: 'Wake up ye gods and dispel the darkness of fear. Assert your own God-given right. Know the truth, and the light of knowledge will reveal everything that is, was, or will be.' It is only fear that holds us confined to vain appearances. Suppose you are told that you are *Brahman*, that you have the possibility of all perfection within you, why does that truth not reveal itself through you instantly? No doubt, it is, because of that destructive force of fear. We are afraid to express ourselves. We are afraid openly to embrace the truth and live it. That is why, being told over and over again, we still do not derive any benefit from the wisdom presented so emphatically by this philosophy of Vedānta.

I had the privilege of sitting at the feet of a great Swami, Swami Turiyananda, (a direct disciple of Sri Ramakrishna) whose very presence radiated strength and fearlessness. My memory goes back to that gigantic lion of spiritual strength and courage. His voice still rings in my ears as he encouraged us by repeating from the Upaniṣads. *'Abhiḥ! Abhiḥ!* have no fear,' he would exclaim. 'It is only fear that is holding you down. Dispel fear, and you will find that you can accomplish anything in this world.' Once he wanted me to go to a place to do some difficult work. I went to him and told him that I had never done any work like that and did not think I would be able to carry it out. My fear displeased him. 'What!' he said. 'You come to me and say you cannot do it! What good has your philosophy done you if even now you are under the delusion that you are weak? What hallucination! Go ahead. Try to do it. You may not be able at first to overpower all the destructive forces, but persist and you will get over the weakness of fear. Then everything you do will manifest great power, strength and vitality.' to make a long story short, let me tell you that I was aroused to a higher consciousness of strength and power, and certainly the very memory of the work I did under his instruction and encouragement gives me a thrill. It uplifted me for the rest of my life.

I would like to tell you a few instances of how he lived that principle of fearlessness in his own life. At one time he was living in a dilapidated old place, forsaken by people as being a haunted house. But there were many students who came to him there for instruction. Once they were having a beautiful discussion about the indestructibility of the soul and other higher truths of Vedānta. In the midst of the discussion an earthquake shook the house. Plaster and bricks were falling all around. Horrified, everyone jumped up and rushed out of the house, through doors and windows. The teacher, led by some instinct, also rose to run away. But as soon as he stood up there rang a distinct voice in his ears, '*Abhiḥ! Abhiḥ!* have no fear! have no fear!' He told me that the voice sounded so sarcastic, as if it was pointing out to him: 'Have you not just now been discussing the indestructibility of the soul? Then how is it that as soon as the house begins to shake you at once go down to the consciousness that you are the body? If an earthquake could demolish anything it would only destroy the physical body. It could not even touch your inner, real Self.' That at once put him into a state of contemplation, and he sat down and remained absorbed in it. When the earthquake was over, the fugitives began to wonder where the teacher was. They saw the ruins and could not recollect if he had escaped from the house. Hurriedly they started to remove the debris and they found him where they had left him, without even a single bruise. He was absorbed in *Samādhi*.

On another occasion he faced a tiger. He was in the Himālayas, in one of those forest retreats, practising meditation and contemplation. One beautiful moonlit night he was sitting on a big boulder on the bank of the river Ganges. He was absorbed in the contemplation of that one fundamental Principle, without beginning, changeless, and free from destruction. Suddenly a huge tiger appeared before him. He felt frightened and his first thought was to run away. Sometimes, you know, old instincts get the better of us. In his case also, the Swami told us that his instinct was to flee to safety, but at once something held him down. 'Run away from whom? Is not the very same *Brahman* present in that tiger?' came the voice of truth from within himself. 'It is duality that always creates fear and enmity.' The Swami said that he sat down again and became absorbed in the thought of the oneness of all things. Suddenly, as if by a miracle, the man-eating tiger was frightened by some noise and it ran away and never appeared again.

In later life this great man suffered from diabetes. At that time there were no effective medicines for this disease and the Swami developed huge carbuncles on his back. These had to be operated upon. But, in every instance, he refused anaesthethic. He withdrew his mind from the body and allowed the surgeon to operate upon these painful boils, much to the amazement of the doctors. They probably thought he was just immune to pain, for one day the doctor who was attending on him decided to cut some more flesh around the wound. Without saying anything to the Swami he cut through with his scissors. The Swami let out a cry of pain. When the doctor enquired about it, the Swami said, 'When I know you are going to operate I withdraw my mind from the body, and then I feel no pain. But this time I was not prepared.' He had perfect control over his mind, whenever he wanted to exert that. Such strength I have never seen or heard of before.

On many occasions I have seen how this great man was above all fear. Those who saw him pass out of his body are convinced that never in their lives will they find a second similar instance of fearlessness. He stared death right in the face. He challenged all the forces of destruction, saying in so many words, 'Death, you can take away my physical body, but over my spirit, the *Ātman*—my real Self—you have no power.' Almost the last words that came out of his mortal lips were, '*Abhiḥ! Abhiḥ!* Have no fear! Strength is God. Strength is *Brahman!*' He proclaimed that God is present everywhere, in the high and in the low, in phenomena as well as outside of it. 'Everything is *Brahman,* everything is real,' he said. 'The world is real, the world is *Brahman!*'

When his attendants saw him trying to raise himself up they gently asked him to lie down, but he said, 'What! I must sit up. I want to sit in the posture of meditation.' He meant that he wanted to pass out of the body in the state of *Samādhi*. This he did. So established was he in discrimination that he could feel the vital energy leaving his body. He observed it as an unattached witness. He watched the death of his body. He was completely detached from it. He saluted his beloved Guru, Sri Ramakrishna, and with a smile of God-realisation illuminating his face he entered into the state of Absolute bliss.

In my estimation there could not be my greater expression of power than I have seen in this great man—power that does not consider any catastrophe, any danger or difficulty as worth anything; power that always remains in touch with that infinite source of purity, beauty and perfection; power that sustains a condition of happiness and effulgence; power that projects peace and bliss, and which cannot be subdued or surpassed by any force that we know of in our experience of the world. I have seen many demonstrations of uncommon physical strength. I have witnessed marvellous feats of mechanical power. I admire them, but compared with the power of the Spirit they are only 'drops in the bucket'.

It is my conclusion that these powers that we call physical or mechanical are only indirect manifestations of the one spiritual power. Power is one, but it can be expressed differently and it can be applied for various purposes. One who sees in a huge engine the power of the Spirit knows the truth. It is not the mass of steel, gas, or fire, or even the sum-total of materials that makes the engine or power-plant so tremendous. It is the power of the Spirit behind, it is the power of man at its back, that makes it mighty. Analyse any manifestation of mechanical or physical power and you will find that directly or indirectly it is the manifestation of the power of man. When that power is focussed on man himself, when its force is applied within man himself, when its force is applied within man instead of outside, man's real nature is revealed to him. He realizes his own Self as the one source of all power, manifest and non-manifest. He becomes free for ever. He attains the kingdom of Infinite existene, knowledge and bliss.

❑❑❑

29

GEORGE SANTAYANA AND VEDĀNTA

A.V. Subramania Aiyar

The object of this paper is to give a short account of the life and the philosophy of George Santayana and to show that in a few of its basic elements it has affinity with Indian Vedāntic thought.

Santayana was born of Spanish parents, both of whom had lived for some years in the Phillippine Islands. His father had sailed round the world and had enough taste for literature to translate Seneca's plays from Latin to Spanish.

He was born in 1863. After a friendly separation from her husband, his mother left for U.S.A. leaving young Santayana with his father in Spain. After living in Spain till his ninth year Santayana went to America to join his mother. He had his secondary education there and his collegiate study at Harvard University. Here he learnt Philosohy under William James and Royce and developed a flair for it. After taking his degree he proceeded for further study to Germany, the country of masters like Kant, Schopenhauer and Hegel, who had profoundly influenced the philosophic thought of the 19th century. In Germany he came into contact for the first time with Greek philosophy, which impressed him very much. Some years later while he was serving as a teacher of Philosophy in his *alma mater* of Harvard he came to England for a specialised study of Plato and Aristotle under Henery

Jackson of Cambridge University. Santayana remained at Harvard as Professor of Philosophy for 23 years along with his masters James and Royce. Though his relationship with William James was not cordial on account of temperamental incompatibility which nothing could overcome, he gained the respect of the discerning public and the admiration of a whole generation of students, who were thrilled by his profound learning and eloquence. Santayana left Harvard in 1912 for Europe and remained there as a lone star among philosophic writers till his death in 1952. Europe saw two world wars during his stay. They deeply perturbed him and influenced his later thought to some extent.

George Santayana was a very voluminous writer. His masterpiece is the *Life of Reason,* which was published in five volumes in 1905 under the titles *Reason in Common Sense, Reason in Society, Reason in Religion, Reason in Art,* and *Reason in Science.* He had written earlier some poems and a number of essays in *Literary Criticism* on subjects like the *Sense of Beauty* and *Poetry and Religion,* which have the Santayana touch. But it was after the appearance of the *Life of Reason* that his fame as a philosopher of the front rank was firmly established. John Dewey, the American philosopher wrote of this book: 'We are grateful to Mr. Santayana of what he has given us, the most adequate contribution America has yet made, always excepting Emerson, to moral philosophy.' The book contains an acute and masterly survey of the achievement of the human intellect and mind throughout history in language of great force and brilliance. He himself spoke of it some years later as 'a presumptive biography of the human intellect, which instead of the *Life of Reason,* might have been called the 'to mance of Wisdom'. In 1913 his *Winds of Doctrine* was published. Ten years later, *Scepticism* and *Animal Faith,* a thought-provoking book, as an introduction to his second masterpiece, The *Realms of Being* (1927 to 1930) appeared. Till the end of his life he was writing essays and critiques on various philosophical subjects. In his lecture in *Ultimate Religion,* which he delivered at the Hague in 1936 during the tercentenary of Spinoza's birth, he gave a distilled essence, as it were, of his mature views on Religion and Philosophy in simple and telling language.

Santayana's Philosophy

Santayana begins his preface to *Scepticism* and *Animal Faith* by saying, 'Here is one more system of philosophy' and adds, 'My system is not mine nor new.' But in fact he has not created any special philosophical system or school nor does his philosophy fit completely into the known systems such as Materialism, Naturalism, Idealism, Transcendentalism, Pragmatism, Instrumentalism, Existentialism, Behaviourism or other innumerable 'isms' of modern western metaphysical thought. Santayana's philosophy is not the less valuable on that account. There is a cogency in the core of his thought, which precludes it from being considered as some kind of eclecticism. The one thing that is evident is that the phenomenal growth of Science and the historic spirit in the 19th century had their effect on his thinking, which however was mostly shaped by the Greek masters among the ancients and Spinoza among the moderns. The many references to Indian Philosophy and thought, found scattered in his works show a clear grasp of their fundamentals, which extorted his admiration, if no full assent.

There is a view that his Philosophy is in essene Materialism and Naturalism, clothed in a religious and romantic literary grab. He himself has said: 'Now in natural philosophy I am a decided materialist—apparently the only one living—and I am well aware that idealists are found of calling materialism too metaphysics in rather an angry tone, so as to cast discredit upon it by assimilating it to their own systems. But my materialism for all that is no metaphysical.' In another place he writes: 'The necessity of naturalism as a foundation for all further serious opinions was clear to me from the beginning.' This does not mean that he is a materialist in the accepted philosophical sense of that word. Materialsim, as Dr. S. Radhakrishnan has said 'is as old as philosophy'. Any one who considers that Matter is a reality, and that modern philosophic thought cannot ignore the conclusions of science and build any system, is not a materialist. Only he who holds that matter and the material world constitute the sole Reality and, repudiating spirit in its cosmic and mundance pervasiveness, postulates that there is nothing beyond what our senses see and nothing after death is an authentic materialist. In this sense the ancient Indian Charvakas and Lokayatikas were pure materialists and were more forthright than their contemporaries, the Greek Atomists or the modern materialists and rationalists of the 19th century. In Indian philosophy itself, there are both theistic and non-theistic schools, which consider matter to be real, eternal and separate without being liable to be called materialistic in their nature.

Santayana, for all the importance he attaches to matter, believes also in spirituality and spirit completely, as the most dynamic influence in the affairs of Man and the Universe. Some of his most beautiful and rhapsodical passages are on the glory of the spirit and its pivotal position in life and existence. He writes : 'Spirituality, then, lies in regarding existence merely as a vehicle for contemplation, and contemplation merely as a vehicle for joy ... Spirit is not an instrument, but a realisation, a fruition. At every stage and wherever it peeps out through the interstices of existence, it is a contemplation of eternal things.' He further points out: 'The first philosophers, the original observers of life and nature were the best; and I think only the Indians and the Greek naturalists, together with Spinoza have been right on the chief issue, the relation of man and his spirit to the universe.' Santayana is also of the view that the final glory of the spirit is its union with the Supreme which he calls Pure Being. About that he says: 'In some sense evidently pure being is the supreme being. May it then be identified with God? I think that a religion is possible, which should have pure being for its object and that it might even become a popular cult. Brahminism seems to be actually such a religion.' He has shown an acute perception here. But he has wavered in other places and hesitated to identify his pure being with the personal God of religion. Santayana has also declared that the way of renunciation is the best and surest for release, though he has a personal preference for a different way. In a fine passage he writes: 'I myself have no passionate attachment to existence and value this world for the intuitions it can suggest, rather than for the wilderness of facts that compose it. *To turn away from it may be the deepest wisdom in the end.'* (italics mine) He has accepted the common Vedāntic view that worldly life is inimical to spiritual life. A careful reading of his works unmistakably shows the Vedāntic tinge of his outlook. He has expressed warm admiration for the best elements of Indian thought and philosophy, though in a few matters pertaining to them, he has, like most western philosophers, misjudged.

Writing about philosophers he observes: 'A philosopher could hardly have a higher amibition than to make himself the mouthpiece for the memory and judgment of his race.' He himself has fulfilled this role with distinction. He is probably the supreme master of English prose among modern philosophers. When it is remembered that he is a foreigner to the language of his choice his achievement is almost a miracle. Competent critics have observed that after Plato, Santayana is the most literary and artistic writer on Philosophy. It is usual to refer to him as a poet-philosopher. His true gift of poesy is reflected in the imaginative texture, the rich cadence and the wealth of metaphor found in his English prose. He has written so much over a period of 50 years that inconsistencies and differences in emphasis may be found, but these are trifles by the side of the solid core of wisdom and thought and penetrating insight into the fundamentals of life and existence, expressed in language of sustained power, brilliance and beauty in his works, which are a joy to read, and ponder over.

30

THE NĀTHA TRADITION

M.P. Pandit

Though the beginnings of this cult are lost in legend, and the innumerable sects into which it has proliferated all over the land have made it difficult to determine the exact form of its original formulation, still there are certain broad features of its philosophy and practice that make it possible to lay hold on the central truths of this important branch of the Indian spiritual effort. There are, indeed, a large number of treatises on the subject in Sanskrit and in the various vernaculars of the regions where it has held sway, notably in parts of eastern Bengal, Nepal, upper India, central and western India, but by and large, they all base themselves on the teachings of Gorakshanatha, which are said to have been expounded by the great teacher himself in the *Siddha-siddhāntapaddhati*. Whether the said work was actually written by Gorakshanatha, and whether all the doctrines therein were enunciated by one person of that name, is a question that cannot be decided with any finality. It is enough for our purpose to note from this treatise that the *Nātha sampradāya* (tradition) has certain basic philosophic postulates and a system or combination of the essentials of different systems of Yoga to translate the knowledge into practice. This tradition looks upon the whole universe as a direct manifestation of the divine Reality on different levels, the many proceeding from the One in purposeful evolution, and posits the goal of life as the full realization of this truth by each individual in oneself. The means to awaken and realize this true state of one's existence is a graded discipline consisting of the main elements of *haṭha-yoga, rāja-yoga, mantra-yoga* and *laya-yoga.*

The Concept of Śiva-śakti

There is one Reality which is the ultimate Truth of all. It is infinite, and has no limits. It alone exists and there is none other than It. It is eternal; It has neither beginning nor end. It is self-luminous and needs nothing else to reveal It. This supreme Reality identical with the *Brahman* of the Upaniṣads, is called Śiva.

Though, thus, absolute and indeterminate Śiva is not bound by this indefinability. He reveals Himself as the all. For the all is nothing else but He; there can be no other besides Śiva, the sole Reality *(advayam).* Śiva has within Himself a Power, by which He moves into manifestation. This Power, Śakti, is not something different or subsidiary to Him. It is Himself. Or, to put it in another way, the same Reality as the immutable, the static, is Śiva; and as the mutable, the dynamic aspect, Śakti. There is no difference . says the *Siddha-siddhānta-saṅgraha* (IV. 37):

Śivasyābhyantare Śaktiḥ
Śaktirabhyantare Śivaḥ;
Antaraṁ naiva paśyāmi
candracandrikayoriva.

'Within Śiva there is Śakti; within Śakti there is Śiva. I see no difference between them; they are like the moon and the moonlight.'

Śakti exists in Śiva and cannot be apart from Him. Śiva always contains His Śakti, which may be active or not active. In either case, the Śakti inheres in Śiva. Similarly, the Śakti always carries Śiva. When it acts, it acts in Him, out of

Him, and for Him. When it does not act, it reposes in Himself, that is, in Śiva. Thus, manifest or unmanifest, the Śiva-Śakti reality is eternal. To put it in other terms, Śiva is the Reality as being; Śakti, the same Reality as becoming. Both are different poises of the One. The universe is a becomig, a self-manifestation of Śiva, worked out through His innate power, Śakti. Creation ensues in the expansive mood of the Śakti, destruction in the mood of withdrawal into Herself, in Śiva. The cause of the entire movement is Śiva-Śakti, *śakti-yukta-śiva*.

Evoution of the Universe

And how is the manifestation of the universe brought about? In the beginning, there is only the absolute, indeterminate, pure Being. There is only the supreme transcendent Śiva, the luminous existent beyond, *aparaṁ paraṁ*. His innate power, *nija-śakti* is there in Him, identical with Him, as His pure will, *icchāmātra*. The will is pure, it wills noth-ing. It is formless, eternal, whole, still, and unrisen.

Next, there arises the impulse to reveal. The Power or the will gets an urge to manifest what is contained within. This power instinct with the will to manifest is *parāśakti*. The same Power, which, as *nija-śakti,* was indistinguishable from Śiva, is now, as *parā-śakti,* distinguishable from the transcendent Śiva. As has been well put, it exists not as Śiva but in Śiva, who is *paramaṁ padaṁ* and cognizant. This *parāśakti* asserts its existence; it is immeasurable and infinite, but yet non-differentiate and unmanifest. The urge to manifest has arisen; it is facing towards manifestation, but as yet there is no movement.

Now there is a stir, a vibration, *spanda* within. The Śakti in which this movement has stirred is calld *aparā-śakti*. The *aparā-śakti* goes one step further from the changeless Śiva in the static poise of Being, and tends towards definite movement of revelation. But as yet, there is no outer movement. It is a stir within. It is vibrant, throbbing, clear, disclosive, and blooming. And along with His Śakti, Śiva, too emerges more clearly as the illuminer of His active will. He becomes the very will, *svecchāmātra,* Himself appears as *śūnyam.*

The fourth stage arrives when there arises the consciousness of 'I' in the whole movement. When Śiva, who was so far an impersonal Spirit, becomes conscious of Himself as the existent, stainless, governing His creative will, as a determining person, His Power assumes the character of His body. The Śakti here is called *sūkṣma-śakti.* She is impartite, unparcelled, immobile, definite, and without distinctions.

In the fifth and the last subtle stage, the Śakti reveals Herself as a power that can know, feel, and will, *vedanaśīlā,* and is called the *kuṇḍalinī-śakti.* She is perfect, irresistible, fronting towards creation, constituting Herself as the Matrix, and reflecting the nature of Śiva in the forms of Her making. All that is to be brought out, all that is to be revealed, is manifested in an ideal state in this step of the Śakti, illumined by Śiva, who poises Himself as the great Self, *Paramātman,* and the Lord of that ideal creation. As the Śakti, in each of Her stations, has different attributes, so also Śiva, in each of His poises, has different characteristics.

The ideal world so created by the Śakti on the move and held by the *kuṇḍalinīśakti* is the cosmic body, *parā piṇḍa,* of Śiva, who, as the soul of this vast body, is called the *Para* Śiva. This cosmic body is also called *anādi-piṇḍa,* beginningless, for it has no beginning as such in time. The ideal creation has no relation with the time of our conception.

From this ideal formulation of the Śakti, there proceeds as a result of further self-variation, self-diversification, self-evolution, the gross creation, *jaḍa-jagat*. 'From the *ādya (anādi-piṇḍa)* comes *mahākāśa;* from *mahākāśa*, the *mahāvāyu;* from *mahāvāyu,* the *mahātejas;* from *mahātejas,* the *mahāsalila*; from the *mahāsalila,* the *mahāpṛthivī;'* And this great material body of the universe is the *mahā-sākārapiṇḍa,* the great formed substance. As the soul of this *sākāra piṇḍa, Śiva* is the *Paramātman.*

Individual Formations and Man

Thus far regarding the cosmos, the universal creation. The next to issue is the *vyaṣṭi piṇḍa,* individualized self-involvements of the manifesting Śakti. Each individual form is a self-creation of Śiva-Śakti, of which Śakti is the body and Śiva the soul. There are, indeed , a million orders in this creation, but this truth of *śakti-yukta-śiva* pervading and constituting each formation is to be found everywhere. In man, this truth arrives at a point of overt expression.

In a sense man, the individual, is the point of return in the curve of the manifestation. The entire cosmos with all its principles and powers is reflected, reproduced, in a miniature scale in his system. All the regions of the created universe are found organized in the human body—the various heavens in the upper body and the nether regions in the lower. The different kinds of beings, viz. gods and goddesses active in the universe are also active in the human body at their respective centres. No doubt, the *Śiva-Śakti* manifestation in the universe is repreated in each individual form, though in different degree of self-revelation. Says the *Sarvasiddhānta-saṅgraha* (III. 40) :

Akhaṇḍaparipūrṇātmā
viśvarūpo maheśvaraḥ;
Ghaṭe ghaṭe citprakāśaḥ
tiṣṭhatīti prabudhyatāmi.

'Awake to the truth that the great Lord, infinite, full,

universal in form, abides in the Light of His Consciouness, in every vessel.'

In man the process arrives at a certain completion. In him, there is a consciousness that has developed and is on the verge of becoming aware of the true nature of its own existence and its purpose. The embodied consciousness begins to perceive and feel that it is but one wave of a mighty pulsation of *Śiva-Śakti* in manifestation. The Śakti developing in the growing consciousness is ready to greet Her Lord once again in the full blaze of manifestation. The body and the soul are close to realizing their identity. In the fulness of manifestation, the Śakti reveals Herself as none other than Śiva Himself. As the *Siddhasiddhāntapaddhati* (IV. 1) says:

Śaivaśaktiḥ yadā sahajena svasmin unmilinya nirutthānadaśāyāṁ vartate tadā Śivaḥ sa eva bhavati—

'When the same Śakti attains to its state of perfect manifestation through its own self-revelation, then She becomes Śiva Himself.'

Further, the moment man awakes to this fact of *Śiva-Śakti* manifestation in himself and the same *Śiva-Śakti* efflorescence in the universe around, and realizes it in his consciousness by an inner identity, he becomes one with the *Paramātman*. The Śakti in manifestation has completed Her round of play and unites once again with the Lord. The finite rejoins the Infinite, the temporal, the Eternal.

The Nātha-Yoga : Its goal and Method

The process to realize this truth of one's existence, to actualize this perception of the unity of one's soul with the Supreme is the yogic discipline built up by several teachers, the *nāthas* of this tradition, *sampradāya*.

All available spiritual knowledge and occult lore is pressed into service. The science of *haṭha-yoga* is utilized and developed in certain directions for this purpose. The various *āsanas* and practices of this *yoga* are resorted to for awakening the latent powers and for a complete mastery of the functions of the body, not only the physical body but also the subtler nervous organism. The body is sought to be perfected in each limb, so as to give the needed foundation and base for the edifice of realization. It is raised to its full potency. There is even an attempt to spiritualize the body in order to provide the proper vehicle for the inner spirit fast realizing itself as the divine Śakti. Once the body is so strengthened and purified, certain methods of *rāja-yoga* are practised alongside to bring the mind under control and still it into silence. It is to be noted that the traditional eight limbs of the *aṣṭāṅga-yoga* acquire in *nātha-yoga* an extended significance : *yama* is the endurance of the suffering of duality; *niyama,* that by which mental movements are controlled; *āsana,* constant settlement in one's natural state; *prāṇāyāma,* what brings stability to *prāṇa; pratyāhāra,* the turning back of the waves of the mental movement from sense objects; *dhāraṇā,* holding to the denial of form to each movement as it rises; *dhyāna,* the inner condition in which is experienced the one *Ātman* delighting in itself; *samādhi* that in which all principles are in equal harmony. *Mantra-japa, nādānusandhāna* (*yoga* of sound), etc. are cultivated under the guidance of the *guru* in order to bring about the *samarasa*, equilibrium, of the *piṇḍa* with the *pada,* to process the consciousness and lead it to become one with the divine consciousness of *Śiva-Śakti (laya)* in all its poises of existence, viz immanent, universal, and transcendent.

❑❑❑

31

APPROACH TO GOD

There is a conception that unless there is awe and fear and the concomitant feelings of submission and servitude, God cannot be approached or worshipped. While it is a fact that this attitude may be one of the approaches to God, it does not necessarily follow that it is the only approach. An everyday and every man's experience in the world should throw some light upon this statement. Whom do we remember most? Those whom we fear or love? Who does command our submission, non-acquisitioned and spontaneous, earliest; one who tyrannizes or one who loves? The only answer can be those whom we love. In fear the burden of submission is irksome, always, and is a compulsion that is sought to be overthrown the moment the subject feels himself strong enough to do so, or to flout it. But in affection, in love, man does not feel it though it may weigh down upon him. There is no groaning under its weight; there is not even the grumbling. Rather, there is a spontaneous joy in such submission. In worship or approach to God also this same rule is applicable. In fact man's feelings, being what they are, cannot be multiplied in number; no fresh type of faculties can be created but they can be extended, expanded, sublimated. And that is what happens in our approach to God. You are not asked to be bereft of your feelings or create new ones but only to turn them Godwards.

Now, what infuses awe or fear into us? Is it not the immensity of the powers or glory of God? And also a feeling of alienation from Him when we do not consider Him as our own? It is those who love glory themselves that think much about the glory of God', says Sri Ramakrishna. Why should we be overwhelmed with His glory? Perhaps, there is a desire for worldly things and glory lurking in ourselves that makes us do so. Perhaps, we want to bargain with Him for some of His glory. This does not, however, mean that one should not appreciate a beautiful scenery or a serene and soul-elevating place or circumstance. But to think of His glory and forget Him is not an aspirant's way. Shri Ramakishna used to say, 'What will you gain by counting the trees and branches and leaves in a mango grove? You have come to eat mangoes. Eat them and be happy'. What will it avail us if we come to know what all are the powers of God? And is it possible to know all? On the otherhand, if we realize God, see Him, talk with Him that will liberate us, make us free. And this freedom is not something like that what we see in the world, momentary and conditioned. It is eternal and unconditioned. It makes us soar beyond the plane of mundane consciousness. It enwraps us in a divine and eternal light, makes us free from fear, free from inhibitions, free of likes and dislikes, free from attachment and hatred. Is not such a state covetable? Worship of God helps us reach this state. Nothing else can.

There is a Sanskrit verse by the poet Bhartṛhari which runs thus: 'In enjoyment there is the fear of disease; in social position, the fear of falling off; in wealth, the fear of kings; in honour, the fear of humiliation; in power, the fear of the foes; in beauty, the fear of old age, in scriptural erudition, the fear of antagonists; in virtue, the fear of calumniators; in body, the fear of death. All things of his world pertaining to man are attended with fear; renunciation alone stands for fearlessness.'[1] We may add that when this renunciation leads to God-realization it opens the flood-gates of bliss eternal leaving no room for the baser motives and fear to assert themselves. That is why one who has touched the source of

Truth, of Light wavers not in his path; fears nothing. He stands like the adamantine rocks which though battered by the waves remain unmoved, undented. Tribulations and trials,miseries and afflictions leave him unperturbed. When we realize God we know Him to be our own, the Soul of our souls, our inmost Being. Can we then call it servitude or submission in the sense we understand worldly servitude? To whom do we submit? Is it not to our own inner Being? Could there be any harm in that? What is more welcome than that we conquer our baser impulses, the turbulent passions, and the still stronger ego and submitting to the Indwelling spirit be at peace with ourself and the whole world? And if worship of God does it, as assured by God-men and men of God, why should we stand away?

All the objections to worship of God seem to arise from the conception that He is an extra-cosmic Being, sitting somewhere in the Heaven, high above the clouds, demanding implicit submission under threats of dire consequences, holding out bouquets and enjoyments to those who follow His commands and punishment of hell fire to those who transgress. But the Hindu view of God—that He is the Indwelling Spirit of every being and at the same time transcends them all—is a very encouraging one. Here the distance between the soul and the Oversoul shrinks, as it were, to an appreciable extent. The strangeness, man at first feels towards God, drops off yielding place to a feeling of appurtenance, belonging. The sages and saints experienced this; the Upaniṣads declare it: The *Chāndogya,* for instance, points out 'that *Puruṣa* which is seen in the eye that is the *Ātman'*.[2]

Bādarāyaṇa in his *Śārīraka-sūtras* removes the apparent ambiguity about the meaning of this passage—whether it refers to the *Jīva* or the *Paramātman*—by two aphorisms: 'The one within (is the *paramātman*); on account of His qualities being declared.'[3] A second passage which refers to the "within" occurs in the same *Upaniṣad* (I. vi. 6) wherein the description of that Being, in the orb of the sun, is given.[4] An objection was raised that this description cannot pertain to the *Paramātman*—He being without form—and therefore must only be for the *jīva,* or the deity representing the sun. This contention is, however, refuted. The highest Lord though without form assumes forms to bestow grace on the *sādhaka* by His own power, *Māyā.*[5] Why does this become necessary? It is well-known that all individuals have not the same capacity of comprehension. Our sages too knew it. So, for such of those who cannot or do not like to think in terms of the formless aspect of God, the forms and qualities are declared.

Any further doubt lingering in one's mind is removed by the next aphorism: 'And there is another one (i.e. the *Paramātman,* who is different from the individual souls animating the sun etc.); on account of the distinction being declared.[6] Where is this distinction proclaimed? The *Bṛhadāraṇyaka Upaniṣad* gives the answer. It is not the deity representing the sun that is meant while referring to the One inside its orb, but the 'One who dwells in the sun, but is within it, whom the sun does not know, whose body is the sun, and who controls the sun from within, that One is the Internal Ruler, your own immortal Self'.[7]

Śruti is never tired of repeating its statements to drive home the truths. It repeats this formula in the case of all elements, all beings, all limbs of man, and his mind and his knowledge. Here we see how close we are to God and yet we know Him not, comprehend Him not. Shri Ramakrishna used to give the simile of the musk-deer. The deer would smell the fragrance of the musk but not knowing that the source of the fragrance was in its own navel would run to all quarters of the forest and at last when tired would lie down and then come to know that what it has been seeking outside in vain was all the time within itself.

Now a question would arise: 'If we are controlled by a higher power residing in us, in what way are we responsible for our actions? Such a question was put to Shri Ramakrishna also. And that question will be repeated for ages to come, by people who would want to shift the responsibility of their wicked deeds on to someone else. Actually, they do not believe it when they repeat that it is the Indwelling Spirit who is working through them. It is only a veil to hoodwink others. In the heart of their hearts they know that they are far far away from believing it themselves. They assert their ego most of the time. 'Well', you may say, yours is a strange logic indeed! You breathe hot and cold at the same time. Once you say that everything is controlled by the Inneer Ruler and again you say that the ego asserts. Then, what type of a ruler is that who cannot resist the force of the ego?' To this we reply, 'True, it seems very incompatible. But haven't you seen a mother,with her benevolence and beneficence, though guiding the steps and conduct of her child, giving way to its unreasonable importunities? Aye, she even sometimes allows the child to burn its fingers in fire though she could, if she would, prevent it in the interest of the child. But then she would take care of its again as soon as it has done with its play, learnt its lessons. For all that, can you insist that the mother was not strong enough to restrain the child? No, Likewise the Inner Ruler *(antaryāmin)* is not a despot. You are given a little free play to use your faculties, to pick your own way, learn your lessons yourselves in the world, when you would not listen to the sane advice that is pouring forth from your own Inner Being. He even allows you the freedom to deny Him. But there it ends, your ego comes into clash with those of others if you will assert it too much. Then you fall back for support on God, on your Inner Being. Where then is the inconsistency in what we have said?' This much about those who would say that they have their free will.

A little digression here is inevitable as the subject of free will has been introduced. Is our will free? The answer is yes and no. We can approach this reply from two standpoints. First of all, as related already, a certain amount of freedom is given to us, just as a cow fetered to a post is allowed to roam about, in a meadow, to the extent the length of the rope round its neck allows it, but no more. We can feel this even in society. Society gives us freedom to develop in our own individual way, of course, subject to certain restrictions. And when we go beyond the set bounds, down comes its mighty arm. The long arm of the law seizes one who transgresses its limits, or enters into others' domains. However much we may like to break these bonds they would not yield, but only chafe us the more. We are not in any way in a dissimilar position as far as 'will to act' is concerned. So many factors press us down: our inherent tendencies, circumstances, environments and the like.

From the second point of view, as long as our will remains distinct from the Cosmic Will it is not free, but when the former runs in concurrence with the latter it has no more bonds. Whatever it wills comes true, for it can have no desire apart from that of the Cosmic Will. Of course, this latter state is possible only when man has attained complete perfection, when not a speck of worldly taint is left in him.

To return to the subject of submission: what about those who simulate submission accepting the existence of a Higher Entity ruling over us? It is a dangerous game they try to play. They are deceiving themselves. Shri Ramakrishna's parable of the *Brahmin*—who killed a cow and who while taking credit for the lay out of his garden and every good and beautiful thing he possessed,imputed the sin of cow-killing to Indra, the presiding deity of the hand—should serve as a very poignant eye-opener. Another example Shri Ramakrishna used to cite was that of Duryodhana.

Duryodhana said to Shri Krishna: 'I know what is righteousness but I have no inclination to practise it, and I know what is unrighteousness but I have no disposition to avoid it. O Krishna, I act as you, dwelling in my heart, make me act.[8] Shri Ramakrishna says that such lip service won't do us any good: 'You know in your heart of hearts that those are mere words. No sooner do you commit an evil deed then you feel a palpitation in your heart.' Again he said be one in your thought, word and deed. For sincerity is the *sine qua non* of spiritual life. A man with a sincere trust in God does not come to grief. 'If you place your trust in a great man he won't let you down. What then to speak of the Lord!' remarks Shri Ramakrishna.

Having said that awe and fear, submission and servitude need not be the only approach to God it devolves on us to point out what other approaches are feasible. We shall leave out the Vedāntic idea of '*Atman* is *Brahman*, as it is not a practicable proposition in the case of all and sundry. Worship implies three things, the worshipper, the worshipped and the act of worship. Let us recall what we said earlier, viz. that God assumes forms for bestowing grace on the aspirant. Everything will be easier to comprehend if we remember this. Now, to God with form, the other forms of approach would be respect, reverence and love. The last one is an intimate relation. We are not devoid of these feelings. We respect and revere those who are good and great, who possess virtues in abundance, and who are pure. Man loves his father, mother, wife, and children. The approach of the Vaiṣnavas is somewhat on this line, and can be followed with profit. There are no conventionalities to be observed, no retrictions to be feared in man's approach to these relations. Man feels one with them. That is the reason why man turns to his home after a hard day's labour or a nerve-racking experience, for rest and sympathy. He is sure of the soothing touch of the beloved ones there. It restores him to cheerfulness, gives him courage to face life again, however terrible a form it may assume.

But very rarely do people come across disinterested love in the world. It is all give and take, a shop-keeping, that is why there is so much of unrest in families. Perhaps, man's love towards God begins that way. He will worship God to get some of his desires fulfilled. In other words, his devotion is *sakāma*. If, however, the aspirant uses his discrimination he will soon understand the emptiness of the enjoyments. Love of God rightly directed is able to generate in us dispassion for these enjoyments. That is the test of the dawn of real love of God. Nothing tempts a man, who has that love, to fall from the ideal. It is love of God for His own sake, not for the sake of 'loaves and fishes'.

Man is obsessed with the idea that everything should be judged by his own standard. He wants to weigh God also in his own moral balance. This shows how anthropomorphic an ordinary man's idea of God is. Nay, even great theologians and scholars commit this mistake. They superimpose their own imperfections, disabilities and drawbacks on the Lord, and posit that such a being does not deserve any worship. But a little thought would satisfy that it is puerile to speak of good and evil in the transcendent. We will bring down the transcendent Lord to the level of man, if we try to impose on Him our standards of morals and the like. Morals and laws are necessary in a world of multiplicity where there is a conflict between interests. But God is one who has no axe of His own to grind, who has no pleasures to seek and is on a plane where there is no multiplicity, no interests to clash. He is ever pure, ever perfect, ever knowing, and ever free. He desires nothing, wills nothing. If such a Being does not deserve worship who else will? Man, wherever he finds greater powers, greater talents and greater virtues instinctively bows down his head in salutation. Then why should he be arrogant towards the highest Being, who is the fulfilment of all virtues and power and glory?

REFERENCES

1. भोगे रोगभयं कुले च्युतिभयं वित्ते नृपालाद्भयं
   माने दैन्यभयं बले रिपुभयं रूपे जराया भयम्।
   शास्त्रे वादभयं गुणे खलभयं काये कृतान्ताद्भयं
   सर्वं वस्तु भयान्वितं भुवि नृणां वैराग्यमेवाभयम्।।
2. य एषोऽक्षिणि पुरुषो दृश्यत एष आत्मा।
   —*Chāndogya Upaniṣad,* VIII. vii. 4
3. अन्तस्तद्धर्मोपदेशात्। —*Brahmasūtra* I. i. 20.
4. य एषोऽन्तरादित्ये हिरण्मयः पुरुषो दृश्यते
   हिरण्यश्मश्रुर्हिरण्यकेश आप्रणखात्सर्व एव सुवर्णः।।
   —*Chāndogya,* I. vi. 6
5. माया ह्येषा मया सृष्टा यन्मां पश्यसि नारद।
   सर्वभूतगुणैर्युक्तं मैवं मां ज्ञातुमर्हसि।।
   Quoted by Śrī Śaṅkara in his commentary on *Br. Sūtra Bhāṣya,* I. i. 20
6. भेदव्यपदेशाच्चान्यः। —*Br. Sūtra,* I. i. 21.
7. य आदित्ये तिष्ठन्नादित्यादन्तरः, यमादित्यो न वेद,
   यस्यादित्यः शरीरम्, य आदित्यमन्तरो यमयति, एष त आत्मान्तर्याम्यमृतः।।
   —*Bṛ. U.* 3.7.9.
8. जानामि धर्मं न च मे प्रवृत्तिः
   जानाम्यधर्मं न च मे निवृत्तिः।
   त्वया हृषीकेश हृदि स्थितेन
   यथानियुक्तोऽस्मि तथा करोमि।।

❑❑❑